Jens Damm,
Isabelle Cheng (Eds.)

Taiwan

Berliner China-Hefte
Chinese History and Society

Edited by
Mechthild Leutner

Editorial Management
Hauke Neddermann

Ostasiatisches Seminar
der Freien Universität Berlin

No. 47

LIT

TAIWAN

Self vs. Other

Edited by

Jens Damm and Isabelle Cheng

LIT

Bibliographic information published by the Deutsche Nationalbibliothek
The Deutsche Nationalbibliothek lists this publication in the Deutsche Nationalbibliografie; detailed bibliographic data are available on the Internet at http://dnb.d-nb.de.

ISBN 978-3-643-90777-6
ISSN 1860-2290

A catalogue record for this book is available from the British Library

Klosbachstr. 107
CH-8032 Zürich
Tel. +41 (0) 44-251 75 05 Fax +41 (0) 44-251 75 06
E-Mail: zuerich@lit-verlag.ch http://www.lit-verlag.ch

Distribution:

In the UK: Global Book Marketing, e-mail: mo@centralbooks.com
In North America: International Specialized Book Services, e-mail: orders@isbs.com
In Germany: LIT Verlag Fresnostr. 2, D-48159 Münster
Tel. +49 (0) 2 51-620 32 22, Fax +49 (0) 2 51-922 60 99, e-mail: vertrieb@lit-verlag.de
In Austria: Medienlogistik Pichler-ÖBZ, e-mail: mlo@medien-logistik.at
e-books are available at www.litwebshop.de

Contents

Taiwan: Self vs. Other

Isabelle Cheng
Which Team Do You Support? Situating the In-between Identity of Immigrant Women in Taiwan 5

Lara Momesso
From Someone, to No-one, to a New-one: A Subjective View of Taiwan's Immigration Policies in the Context of Multiculturalism 24

Feng-yi Chu
Benevolent Self vs. Malignant Other: The East-West Antagonistic Narrative of Taiwanese People's Chinese Identity 37

Ek-hong Ljavakaw Sia
Crafting the Taiwanese Nation: Exclusivist and Inclusivist Theses of the Post-war Taiwanese Nationalism 56

Jens Sejrup
One or the Other: Synecdoche and Representation in Taiwan-Japan Controversies 85

Barbora Platzerova
Bigamy in Chinese Law in the 20th Century: Conflict between Laws and Special Cases of Bigamy 105

Jens Damm
The Contemporary Political and Public Discourse on the Xinhai Revolution in Taiwan in the Context of the Centennial Celebration of the ROC 122

Conference Reports / Konferenzberichte

China's International Relations in Historical Perspective, Konfuzius-Institut an der Freien Universität Berlin. 27.-28. November *(Ryanne Flock)* 140

International Workshop China Studies in a Global Context, Konfuzius-Institut an der Freien Universität Berlin. 16.-17. Oktober 2015 *(Susanne Kuß)* 141

Notes on Contributors 146

Isabelle Cheng

Which Team Do You Support? Situating the In-Between Identity of Immigrant Women in Taiwan

The link between sports events, national identity, and nationalism is a well-known modern phenomenon in contemporary social and political life. The act of supporting a national team or an individual athlete who is competing in the international arena is often perceived as expressing or performing national identity (Houlihan 1997; Maguire and Tuck 1998; Lu 1999; Dyreson 2003; Smith and Porter 2004; Xu 2006). In international events such as the Olympic Games, the performance of national teams or individual athletes is viewed as the delegation of national power and they are praised for radiating national glory. Thus, the achievements of a nation-state in sport are employed by some as a measurement of national pride (e.g. Smith and Jarkko 1998). At sporting events, the unity of the nation is imagined and consolidated through the shared sentiments of the viewers in the arena or in front of the TV – at home and abroad. However, migration, and the resultant inclusion of the immigrant community within the host state, challenges the comfortable assumption that a member of the national community will identify himself/herself exclusively with his/her nation. Translated into support for national teams, this assumption was embedded in the 'cricket test' invented by the British Conservative Home Secretary, Norman Tebbit, in 1990. According to Tebbit, immigrants from the West Indies, Pakistan and India would be failing to show loyalty to Britain if they cheered for the West Indian, Pakistani and Indian teams rather than for the English national cricket team. (Smith and Porter 2004: 8). This paper challenges the demands for such exclusive and singular loyalty. Female marriage immigration to Taiwan is used as a case study to argue that any such 'cricket test' that demands an 'either-or' answer misses an opportunity to explore how immigrant women implicitly express their sense of belonging with sophistication and on various occasions, such as sports events. Thanks to the multiple origins of immigrants in Taiwan and the different national sports of their countries of origin, this paper underlines the fallacy of the 'cricket test' in that the embedded assumption denies the existence and authenticity of any fluid and ambiguous dual identity. By examining the ways in which immigrant women express their support for Taiwan *as well as* for their countries of origin, this paper argues that they experience the fluidity of dual identity in their daily lives. Moreover, by defining the situation envisaged by the 'cricket test' as 'in between', this paper argues that the usual label of 'dual identity' is insufficient to grasp the experiences of dynamism and the fluidity of immigrant women's national identity. Emerging from the in-between situation is an 'in-between' identity in which immigrants live within the ambiguity, fusion, and conflict of the two pulling forces from both ends of their migration journey. This paper argues that a sports event where immigrant women experience the tug of war between two competing nation-states with which they establish a real and emotive link is an embodiment of the in-between identity. The casual and mundane experiences described during the interviews underline the often overlooked and understated commonness, rather than the oddness of in-between identity. The caution, reluctance or ambiguity of expressing the in-between identity is in fact the testimony of the pressure of conforming to the imposed norm of exclusive and singular national identity. The varying responses presented in this paper are the strategies arising from immigrant women's mundane practices where they negotiate with the hegemonic norm in their everyday lives.

This paper will first of all briefly introduce the settlement of marriage immigrant women from China and Southeast Asia and sketch out the national sporting pastimes in their native countries. It will then move on, to explain the research questions, the framework within which the case of in-betweenness and the qualitative method that is employed to conduct this research. Next, there is a detailed analysis of the findings drawn from the responses of immigrant women to three questions concerning their experiences of expressing national identity, focusing on the ways in which immigrants articulate the fluidity and ambiguity of their competing dual identity. That is, why they support Taiwan and their countries of origin, and how they negotiate the in-between situation. Most importantly, this paper argues that their in-between identity is embedded in their daily life experiences, such as occasional sport events, which projects their relational identity derived from the gendered role as a mother, the enduring influence of primordial identity, and the construction of national identity engineered by the nation-state.

New Members and Different National Sports

Since the early 1980s, married immigrant women from Indonesia, Thailand and the Philippines have been taking up residence in Taiwan, (Hsia 1997: 3, 40), despite the fact that the island state was largely closed to international migration during the Cold War (Seyla 2004: 307). Ethnographic research suggests that those from Indonesia were of Chinese ethnicity, and that some of them married military personnel who were fleeing from China with the retreating Guomindang (GMD, also: Kuomintang, KMT) government around 1949 (Cheng 2013a). From the late 1980s onwards, however, the rather insignificant female marriage immigration began to gather pace as a result of the resumption of contact with China and the increased overseas investment in Southeast Asian countries, later officially known as the *Go South* policy (Wu 19955; Leifer 2001; Cai 2008: 143;). Thus, the two streams of female marriage migration to Taiwan began to take shape.

One stream has come from Mainland China, the Peoples' Republic of China (PRC). In November 1987, the government of Taiwan lifted the ban on travelling to China after nearly four decades of disrupted contact between the peoples across the Taiwan Strait. The resumption of contact started a trend towards marriage between the people living on the two sides of the Strait. At first, the marriages were mainly between men who had fled China around 1949 (known as Mainlanders [*waishengren*] in Taiwan) and Chinese women who were widows or divorcees. In recent years, as the contact between both sides has expanded rapidly and considerably, marriages between older couples, and second marriages, have become a minority[1]. They have been outnumbered by younger couples whose relationships have been initiated by commercial brokering, social matchmaking, and online dating, as well as by couples who have become acquainted with each other on social occasions through work, tourism or study courses (Cheng 2013b: 1).

1 A national census found that 9.5 per cent of Chinese wives relied on their husbands' pensions as the main family income (Neizhengbu 2004). This may be taken as an indication of the number of marriages between older couples.

The other stream has arrived from Southeast Asia. The reasons for the earlier patterns of marriage migration from Indonesia have not yet been subjected to thorough research, but my fieldwork results suggest that these marriages came about via transnational connections. This social matchmaking was later overtaken by commercial brokering, which was correlated to the rapid expansion of Taiwanese investment in Southeast Asia after the late 1980s (Hsia 1997: 40). As part of their business portfolio, small-sized Taiwanese businesses began to operate commercial brokering services, charging fees for making travel arrangements and applying for documentation (Wang and Chang 2002). Brokering services took off in Indonesia, thrived in Vietnam and later expanded to Cambodia.

Statistics show that female marriage migration is one of the main reasons that foreign-born citizens move to the island nation-state. From 1987 to February 2013, a total of 293,631 women from the People's Republic of China (PRC) had residential status in Taiwan as the spouses of local citizens. At the same time, a total of 131,764 women from Vietnam, Indonesia, the Philippines, Thailand and Cambodia had the same status (Ru-chuguo yimin shu 2013)[2]. A nation-wide census conducted by the Ministry of the Interior in 2003 found that the mean age of Chinese wives was 33, and that half of these became mothers in Taiwan, whereas the mean age of foreign wives (the great majority of them are of Southeast Asian origin) was 27, and nearly 71 per cent of these became mothers in Taiwan. Amongst the PRC Chinese, 18.9 per cent had married for the second time, a ratio six times higher than that found among their Southeast Asian counterparts (Neizhengbu 2004). By settling and establishing families, immigrant women have become new members of the national community. Becoming acquainted with the local sports scene has been a part of their life experiences since migrating to Taiwan.

In Taiwan, the dominant national sport is baseball. Introduced by Japan as a means of sustaining its colonial dominance and strengthening the assimilation of the colonised peoples, baseball became the symbol of the resistance of the islanders against their oppressors (Lin and Lee 2007). At the peak of the Cold War, when the survival of the GMD regime hinged on its security alliance with the United States in East Asia, baseball, particularly the successes of the Maple Leaf and the Tainan Giants Teams in the Little League World Series in the US, was appropriated by the GMD government as a vehicle for consolidating national identity. The game constructed a field where the islanders collectively espoused their identity under the banner of the Republic of China (ROC) (Morris 2006:70-73).

After the change in ruling party in 2000, baseball, particularly the hosting of the Baseball World Cup in 2001, was again utilised for promoting Taiwanese nationalism by the Democratic Progressive Party (DPP) government (Lin et al 2010). Consequently, the success of Taiwanese baseball players in that game attracted the attention of the international media (ibid: 2252). The success in baseball is so tightly woven into the national sentiments that players who reached stardom in the US professional leagues, such as Wang Jianmin (Wang Chien-min 王建民), were crowned as the 'Glory of Taiwan' (*Taiwan zhi guang*). The positive international publicity generated by baseball - a sport central to Taiwan but peripheral to China (Yu and Mangan 2008: 840) - was such that speculation arose over whether Beijing had pulled strings to have baseball removed from the 2008 Beijing Olympics (Lin et al

[2] In total, 87,364 Vietnamese, 27,325 Indonesian, 7,045 Filipino, 5,748 Thai, and 4,282 Cambodian wives are resident in Taiwan, either with residency permits or through obtaining citizenship.

2010: 2250). It is believed that Beijing's aim was to block the possibility of Taiwan outperforming and thus embarrassing China. In spite of the distrust of China, the idea that both sides could co-host some events of the 2008 Olympics Games was entertained in 2000 and 2001. The fact that the North and South Koreans appeared as one team in the opening ceremony of the 2000 Sydney Olympics gave fresh impetus to this possibility (Chen 2002: 144-147). Nevertheless, Beijing's insistence on restricting the display of ROC symbols during the torch relay in Taiwan was rejected by Taiwan since this restriction was regarded as Beijing scoring a goal by denying the sovereignty of Taiwan (Bairner and Hwang 2011: 241). Although, in the end, baseball was not removed from the 2008 Olympics, Taiwan's unexpected 8-7 defeat by China was lamented by the Taiwanese media as a 'national humiliation'. The degree of injury to national pride this defeat caused was compared with the loss of the ROC's seat in the United Nations in 1970 (An and Loh 2010: 59-62).

Unlike cricket, which is also popular in the West Indies and on the Asian subcontinent, the binding national passion for baseball is not widely shared by immigrants from Southeast Asia. For those from the Philippines, the attraction of baseball has given way to basketball as part of the postcolonial transition from the 1910s to the 1960s. Both sports were introduced by the US, but the former is closely associated with the image of an 'occupation force', whereas the latter tends to be seen as conveying the image of a 'benevolent America' (Antolihao 2012). In Vietnam, (and for the Vietnamese community in Poland), football is the national sport played at home and abroad (Grzymala-Kazlowska 2002: 7). The outpourings during the mass celebrations after Vietnam beat Indonesia in the Asian Games in 1997 and after the semi-final victory in the 1998 Tigers Cup drew the attention of the authorities because it led to the disruption of public order (Thomas 2001). As shown later, the fact that one Vietnamese interviewee proudly mentioned the similar success of the Vietnamese football team in the Southeast Asian games highlighted the nationalistic connotations of the sport.

Although football is also popular in Indonesia (Colombijn 2000, cited in Brown 2006: 72), badminton comes a close second, since it is 'part of life and identity, and also a "religion".... [It] eliminates sadness, suffering, poverty, powerlessness and injustice' (Sunito 2003, cited in Brown 2006: 73). It is perhaps more so for the Indonesian Chinese, who started to dominate the sport from the 1930s onwards (Brown 2006: 74). As discussed below, the fact that one older interviewee praised the success of Rudy Hartono and Susi Susanti and that a younger interviewee mentioned her early experiences of watching badminton games between China and Indonesia gave rich nationalistic meanings to the sport. Stardom achieved in international games allowed some successful badminton athletes of Chinese origin, such as Rudy Hartono Kurniawan and Lucia Francisca Susi Susanti, to speak out about the anti-Chinese riots in 1998 (Brown 2006: 92), the violence of which was one of the primary motives for Indonesian Chinese women to seek marriage migration to Taiwan (Cheng 2014).

The overview of the varying national sports of the immigrants underlines the differences between the host societies and the immigrants. The highly emotional attitudes and reactions to international sporting events do not simply derive from personal interest, but from the origins and the historical roots of these national sports. As shown below in the analysis of their identity, the cultures behind the sports and the immigrants' keen awareness of their disadvantaged position in the host society interweave and generate a range of implicit, subtle and sophisticated strategies for expressing their sense of national belonging in a way that will help them to avoid the intrusive demands of an exclusive and singular identity.

Framework of Analysis: Performing Identity in In-Between Situation

The 'cricket test' was founded on the firm belief that loyalty towards the nation is exclusive and singular. Tebbit explained that 'one cannot uphold two sets of ethics or be loyal to two nations, any more than a man can have two masters. Youngsters of all races born here should be taught that British history is their history, or they will forever be foreigners holding British passports' (The Guardian, 8 October 1997, cited in Kofman 2005: 461). This can be seen as an attempt of the nation-state to monopolise the loyalty of all citizens, including immigrants who have become citizens. However, theories such as transnationalism (Basch et al 1994) and flexible citizenship (Ong 1999) have recognised the existence of a multilayered identity. A study conducted on Korean women who married US servicemen and emigrated to the US found that these Korean wives insisted on retaining their tenuous Korean identity whilst simultaneously laying claim to America as home (Yuh 2002). Similarly, as a symbol of loyalty to the receiving state, the requirement to renounce the former nationality in order to become eligible for citizenship paradoxically underlines immigrant women's dual identity. A study on the renunciation of the former nationality by immigrant women in Taiwan found that their identification with Taiwan and their native country is *mediated* by their gendered roles as chaste wives, caring mothers and dutiful daughters. That is, their identification with Taiwan grows partly because of their wifely and motherly duties towards their husbands and children in Taiwan. Meanwhile, they retain identification with their country of origin partly because of their daughterly duties towards their parents in the native country. The relinquishing of their former nationality is perceived as the result of being forced by the state of Taiwan to prioritise the role of wife-mother over the role of daughter. As their gender-defined commitment and duty is hard to divide, the forced prioritisation creates a tug of war between their two senses of belonging (Cheng 2013a). Immigrant women are therefore trapped in their dynamic, gendered and role-defined dual identity.

The influential constructivist approach has given rise to the cliché that individuals have multiple identities, and that identity is fluid, unstable, fragmented and negotiated (Brubaker and Cooper 2007: 11). Although this stance may have become meaningless, the challenge of discovering exactly how identity is thrown into flux remains. As a result, the impact of fluid identity on individuals' everyday lives is less well understood. As mentioned above, the renunciation of the former nationality creates a tug-of-war situation that demands the prioritisation of immigrant women's dual identity. In this paper, by challenging the 'cricket test', I will show how similar tension also arises at sporting events. Similar to the renunciation requirement that generates forced prioritisation because the host state demands singular and undivided loyalty, the 'cricket test' also presumes the singularity and exclusiveness of national identity. However, as shown in the following pages, if this presumption is set aside and other scenarios (other than the one in which the host countries and countries of origin play against each other) are provided, we will see how immigrants develop different strategies to negotiate the fluidity of their dual identity and the external pressure of conforming to a fixed singular identity. In scenarios where the country of origin and the host country play against a third country, their dual identity sees them comfortably offering support to both. However, when the host countries and the countries of origin play against each other, those who feel torn apart by two senses of belonging experience an 'in-between identity' that is underlined by tension, conflict, ambiguity and *liminality*. Stripping the cricket test's intent of pressing immigrants to prioritise their dual identity, this paper delves into the uneasy in-between situation in order to underline immigrant women's autonomous agency in asserting their national identity in the *mundane* practices of daily life. Their subjective interpretation of the in-between situation, the strategies they employ to relieve the prioritisation pressure, and the decisions they make to encounter the in-betweenness will contextualise and deepen our comprehension of the impact of identity embodied in occasional and mundane incidents on our daily lives.

Research Questions, Method and Reflections on Conducting Fieldwork

For the purpose of analyzing the uncomfortable state of in-betweenness, the following three research questions were formulated: (1) how would immigrant women express their national identity in the country of settlement and the country of origin at sporting events? (2) How would immigrant women respond when they are placed in an in-between situation where the two countries are in competition? (3) How would their responses be affected by the socio-political environment in their countries of origin and the host countries? This research employed qualitative methods to obtain findings of rich and subtle meanings, rather than to achieve statistical representativeness. Semi-structured in-depth interviews were used to collect data related to the national identity of immigrant women. Conducted in March 2009 - June 2009 and January 2010, this paper presents the findings of interviews with 98 women in urban and rural areas in Taiwan and Penghu, including 39 Chinese from Mainland China (henceforth PRC Chinese), 26 Vietnamese, 13 Filipinos and 20 Indonesians who are of Chinese ethnicity (and will henceforth be referred to as Indonesian Chinese). The sampling method used was purposeful sampling and snowballing. Interviews were conducted at home, in cafés, workplaces, restaurants, churches, at evening Mandarin classes, and in parks. The languages used in the interviews were English with Filipino immigrants, as they requested, and Mandarin with immigrants of all other nationalities. Owing to my inability to speak Tagalog, Visaya (spoken in Cebu), Vietnamese and Indonesian languages, and since there was no funding available to employ interpreters, English and Mandarin were the only communication tools available to facilitate the interviews. The fact that the interviews were conducted in Mandarin rather than in the immigrants' own languages limited, to some extent, the depth and quantity of the narratives, and this is an acknowledged limitation of the fieldwork findings.

All the interviewees were given pseudonyms. The names of PRC Chinese interviewees are spelled in accordance with the Hanyu Pinyin system. Filipino interviewees were given English names because of their preference for speaking English. Vietnamese interviewees were given Vietnamese names with or without the gender signifier '*Thi*'. Depending on their language habit in Indonesia, most of the Indonesian Chinese interviewees were given Chinese names pronounced in Hokkien (Fujian), Teowchew (Chaozhou), Hakka or Cantonese dialects. Some younger interviewees were given Indonesian names if they confirmed that they had adopted Indonesian names or if they were introduced to me under their Indonesian names. Applying different naming methods to Indonesian Chinese is to highlight their diasporic and hybrid identity (see below).

As part of a research project on in-betweenness experienced in daily life with regard to citizenship, language proficiency and motherhood, the interviews for this present paper focused exclusively on three questions:

1. If Taiwan played against Japan in an international match, which country would you support? Why?
2. If China (or the Philippines, Vietnam, Indonesia) played against Japan in an international match, which country would you support? Why?
3. If Taiwan played against China (or the Philippines, Vietnam, Indonesia), which country would you support? Why?

Given that the most popular sports in Taiwan and the immigrants' countries of origin are different, the fictional matches in these three scenarios were accordingly adjusted to the most popular sport. Considering the intensive media coverage of the baseball match between Taiwan and China at the 2008 Olympics, the fictional match was baseball for the PRC Chinese interviewees. For the Filipino, Vietnamese and Indonesian Chinese interviewees, it was basketball, football, and badminton respectively. For the second question, Japan was chosen for the fictional competition since Japan enjoys high international visibility in East Asia. As discussed later, assigning the role of opponent to Japan had the unexpected effect of evoking some interviewees' war memories, although none of these interviewees had had any personal experience of the war.

It is worth noting that this research recognises the pressure felt by immigrants when their national identity was investigated by a researcher. This pressure was clearly raised by Pham Thanh Van. When contemplating how to respond to the third question, she explained that she was cautious about how her answers might be judged. Her replies would be measured by an array of variables, including where the question was asked (in Taiwan or Vietnam), who asked the question, and in what kind of manner the question was asked. Although she was at ease with being approached by an academic researcher, it would create pressure if the question were raised by a Taiwanese or Vietnamese official (interviewed in Taipei on 15th April 2009). Thanh Van's replies send a strong message that studying identity is not only to ascertain who one is but also analyse what one does in what kind of context and how one is *'othered'* by the social environment in everyday life. For this reason, instead of portraying immigrants as 'disloyal' or regarding their dual identity as 'unauthentic', this paper highlights the fact that their seemingly ambiguous responses testify to their awareness of the pressure of showing loyalty that is embedded in their daily life when they interacted with their in-laws and the host society.

In the following pages, I will show how the interviewees describe their dual identity, and how some of them develop strategies to negotiate the in-between situation. After outlining the commonality shared by all interviewees, I will further discuss the narratives of the Indonesian Chinese and the PRC Chinese since their reactions and strategies bear specific political references. For the former, their experiences mirror the evolution of their diasporic and hybrid identity in Indonesia; for the latter, their experiences reflect the intensified antagonism between Taiwan and China and the prevailing 'China-bashing' in Taiwan. Their narratives once again highlight the political undercurrents of sporting events.

Relational Identity: Identifying with Taiwan as a Mother

In the first scenario, with the exception of a few who were a little hesitant, the great majority of interviewees supported Taiwan. The popular pitcher, Wang Jianmin, was praised by Peony because he 'carried the name of the nation' (interviewed in Pingdong [Pingtung] on 27th January 2010). Sometimes, the familiarity with Taiwanese star players was one result of their children's enthusiasm. Nguyễn Thi Xuân Mai, the mother of two school-age children, had little leisure time because she had to work long and laborious hours in a factory. Her knowledge of Wang's performance was gained through her son, who provided his exhausted mother with details partly to entertain her in the late evening.

A common explanation for their identification with Taiwan, as Peggy said, was 'Because I live here, I feel for the Taiwanese' (interviewed in Pingdong on 27th January 2010). At first glance, this seems to echo the findings of Manning and Roy whose research interest in immigrants' national identity seems to be also partly aroused by Tebbit's cricket test (Manning and Roy 2007: 3-4)[3]. They report that third-generation immigrants are more likely than second-generation immigrants to think of themselves as British, and that newly arrived immigrants never think of themselves as British; however, the longer they remain in the UK, the more likely it is that they will eventually feel themselves to be British (ibid: 23). The responses provided by my interviewees showed that residency alone did not *independently* explain how the sense of belonging to the country of residence evolved. What was critical to this evolution was the transition of the personal life course. In the case of the immigrant women, one of the most significant transitions was becoming a mother. Echoing *relational* feminism which argues that women's identity is constituted by her roles in relation to family members (Knop 2001: 57-58), their identification with Taiwan is *mediated* from their self-identity as a mother. They internalised the gender norms and regarded caring for children as their duty. This *gendered* sense of belonging was typified by 42-year-old Hoàng Minh Suong:

My home is where my children are. I'm beginning to feel more and more Taiwanese because of my children. At first, I wanted to go back (to Vietnam), but day by day, I watched my children growing up. It's like a small tree growing taller and taller, you've got to support it. Then you don't want to go' (interviewed in Jinshan on 2nd June 2009).

The gendered sense of belonging developing alongside the sense of caring duty was commonly narrated by Filipino, Indonesian Chinese and younger PRC Chinese interviewees (older PRC Chinese interviewees in their second marriages were the exception in this regard since they had not given birth to children in Taiwan).

Primordial Identity Reinforced by the State's Construction: Identifying with the Country of Origin

The second scenario gave rise to an occasion when the immigrants were invited to speak about their identification with the country of origin. It was on this occasion that Hồ Minh Mai, a French literature graduate from Hanoi University, proudly announced Vietnam's victory in the 2009 ASEAN Football Championship. Minh Mai also likened the French influence on football in Vietnam to the Japanese influence on baseball in Taiwan. With no

---

3 Manning and Roy mentioned a case in which Mexican-Americans booed the US soccer team when the latter played against the Mexican team in Los Angeles in 1998. The booing of the Mexican-Americans was regarded as showing disloyalty towards the US by Samuel Huntington (2007: 4).

exception, the interviewees attributed their identification with the country of origin to the fact that they had been 'born and bred there'. The deeply imprinted primordial identity would not be removed from their sense of self, although they had begun to develop feelings for Taiwan and to think of themselves as Taiwanese. This enduring primordial link was explained by Hoàng Minh Suong, who also identified with Taiwan because of her motherhood: 'We came from Vietnam. When we returned to Vietnam, we thought of our childhood years and felt that this was indeed where we had been born'. The resilient primordial identity was found universally amongst Chinese, Filipino, Vietnamese and Indonesian Chinese interviewees.

The interviewees' replies also revealed the role that 'the other' played in their national identity and how this role could be reified by the state. As explained above, in the second question, Japan was picked as the common opponent for practical reasons. Nevertheless, this evoked nationalist sentiments in some interviewees. For Zhang Jie, a 42-year-old Sichuan native who had been educated up to junior secondary level, her support for China was not only based on her primordial identity but also framed in war history: 'I hope China will win. In my hometown, we saw films about how Japan savaged China during the war. My granddad and great granddad also told me about their brutality' (interviewed in Taibei [Taipei] on 15th April 2009). During Jie's youthful years, the Chinese cinema was utilised to indoctrinate the nation with nationalism and patriotism (Lu 1997: 6-7). Thus, her testimony conveyed the enduring message that the state construction was interwoven with personal 'memories' that were passed down from generation to generation within the family. In addition to Zhang Jie, one Indonesian Chinese interviewee also placed Japan as the historically hostile *other* to Indonesia (as well as China) in her reply to the second question (see below).

Fluidity of Identity: Strategies for Negotiating the In-Between Situation

Having a real link with both countries, the interviewees were emotional when responding to the first two questions. They endeavoured to seek a strategy to negotiate a way out of the sticky and murky in-between situation. In the following section of this paper, I will discuss the strategies that they employed to manage this emotional in-between situation.

Bandwagoning

Bandwagoning, or identifying with the winner, was one common strategy that was employed. That is, instead of prioritising their support for Taiwan or the country of origin, interviewees supported the winning country. It is argued that identifying with the winner is common behaviour, since fans prefer to 'bask in reflected glory' (End *et al* 2002). However, when the match seemed to represent a showdown between the two senses of belonging, their motivation for supporting the winner was certainly driven by more than a desire to 'bask in reflected glory'.

When there was an acknowledged competence gap between Taiwan and the country of origin, bandwagoning became a rational and logical strategy. This was typified by the analysis of Nguyễn Thanh Xuân, a 30-year-old mother of two who was born and bred in Kien Giang where she had attended primary school for five years. After living in Taiwan for eight years, and realising that football was not popular in Taiwan, Thanh Xuân argued that Taiwan might not be able to defeat Vietnam due to a lack of skill and talent (interviewed in Penghu on 15th June 2009). Likewise, 36-year-old Wong Hong, who was a primary school teacher in Hubei, argued that Taiwan was far more advanced than China in baseball. Therefore, 'it was merely reasonable that one would not support the weaker side' (interviewed in Taipei on 18th March 2009). Siding with the stronger country was therefore a legitimate exit strategy that set them free from the in-between situation.

Withdrawing

Another common strategy is to withdraw from the scenario, or to play the 'indifference card'. The response of Nguyễn Kanh Van, a university drop-out who later worked in a factory in Taiwan before she was married, is a case in point. Kahn Van explained that women in Vietnam also watched football, and that football matches were like a street party where young spectators would race through the streets on their scooters waving the national flag. In the first and second scenarios, she would 'of course, cheer for Taiwan', and cheer for Vietnam. However, when asked what she would do if the match was between Taiwan and Vietnam, she had to ponder a few seconds and then announced: 'This is rather difficult… I'm not that crazy about football anyway, I'd be happy no matter who won' (interviewed in Taibei on 15th April 2009). The conscious disengagement was in strong contrast to her previous enthusiastic support for both countries. This withdrawal, similar to bandwagoning, developed from her awareness of the tug-of-war situation in which she was pressed to divide and prioritise her dual identity.

'I'm Sitting in the Middle'

Nguyễn Kanh Van was not the only one who spoke about the difficulties arising from the in-between situation. The dual identity, the image of a 'tug of war', and the sentiment that their dual identity was tugging them in two different directions was expressed in the following replies:

'The Philippines is my nationality, but I'm here because of my family' (Jennifer);

'My country is the Philippines but I now live in Taiwan, I'm sitting in the middle, I wouldn't want to see them playing, I would run away' (Beth);

'Half of me supports Taiwan and the other half supports Indonesia because I won't forget we're from Indonesia' (Choi Kim Chai);

'I feel both countries are my own land, I wouldn't cheer for either side, I'm in the middle' (Hoàng Minh Suong). (Jennifer and Beth interviewed in Pingdong on 27th and 28th January 2010; Choi interviewed in Penghu on 15th June 2009; Hoàng interviewed in Jinshan on 2nd June 2009).

Unlike those who tried to project themselves as rational and logical beings by bandwagoning or withdrawing, these interviewees emphasized their in-between identity. They expressed the notion that the in-between identity was a result of the interplay of the different driving forces of national identity. One strand of these forces is the primordial identity of the country of origin, whereas the other strand is to identify with Taiwan as their adopted home. As mentioned above, the latter is their relational identity that affiliated them with Taiwan because of their gendered role as a mother. By associating Taiwan with home and family and juxtaposing Taiwan with the country of origin, the difficulty of acting in a tug of war situation, such as a sports event, was explained: one could not prioritise one home over the other. Home is 'there' (the Philippines, China, Vietnam, Indonesia) where one was born and bred; home is also 'here' (Taiwan) where we have built a home and are responsible for the family's wellbeing. Confronting the sticky and murky in-between situation head-on, their in-between identity became one of *liminality*.

The above analysis clearly shows that immigrant women developed a dual identity after emigrating to Taiwan. Expressed via their responses to fictional sports events, the two senses of belonging derived from their primordial attachment to the natal country *as well as* their internalisation of the gendered duty of motherhood fulfilled in Taiwan. For the former, in some cases, it was enhanced by the state's indoctrination or the inheritance of generational memories. The fluidity of their dynamic dual identity was ambiguously pronounced by their strategies for evading or confronting the in-between situation. Whilst there were rational strategies of bandwagoning or withdrawing in order to relieve the tension built into the situation, the in-between identity was expressed by those who were conscious of the difficulty of prioritisation and were therefore reluctant to divide their dual identity.

In the ensuing section, my focus is on the socio-political environment from which immigrant women drew referents to fathom their strategies for negotiating the in-between situation. The cases investigated are the unique experiences of Indonesian Chinese and PRC Chinese. The former is correlated partly to the evolution of their diasporic and hybrid identity as the *ethnic other* in Indonesia, and partly to the discrimination they endured in Taiwan. The latter is overshadowed by the stand-off between Taiwan and China and the overwhelming China-bashing discourse.

Recalling the Memories of Being the Ethnic Other: Indonesian Chinese

The reactions of the Indonesian Chinese to the three scenarios were similar to those discussed above. Nevertheless, for some of them, as the *ethnic other* in Indonesia, their experiences of watching badminton games where ethnic Chinese enjoyed historical dominance gave them distinctive referents with which to respond to the second and third questions.

For 55-year-old Ng Siew Day, the problem of watching Indonesia competing against Taiwan could be resolved if the Indonesian athlete was also ethnic Chinese. Siew Day had a strong diasporic Chinese identity, which was rooted in the Chinese-language education that had been chosen for her by her Fuzhou-origin father. For her, the Cold War legacy remained in that Taiwan was 'Free China' as opposed to 'Communist China' and the people of Taiwan were part of the Chinese nation, hence she did not experience any difficulty in supporting either side because 'both players are Chinese'. She proudly mentioned that the 8-times badminton gold medallist 'Rudy Hartono was Chinese but indigenous Indonesians were very jealous about his success' (interviewed in Tucheng on 28th March 2009). However, if the Indonesian athlete were indigenous Indonesian, she would support Taiwan. So would 63-year-old Choi Sook Yin, for exactly the same reason. For Siew Day and Sook Yin, it was a matter of intuition: their diasporic Chinese identity drove them to support the Chinese – be they ethnic Chinese in Indonesia or Chinse in Taiwan. As a result, their strong diasporic Chinese identity enabled them to prioritise Taiwan over Indonesia; they were not burdened by an in-between identity.

Support for Taiwan found another outlet in 45-year-old Chong Lian Fa. Lian Fa migrated to Taiwan in 1984 when she was nineteen, after her mother's re-marriage to a Mainlander in Taiwan. After living in Taiwan for 26 years and establishing her family there, she considered herself entirely Taiwanese. When asked about badminton, she reminded me that her favourite sport was baseball rather than badminton. However, like Siew Day and Sook Yin, Lian Fa also embraced a strong diasporic Chinese identity that was underpinned by the Cold

War legacy. When she stated that one reason for the Indonesian Chinese people's moving to Taiwan in the 1960s-1980s was that they had 'wanted to return to China', she was narrating a stance once firmly upheld by the government of Taiwan. That is, under Chinese nationalism, the people of Taiwan were said to be Chinese; the KMT government claimed that it was the legitimate government of China and that Taiwan was the spiritual homeland of the Chinese nation. Their diasporic identity epitomised a bygone era when Taiwan under the ROC title of '*Free China'*, competed with the PRC ('*Red China'*) for the political loyalty of Overseas Chinese (Cheng 2014). Lian Fa's diasporic Chinese identity made her response to the second question particularly noteworthy. She explained that she supported Indonesia, but it was not because she had been born and bred there, as her fellow immigrants had claimed. Rather, it was because 'during the war, Japan invaded Indonesia and China, so I'd hope Indonesia would win' (interviewed in Pingdong on 29th January 2010). In other words, the shared victimhood of Indonesia and China directed her diasporic Chinese identity to empathise with Indonesia.

However, a generational change has occurred to the identity of Indonesian Chinese. For 29-year-old Yenny Wong, who was a university graduate, the diasporic Chinese identity was a source of confusion. For Siew Day and Sook Yin, the diasporic Chinese identity was partly rooted in their childhood experiences of the aftermath of the anti-Chinese riots triggered by the failed 1965 military coup of the Indonesian Communist Party (Beijing was suspected of being behind the plot; for information on the military coup, see Anderson and McVey 1971). This political turmoil had a long-lasting impact on their lives since it eventually resulted in their not having access to independent education conducted through the medium of the Chinese language. Not only were they both deprived of education in the Chinese language, but they also found it impossible to attend state schools[4] (for the gradual closing down of independent Chinese schools, see Willmont 1961: 73; 86-87, Tan 1991: 117). In contrast, Yenny was educated at a state school, where the national curriculum was presented through the medium of Indonesian language. One result widely recognised by Yenny and other younger Indonesian Chinese interviewees was their hybrid identity (for the development of the hybrid identity of the Indonesian Chinese, see Handoko 2009). At a young age, while watching a televised badminton match, Yenny had experienced the conflict between diasporic and hybrid indentities at home in her interaction with her family:

'I used to live with my granny and three uncles when I was little. At that time, there was a badminton match between Indonesia and China (the PRC). Without any doubt, I cheered for the Indonesian player, but my uncle scolded me: "Who are you?!" I was thinking, "Am I not living in Indonesia? How can I support players from another country?" I think I'm Indonesian. I have an Indonesian passport. I grew up in Indonesia. Would Mainland China accept us as Chinese? If they don't, why should we consider ourselves as Chinese? Well, in fact, in Indonesia, we're not completely accepted as Indonesian, either. It's rather pathetic for the Chinese in Indonesia – we aren't entirely Chinese, nor are we entirely Indonesian. Nevertheless, at sports events, I still support Indonesia' (interviewed in Gaoxiong [Kaohsiung] on 25th March 2009).

Yenny voluntarily mentioned this childhood memory before I raised the three questions. For Yenny, her knowledge of the 1965 coup, the anti-Chinese riots, and all the consequences

4 Siew Day was ineligible to attend state school because she was not of Indonesian nationality. Sook Yin dropped out of a state school as a result of being bullied by indigenous Indonesian kids.

(including the ban on private education provided through the medium of the Chinese language) had largely been drawn from textbooks while she was being educated in the state system. She was frustrated that in spite of her subjective identification with Indonesia, she and her fellow Chinese were still considered as *the other* in Indonesia.

At a later stage in the interview, I raised the three questions with Yenny. Whilst supporting Taiwan and Indonesia in the first and second scenarios, Yenny prioritised her support for Indonesia over Taiwan in the third scenario - she was not burdened by an in-between identity. Yenny's replies to the three questions were shared by the 37-year-old university graduate, Susani Halim, and the 39-year-old former guest worker, Hoh Foon Lian. Their lack of an in-between identity was a consequence of the condescending and discriminatory attitudes held by the locals towards Indonesia. For Yenny, the discrimination was symbolised by the locals' offensive descriptions of Indonesia ('poor and backward') and indigenous Indonesian domestic workers ('dark and ugly'). For Susani, the feeling of exclusion occurred at market stalls where she was often singled out as a foreigner because of her Mandarin accent. In addition to the exclusion, she also suffered from discrimination in her workplace. She was the director of a community service centre, but drop-in clients often ignored her greeting, and went straight to her Taiwanese friends for consultations. Susani attributed their conscious selection to her Mandarin accent which revealed her Southeast Asian origins. The combination of exclusion and discrimination made Susani's identification with Taiwan only 'half-way': 'I wouldn't cheer for Taiwan 100 per cent unless I were accepted by you (local Taiwanese)'. Foon Lian would hope to see an Indonesian victory over Taiwan so that 'people in Taiwan would know Indonesia isn't that bad, and they wouldn't look down on Indonesia!'(Susani interviewed in Keelung on 23rd March 2009; Foon Lian interviewed in Pingdong on 29th January 2010). They could certainly empathise with Annabelle who 'felt sad' after watching a real basketball match in which the Philippines lost to Taiwan (interviewed in Pingdong on 27th January 2010).

Their testimonies showed clearly that although they held dual identity (supporting Taiwan and Indonesia), they were not subject to the pressure of in-betweenness and encountered very little difficulty in prioritising their Indonesian identity over their Taiwanese identity. This was in strong contrast to the older generation's reaction. Although both recognised their status as *the other* in Indonesia, the older generation prioritised their identity with Taiwan because of their diasporic identity which led them to see themselves as part of the Chinese nation, whereas the younger generation chose the opposite because of their hybrid identity and *also* because they were keenly aware of being excluded and discriminated against by the host society. Sporting events – both real and fictional – became an arena where the generational change in national identity couild be observed, and, more importantly, the environment in which this shift took place.

Sport and Its Political Undercurrents: PRC Chinese

If the political stand-off across the Taiwan Strait is viewed as an enduring match, Taiwan and China have been in a fierce competition for more than six decades in front of domestic and international audiences. During the 1970s, after Taiwan lost its seat at the United Nations in 1970 and it diplomatic relations with the US were severed in 1979, Taiwan was gradually defeated in the race to claim itself as the representative of real China and the Chinese homeland. Nevertheless, after the late 1980s, in the wake of democratisation, Taiwan started to assert itself as a separate and independent political entity. Backed by a purposeful military build-up, however, China appeared to be winning this political competition, since it persistently rejected Taiwan's *de facto* independence. In Taiwan, a discourse on the China Threat was in wide circulation and hostility to China's belligerent posture developed (Chen 2008). The hostility was intertwined with contempt being shown for the allegedly sub-quality made-in-China products (Cheng 2013b: 11). As a result, as shown below, the PRC Chinese immigrants were confronted with unfriendly attitudes which were rooted in domestic electoral politics.

The impact of the strained Taiwan-China relationship and the local hostility showed in the *measured* reactions of Zhu Yongli and Long Yun in their daily lives in the home and workplace. Their responses were marked by their disengagement with the scenario, one result of their keen awareness of the partisan politics underpinned by anti-China sentiments. At home, Yongli, who was the mother of two school-age children, was confronted with anti-China hostility from her condescending and discriminatory Taiwanese-speaking mother-in-law, who instructed Yongli to vote for the pro-independence DPP (Cheng 2013b). As a consequence, Yongli was indifferent to the competition between China and Taiwan: 'Whoever wins or loses means the same to me. If the Mainland wins, the Chinese are happy and you may enjoy basking in their glory (*zhanguang*, 沾光), but the Taiwanese will hate you! Does it matter if you bask in their glory (*zhanguang you zenyang*, 沾光又怎樣)? Will hatred do any good? Whoever wins is really irrelevant to me' (interviewed in Taibei on 21st April 2009). Youngli's withdrawal was a strategy that she employed to prevent herself from being affected by the backlash against Chinese immigrants in Taiwan.

Long Yun, however, endeavoured to maintain a rational and balanced position in the in-between situation. Shanghai-born Long Yun was 42-years-old and the mother of one school-age girl. She held a doctoral degree in science from a foreign country and was offered employment by a publicly-funded research institute after moving to Taiwan. This interview presented her with the opportunity to express her disagreement with the mutual denunciation of the Taiwanese and PRC Chinese. On the one hand, she disapproved of her Taiwanese colleagues for mocking the presumed low-quality China-made laboratory equipment, but on the other, she also disapproved of the popular stigmatisation of the Taiwanese in China:

'I don't particularly want the Mainland to win. The Mainland won [the Olympics baseball match], and they showed off too much. This was really unnecessary. The loser [Taiwan] didn't really need to feel so upset; people in Taiwan shouldn't take it out on their players. If a small team defeated a big team who were supplied with a huge pool of talent, that'd really be a great achievement. I'm not particularly happy about the Mainland's victory.

I don't think I need to be on the side of the Mainland all the time. Sometimes, I feel I should be on the side of Taiwan. [In China] people say that Taiwanese businessmen are stingy and they would stab you on the back; Taiwanese businessmen have earned themselves an unflattering nickname 'taibazi' (台巴子) in China[5]*. I don't really agree with this. I think the Taiwanese are charitable and they gave a lot of donations after the Sichuan Earthquake [in May 2008]. On the other hand, it's true that businessmen can be stingy. I also heard*

5 Originating from the Shanghai dialect, the term '*bazi*' is used to refer to rowdy, stupid, unsophisticated country bumpkins. After *taibazi* gained wide currency in colloquial Mandarin in China, this term acquired distinctive derogatory connotations with regard to Taiwanese people.

about Taiwanese businessmen's extra-marital affairs in China and other things that are beyond [my] imagination' (interviewed in Miaoli on 24th March 2009).

The above statements by Yongli and Yun show that political competition across the Taiwan Strait creates a permanent in-between situation for PRC immigrants in Taiwan. For Yongli, the pressure to prioritise (vote for the DPP) was imposed by her mother-in-law; for Yun, the anti-China hostility was overwhelming in the workplace. Indifference and neutrality presented a way for them to keep their heads above the troubled waters of in-betweenness that had become a constant parameter affecting their relationships with their families at home and their colleagues in the workplace.

Acquiring an Inclusive Identity: Motherhood

The escapism of Yongli and Yun contrasts strongly with the gendered exit strategy adopted by Zhang Jinhua. Jinhua was a former school teacher from Guangxi and an eloquent activist in campaigns to improve the legal treatment of Chinese women in Taiwan. Whilst supporting Taiwan and China in the first and second scenarios, she assigned herself an inclusive identity which embraced the in-betweenness in the third scenario:

'This was like a match fought between my two sons. I wouldn't regard the defeated one as a loser, and I'd be happy whoever won. I hope they enjoyed the match for fun rather than treating it as a life-and-death race. I watched a wrestling match fought between two British brothers. Could you imagine how their mother would feel?' (interviewed in Taibei on 10th March 2009).

By subjectively acting as a caring mother, Jinhua consciously relieved herself from the confrontation of the either-or prioritisation and placed herself in an embracing role that transcended the competition and division. Instead of being confined by the decades-long antagonism between Taiwan and China, Jinhua adopted an inclusive and nurturing identity without being pressed to conform to the norm of singular and exclusive identity. She transformed her presumed subordination to one side or the other as a member of the national community into the un-dividable affection of a caring mother. In her self-claimed role as the mother of the nation, she placed herself in a higher position than Taiwan or China, who were said to be of the same origin. In this gendered position that focuses on mutual wellbeing, there is no room for in-betweenness that is grounded on prioritisation, division and confrontation.

Conclusion

By exploring immigrant women's experiences on the casual occasion of sports events, this paper has revealed the understated complex and mundaneness of performing identity in the personal interaction in the home and workplace. The fact that some interviewees spontaneously mentioned certain sports events that bore varying degrees of significance or relevance to their personal lives suggests that experiences gained at sports events could be evoked as meaningful presentations of their fluid identities. The findings of this paper challenged the blindness of the 'cricket test' with the existence of dual identity and its hegemonic pressure on immigrants to prove their singular loyalty to the host nation-state. This paper recognised the legitimacy of dual identity and found that it was formed by the intertwined primordial identity of the country of origin and the gendered identity that derived from the immigrants' motherhood which saw Taiwan as the adopted home. The experiences of immigrant women in Taiwan showed that the fluidity and contingency of dual identity was most pronounced when they were caught in an in-between situation that was embodied by a sports event. To navigate themselves through the in-between complex, they employed a bandwagoning strategy in order to appear logical and rational, or withdrew from the situation in order to free themselves from the prioritising pressure. The dual identity led to an in-between situation when the immigrants subjectively felt the difficulty of prioritising or dividing their dual identity. The subtlety, ambiguity and sophistication of the strategies that they employed underlined their cautious efforts to negotiate an escape route when placed under pressure to show undivided loyalty and to avoid appearing inauthentic or contradictory.

This paper also showed that the expression of national identity at sporting events was not isolated from the macro socio-political environment. The experiences of the Indonesian Chinese and the PRC Chinese can be seen as a case in point, and highlighted the fact that their responses to the fictional matches derived from historical and political contexts. The narratives of the Indonesian Chinese were testimony to the shifting national identity amongst the ethnic Chinese in Indonesia. Since they were not weighted down with the burden of in-between identity, the diasporic Chinese identity of the older generation led them to identify with Taiwan, but the hybrid indentity of the younger generation led them to identify with Indonesia. For the PRC Chinese, in-betweenness was a reality experienced in daily life in the home and in the workplace, given the unceasing confrontation between China and Taiwan. Although disengagement and escapism might prevent a backlash, a gendered position – projecting oneself as the mother of the nation – could help to transcend the in-betweenness. These findings do not only deepen our understanding of the way that identity may be thrown into flux, but also, and more importantly, they *contextualise* the existence of dual identity, the situation when dual identity becomes in-betweenness, and the real difficulties that arise from prioritising or dividing dual identity.

To conclude, this paper showed that 'self-other' and subjective identification-objective inclusion forms the axis for immigrant women to position themselves in the host society. If the 'cricket test' has any remaining value for probing immigrants' national identity, it is as a means of deepening our understanding of how a subjective identification with the host country develops and how the identification with the country of origin is sustained; it should be used to assess the kinds of constraints that force immigrants to adopt specific strategies to deal with the complexities of in-betweenness. These findings would help us to understand how national identity can be expressed, challenged, sustained or reaffirmed through the activities undertaken in our everyday lives.

References

Anderson, Benedict and McVey, Ruth (1971) *A Preliminary Analysis of the October 1, 1965 Coup in Indonesia*, Ithaca: Cornell University Press.

An Biyun (An Pi-yun 安碧芸) and Luo Bilian (Loh Phail-lean 駱碧蓮) (2010) 'Bangqiu buneng chengshou zhi zhong: 2008 Beijing aoyun bangqiu sai guozu yishi baodao fenxi' 棒球不能承受之重：2008 北京奧運棒球賽國族意識報導分析 [The unbearable heaviness of baseball: An analysis of nationalism in the 2008 Beijing baseball competition news coverage] *Chaoyang renwen shehui xuekan [Chaoyang journal of humanities and social sciences]* 8(1) (June): 34-70.

Antolihao, Lou (2012) 'From Baseball Colony to Basketball Republic: Postcolonial Transition and the Making of a National Sport in the Philippines', *Sport in Society: Cultures, Commerce, Media, Politics* 15(10): 1396-1412.

Bairner, Alan and Hwang, Dong-Jhy (2011) 'Representing Taiwan: International Sport, Ethnicity and National Identity in the Republic of China', *International Review for the Sociology of Sport* 46(3): 231-248.

Basch, Linda *et al* (1994) *Nations Unbound: Transnational Projects, Postcolonial Predicaments and Deterritorialized Nation-States*, Langhorne: Gordon and Breach.

Brubaker, Rogers, and Cooper, Frederick (2007) 'Beyond Identity', *Theory and Society* 29: 1-47.

Brown, Colin (2006) 'Playing the Game: Ethnicity and Politics in Indonesian Badminton', *Indonesia* 81 (April): 71-93.

Cai, Kevin (2008) *The Political Economy of East Asia: Regional and National Division*. Basinstoke: Palgrave Macmillion.

Chen, Ching-chang (2008) The 'China Threat' in the Eyes of the Taiwanese: A Reflection on Taiwan's Security Policy, 1988-2008, PhD thesis, Aberystwyth: University of Wales.

Chen, Gerald (2002) 'From the "Olympic Formula" to the Beijing Games: Towards Greater Integration across the Taiwan Strait?', *Cambridge Review of International Affairs* 15(1): 141-148.

Cheng, Isabelle (2013a) 'Making Foreign Women the Mother of Our Nation: The Exclusion and Assimilation of Immigrant Women in Taiwan', *Asian Ethnicity* 14(2): 157-179.

Cheng, Isabelle (2013b). *Ballot Paper as the Weapon of the Weak: Resistance of Immigrant Women in the Private Home in Taiwan*, China Policy Institute Blog, University of Nottingham. Available at https://blogs.nottingham.ac.uk/chinapolicyinstitute/2013/09/17/ballot-paper-as-the-weapon-of-the-weak-resistance-of-immigrant-women-in-the-private-home-in-taiwan/ (accessed on 23rd April 2015).

Cheng, Isabelle (2013a) 'Home-going or Home-making? The Citizenship Legislation and Chinese Identity of Indonesian Chinese Women in Taiwan,' in Chiu, Kuei-fen, Fell, Dafydd, Lin, Ping (Eds.) *Migration to and from Taiwan*, London: Routlege; 135-158.

Cheng, Isabelle (2013b). Bridging across or Sandwiched between? The Political Re-socialisation of Chinese Immigrant Women and Their Encounter with Taiwanese Identity, *Asian Ethnicity*, DOI 10.1080/14631369.2014.973003: 1-21

Colombijn, Freek (2000) 'The Politics of Indonesian Football,' *Archipel* 59: 171-199.

Dyreson, Mark (2003) 'Globalising the Nation-Making Process: Modern Sport in World History', the International Journal of the History of Sport 20(1): 91-106.

End, Christian M, *et al* (2002) 'Identifying with Winners: A Reexamination of Sport Fans' Tendency to BIRG', *Journal of Applied Social Psychology* 32(5): 1017-1030, May.

Grzymala-Kazlowska, Aleksandra (2002) 'The Formation of Ethnic Representation: The Vietnamese in Poland', *Sussex Migration Working Paper No. 8, Sussex Centre for Migration Research*, University of Sussex.

Handoko, Francisca (2009) 'Education, Language Use and Shifting Identities among Ethnic Chinese in Indonesia', *Chinese Southern Diaspora Studies* 3: 183-192.

Hourlihan, Barrie (1997) 'Sport, National Identity and Public Policy', *Nations and Nationalism* 3(1): 113-137.

Hsia, Hsiao-Chuan (1997) *Selfing and Othering in the 'Foreign Bride' Phenomenon : A Study of Class, Gender and Ethnicity in the Transnational Marriages between Taiwanese men and Indonesian Women*, PhD Thesis, University of Florida.

Knop, Karen (2001) ‚Relational Nationality: On Gender and Nationality in International Law', in Aleinikoff, T. Alexander, Klusmeyer, Douglas (eds.) *Citizenship Today: Global Perspectives and Practices*, Washington D.C.: Carnegie Endowment for International Peace, 89-124.

Kofman, Eleonore (2005) 'Citizenship, Migration and the Reassertion of National Identity', *Citizenship Studies* 9(5): 453-467.

Leifer, Michael (2001) 'Taiwan and South-East Asia: The Limits to Pragmatic Diplomacy', *The China Quarterly* 165: 173-185.

Lin, Chien-yu, Lee, Ping-Chao (2007) 'Sport as a Medium of National Resistance: Politics and Baseball in Taiwan during Japanese Colonialism, 1895–1945', *The International Journal of the History of Sport* 24(3): 319-337.

Lin, Chien-yu et al (2010) 'Taiwan and the 2001 Baseball World Cup: The National Impact of a World Sporting Event', *The International Journal of the History of Sport* 27(13): 2234-2254.

Lu, Sheldon Hsiao-peng (1997) *Transnational Chinese Cinemas*, Hawai'i: University of Hawai'I Press.

Lu, Suping (1999) 'Nationalistic Feelings and Sports: The Incident of the Overseas Chinese Protest Against NBC's Coverage of the Centennial Olympic Games', *Journal of Contemporary China* 8(22): 517-533.

Maguire, Joseph, Tuck, Jason (1998) 'Global Sports and Patriot Games: Rugby Union and National Identity in a United Sporting Kingdom since 1945', *Immigrants & Minorities* 17(1): 103-126.

Manning, Alan, Roy, Sanchari (2007) *Culture Clash or Culture Club? The Identity and Attitudes of Immigrants in Britain*, CEP Discussion Paper No. 790, London: Centre for Economic Performance, London School of Economics and Political Science.

Ministry of the Interior (MoI) (2013) *Statistical Yearbook of Interior* (Acquirement of the R.O.C. Nationality by Causes) at http://sowf.moi.gov.tw/stat/year/list.htm (accessed on 5th April 2013).

Morris, Andrew (2006) Taiwan: Baseball, Colonialism, Nationalism, in Gblech, George (ed.) *Baseball without Borders: The International Pastime*, Lincoln: University of Nebraska Press, 65-88

Neizhengbu (Ministry of the Interior (MoI) (2004) Waji yu dalu peiou shenghuo zhuangkuang diaocha 外籍與大陸配偶生活狀況調查) [*The census on the living conditions of foreign and mainland spouses*. Taibei: MoI.

Ru-chuguo yimin shu 入出國及移民署 (National Immigration Agency (NIA)(2013) Waiji peiou renshu u dalu (han Gang-Ao) peiou renshu 外籍配偶人數與大陸(含港澳)配偶人數 [Numbers of foreign spouses and mainland Spouses (including spouses from Hong Kong and Macao), February, at http://www.immigration.gov.tw/ct.asp?xItem =1186477&ctNode=29699&mp=1 (accessed on 4th April 2013).

Ong, Aihwa (1999) *Flexible Citizenship: the Cultural Logics of Transnationality*, Durham: Duck University Press.

Selya, Roger Mark (2004) *Development and Demographic Change in Taiwan*, Singapore: World Scientific.

Smith, Adrian, Porter, Dilwyn (eds.) (2004), *Sport and National Identity in the Post-War World*. London: Routledge.

Smith, Tom W., Jarkko, Lars (1998) *National Pride: A Cross-Country Analysis*, Chicago: National Opinion Research Center, University of Chicago, May.

Sunito, Ignatius (2003) 'Birmingham Menanti Ukiran Prestasi Bulutangkis Indonesia' *Bola Sportsline*, at http://www.bolanews.com/sunito/6740.php, 18 July.

Tan, Mely G. (1991) 'The Social and Cultural Dimension of the Role of Ethnic Chinese in Indonesian Society', *Indonesia* 51: 113-125.

Thomas, Mandy (2001) 'Public Spaces/Public Disgraces: Crowds and the State in Contemporary Vietnam', *Sojourn: Journal of Social Issues in Southeast Asia* 16(2) (October) 306-330.

Wang, Hong-zen , Chang, Shu-ming (2002) 'The Commodification of International Marriages: Cross-border Marriage Business in Taiwan and Viet Nam', *International Migration* 40(6): 93-116.

Willmott, Donald E. (1961) *the National Status of the Chinese in Indonesia: 1900-1958*. NY: Cornell University.

Wu, Yu-Shan (1995) 'Taiwan in 1994: Managing a Critical Relationship', *Asian Survey* 35(1): 61-69, January.

Xu, Xin (2006) 'Modernizing China in the Olympic Spotlight: China's National Identity and the 2008 Beijing Olympiad', The Sociological Review 54 (Issue Supplement s2), December, 90-107.

Yu, Junwei et al (2008) 'Dancing around the Elephant: The Beijing Olympics – Taiwanese Reflections and Reactions', *the International Journal of the History of Sport* 25(7): 826-850.

Yuh, Ji-Yeon (2002) *Beyond the Shadow of Camptown- Korean Military Brides in America*, New York: New York University.

Lara Momesso[1]

From *Someone*, to *No-one*, to a *New-one*: A Subjective View of Taiwan's Immigration Policies in the Context of Multiculturalism

Since the 2000s, the Taiwanese government has undertaken significant efforts to encourage social integration and the recognition of immigrants in the expectation that local communities would follow their lead. A number of scholars have, however, criticised Taiwan's multicultural policies, claiming that these are based on an assimilationist model that is focused on educating migrant communities on local habits and heritage rather than on recognising the migrants' original cultures. In this paper, I argue that assessing migrants' integration and encouraging their recognition in receiving societies should not only entail analyses of governmental policies and social responses to these; it is also important to consider the heterogeneity of identities and interests co-existing within immigrant communities, the possible changes in an individual's status during the process of migration, and the migrants' responses to the structural system that is shaping their lives.
This paper draws on critical literature that takes into consideration the diverse needs and interests that make up ethnic and national communities to present an analysis of the impact of immigration policies on individuals whose backgrounds differ from the average expected from the category to which they belong. In this context, migration is perceived and examined as a long-term process of transformation that starts before the actual departure and continues after arrival. The subjective experiences of migration and adaptation in the receiving society of the three marriage migrants from the People's Republic of China that are described here seem to suggest that multiculturalism should be assessed according to the way in which the individual negotiates a path through the structural inequalities that he/she encounters, depending on the different positions in the social hierarchies that he/she occupies. The results obtained here show that immigrants who have previously held an established position in their country of origin and have enjoyed a high level of social recognition do not always find this helpful when they are going through the process of adaptation and trying to gain recognition in the receiving society.[2]

A Subjective Perspective of Multiculturalism

Since the late 1960s, multiculturalism has emerged amongst Western democracies as a response to the struggles of national minorities and immigrant populations for recognition and the accommodation of ethnic diversity (Kymlicka 2012: 8). The earlier experiments have generated a scholarly debate that theorises on multiculturalism in the light of more or less successful empirical cases. On the one hand, Kymlicka's works (1995, 2007, 2012) offer evidence to the effect that multiculturalism could result in positive examples of civic integration and democratic citizenship, but on the other, scholars such as Parekh (2000), Stjernfelt (2012) and Shachar (2001), shed light on the pitfalls arising from multicultural practices

1 I am grateful to the three respondents who shared their experiences and thoughts with me. I also thank the anonimous reviewer, as well as Professor Anthony Fielding, Dr Isabelle Cheng and Dr Bonny Ling for the helpful suggestions and comments at different stages of this paper writing.

2 All the names used in this paper are pseudonyms.

when these are limited to cultural and/or folkloristic traditions rather than in favour of social and political integration.

One line of criticism is that multiculturalism neglects personal interests in order to accommodate group interests. In Shachar's words (2001: 2), multicultural policies that aim to level the gap between minority communities and the wider society 'allow systematic maltreatment of individuals within the accommodated group', nullifying his/her rights. The author refers to this phenomenon as the 'paradox of multicultural vulnerability', since individuals within the group can be injured by the reforms that are designed to promote their status as a group members in the state (Shachar 2001: 2). Yuval-Davis (1997) also criticises multiculturalism for sometimes constructing migrant populations in terms of ethnic and racial collectivities with no regard for the needs and interests of the individual. These scholars suggest that a government's actions, aimed to favour (or disfavour) social inclusion and recognition and based on a categorisation of society in sub-collectivities along shared cultural or ethnic features, could be problematic. It is important to consider the gaining of social inclusion and recognition as a process rather than as fixed events in the life of an individual and it is equally important to look at the various forms of social positioning, powers, and interests that exist within socially constructed sub-collectivities. For instance, as Mahler and Pessar (2001: 445-446) suggest, by looking at migrants' positioning in the social hierarchy of the sending society and how this changes after they have moved into the receiving country, it is possible to deconstruct the biased understanding of social categories.

Building on these reflections, this paper explores the uneven path towards inclusion in the receiving society that was undertaken by three immigrants from the People's Republic of China (PRC) who arrived in Taiwan at a time when the Taiwanese government was promoting multiculturalism to foster the image of Taiwan as a democratic and inclusive nation. The struggle over issues related to the sovereignty of Taiwan between the PRC and the Republic of China (ROC) was one of the reasons for the selection of this sub-category of marriage migrants, since they were subjected to exceptional treatment in Taiwan, but the homeland background of the three selected informants, who are young, highly-educated professionals, constitutes the main reason for focusing on them, because in this they seem to differ from the average PRC marriage migrants described in the literature. This paper is based on the results of broader ethnographic research that was carried out between May 2008 and October 2011, including in-depth interviews and participant observation with more than 100 individuals, including marriage migrants and their family members, civil society practitioners, and government officials.

As the narratives of my respondents will show, their experiences of social integration and recognition in Taiwan could not be isolated from the social positions that these migrants had held before moving to Taiwan. Neither could their experiences be seen as a single event in their lives, since the gap between the 'someone' that they had been in their homeland and the 'no-one' that they became in Taiwan tended to be levelled out after they had acquired citizenship rights in the following years. This paper suggests that patterns of inclusion and the recognition of immigrant communities should be assessed in the light of the systemic inequalities shaping these social groups, their individual positions in society and their personal strategies for negotiating through the surrounding environment. In the next section of this paper, before entering into the specificity of the lives of my respondents, I will explore the emergence of multiculturalism in Taiwan and, in opposition to this, the unequal treatment reserved for marriage migrants from the PRC as potential enemies of the nation.

Marriage Migrants and Multiculturalism in Taiwan

In 1997, the Taiwanese government revised the constitution to claim that the ROC recognised and supported multiculturalism. The values of multiculturalism were originally applied to national minorities, such as aboriginal and Hakka communities, and they became an imperative for the Taiwanese state, interpreted as a way of fostering its image of a modern, democratic and friendly country (Wang 2004: 306; Wang 2005: 174-175; Cheng and Fell 2014: 77). Taiwan's social demography has, however, changed extensively since the late 1980s. A labour shortage on the island motivated the arrival of foreign workers from Southeast Asian countries (Philippines, Thailand and Indonesia), and a shortage of marriageable women in a society with a high male-female ratio motivated the increasing presence of foreign spouses, mainly from the PRC, Vietnam and Indonesia (Kim and Oh 2012: 115). This massive influx of immigrants for labour and marriage posed significant challenges to the discourse on 'multicultural Taiwan'.

In the early 2000s, therefore, when the presence of immigrants in Taiwanese society could no longer be ignored, the Taiwanese government extended the principles of multiculturalism to include the new immigrant populations. A number of positive actions were introduced for the purpose of increasing awareness of the immigrant populations and favouring their social inclusion (Bélanger et al. 2010: 1114; Kim and Oh 2012: 120; Wang 2005: 175). Great emphasis was placed on marriage migrants because, differently from the majority of labour migrants, they would live permanently on the island and contribute to the growth of the nation by giving birth to Taiwanese children. Furthermore, legislative reforms were enacted to improve marriage migrants' access to citizenship rights, a more sensitive and less discriminative language was introduced to address this group, and a network of services and institutions was developed to advance their social and cultural rights (Bélanger et al. 2010: 1114).

Despite these top-down efforts to favour inclusion, a number of problems still persisted with regard to marriage migrants. Seen as causes of Taiwan's social problems, such as prostitution and broken families, they were believed to have a negative impact on 'population quality' in Taiwan (Hsia 2007). Presumed to come from culturally inferior countries, they were expected to adopt the Taiwanese culture and identity and abandon their own. Since the majority were women, they were constructed as mothers, daughters-in-law and wives, and they were ascribed mainly to the reproductive sphere of the family (Tsai and Hsiao 2006; Bélanger et al. 2010; Wang and Bélanger 2008; Sandel and Liang 2010). These discrepancies show a tension, in Taiwan, between the imperative to respect diversity, integration, hybridity, and the expectations, imposed on migrants, to transform themselves into citizens suited to Taiwanese cultural and social standards.

With regard to marriage migrants from the PRC, the above reflections are further enriched by political and cultural connotations that are unique in the cross-Strait cultural, economic and political context. On the one hand, due to shared ethnicity, language and cultural traditions, PRC spouses did not face a number of the challenges that were experienced by other Southeast Asian spouses, such as difficulties in communicating with family members and the local community, and understanding Chinese culture and the Mandarin language. On the other hand, in a context that was dominated by the struggle for sovereignty over the island of Taiwan between the governments of the PRC and the ROC, the logic of nationalism constructed PRC marriage migrants as a threat to national security and sovereignty (Shih 1998: 293). For this reason, although some financial resources were allocated to facilitate PRC marriage migrants' integration and well-being in Taiwan, the immigration policies and public discourse related to this sub-category did not match the multicultural ideals that had been promoted by the Taiwanese state since the early 2000s. Quotas for the various steps in the documentation process produced extensive waiting periods for entering the island, while complex visa and residency requirements restricted the migrants' freedom of movement and actions (Cheng and Fell 2014; Friedman 2010a; King 2011; Yang and Lee 2009). The media discourse further legitimised this unfair treatment. According to Shih (1998), in the 1990s, certain Taiwanese media portrayed PRC marriage migrants in negative terms, presenting them as a potential threat to national security (p. 300). This continued until the first half of the 2000s. For example, a green-leaning newspaper associated Chinese spouses with prostitution and the spread of disease, viewing them as a threat to national security and describing their children as a social problem for Taiwan (Taipei Times 2003a, 2003b, 2003c).

The literature abounds with accounts of the consequences of these systemic inequalities that positioned PRC marriage migrants differently to other marriage migrants in the political discourse as well as in the collective imagination (i.e. Liao 2007; Friedman 2010a; Friedman 2010b; Tseng et al. 2013; Yang and Lee 2009). As King (2011: 185-186) suggests, this was a 'nationalistic framework' that burdened marriage migrants and their families with a biased social identity and placed them under financial and family stress. Friedman (2010a: 92) also argues that the regulatory system forged the migrant population's exceptionality, undermining the principles of equality embedded in the constitution. These accounts challenge the authenticity of multiculturalism in Taiwan and offer a clear overview of the systemic structures that shaped PRC marriage migrants as a social category. They do not, however, succeed in informing the reader on how this exceptional treatment can affect single individuals, especially when their status does not correspond with the average expected from the category with which are associated.

As a matter of fact, most of the mainstream literature starts from the assumption that the PRC spouses are women from less-advantaged social classes who arrived in Taiwan in the early 2000s. There are however other cases that deserve mention, not only because cross-Strait marriage migration, during the last decade, has diversified extensively in terms of the actors, trajectories and motivation for migrating, but also because of the increasing statistical presence of other categories of migrants (Momesso 2015a, 2015b; Friedman 2012).

In the following sections of this paper, I will present the lived experiences of three marriage migrants whose personal and family backgrounds differ from those presented in the mainstream literature. My main objective is to problematise the sub-category of PRC marriage migrants and the impact that external factors can have on their social recognition and inclusion. Ultimately, this analysis offers significant insights into multicultural practices in Taiwan.

Three Ordinary Stories

Earlier marriages across the Taiwan Strait, often involving middle-aged women from the PRC who married older men retired from the Nationalist Army, reflect a context in which the PRC was still affected by widespread poverty, and mobility across the Taiwan Strait was still relatively limited. In these circumstances, marriage was often seen as a strategy for increasing a person's mobility and access to life opportunities (Momesso 2015b: 60). Since the early 2000s, however, the situation has gradually changed. A more dynamic social and economic reality has emerged in the PRC that offers new opportunities for its citizens. Not only has the liberalisation of movement across the Taiwan Strait occurred as a consequence of improved cross-Strait relations, but the international position of the PRC and Taiwan has also transitioned through a process of reconfiguration, with the PRC ascending as a global economic power and Taiwan descending the global ladder. One immediate consequence was the greater heterogeneity of those who married across this border, the reasons why they married and their family arrangements (Momesso 2015b: 61; Friedman 2012: 231). The identities of Chengjie (interviewed on 19 July 2011), Linuo (interviewed on 17 June 2008 and 22 June 2011) and Xingmei (interviewed on 8 October 2011), the three informants on whom this paper is based, reflect the heterogeneity of citizens from the PRC, newly-arrived in Taiwan. Chengjie, a young man from Inner Mongolia, used to work as a professional tour guide in China; Linuo, a woman from Beijing, used to work as a government civil servant; Xingmei was an elementary school teacher from Jinan, the capital city of Shandong province. The accounts of Chengjie, Linuo and Xingmei show three possible identities among the PRC citizens married to Taiwanese citizens, which, as of January 2015, reached a total of 323,722 individuals (Ministry of Interior 2015).[3]

Chengjie was working as a tour guide in the PRC when he met Xuefei, the woman he fell in love with at first sight. She was a student of law in Taipei, and had travelled to China on a school trip that had been organised by her university; Chengjie happened to be the tour guide for her group. The two of them remained in contact with each other, keeping in touch through emails, phone messages and phone calls for several years. Then, since it had become difficult to maintain contact while living apart, they decided to marry. For Chengjie, who had grown up in a modest family in China, life was not easy back home. Without the proper contacts, it was hard for Chengjie to achieve anything, especially in terms of work opportunities. Filled with contempt towards his own country for not offering him enough opportunities, he was glad to have a good reason to go to a place where he would experience more equality. His hope was that, in Taiwan, he would be able to achieve what he had not had the opportunity to do back home. For Chengjie, therefore, marriage was not simply a matter of love, it was also the first step towards acquiring freedom and accessing new life opportunities. Chengjie moved to Taiwan in 2003.

Linuo, a happy, confident woman, lived in her own apartment in Beijing, where she led an independent and successful life. With a degree from Zhejang University's College of Economics, she was working as a civil servant when she met her future husband, a man from Taiwan on a business trip to the PRC. As Linuo recollected,

When he went to Beijing, I was in the USA for work. For several reasons, I had to go back earlier to China and we eventually met at a friend's gathering. He immediately told me he liked me. I liked him too. He is a talkative person with a good sense of humour and interesting. In four-five months we understood that we really liked each other, so we decided to marry and I moved to Taiwan. I tried to insist to him that we should stay in Beijing. I already had my house, friends and career over there. But he really didn't want that. It was mostly a

[3] Citizens from Hong Kong and Macao are not included.

question of pride: he said 'I am the one who should have to take care of the family.' So I had to compromise.

In June 2004, Linuo, just turned forty, resigned from her prestigious job and moved from the political and cultural centre of the PRC, to Xinzhu (Hsinchu), a relatively small city on the west coast of Taiwan.

Xingmei was living a relatively serene life in Jinan, the capital city of Shandong province. In her mid-twenties, she was surrounded by her friends and family, and did not feel any urge to find a boyfriend. She met Yijun, the man who later became her husband, thanks to a relative who acted as a mediator. Although it was not love at first sight, the two young people kept in touch and eventually decided to become a couple. Given that in the early 2000s, only specific categories of citizens from the PRC were permitted to enter Taiwan, when the couple had to switch from virtual to physical reality, their meeting points were mostly restricted to Chinese territory. Therefore, the only opportunities they had to further their acquaintance were on Yijun's visits to Jinan, which were always too short and never enough to satisfy the two lovers' desire to be together. In September 2008, the two of them decided, as Yijun stated, to 'take the risk' of marrying someone they thought they knew well, whose relationship, however, had mainly developed through online chats, short visits, and phone calls. The year that Xingmei turned twenty-eight, she gave up her job, her family, her friends, and all her security to follow her new husband to a place she had never had the chance to see before. Her dream, their shared dream, was that with Yijun close to her, she would be able to overcome any difficulty.

The accounts of Chengjie, Linuo and Xingmei depict three relatively ordinary love and life stories, where personal hopes and dreams intermingled with the uncertainties of real life. These identities and romances, however, meant little to the Taiwanese state, where the main concern was with the dramatic increase in cross-Strait marriages which were believed to be motivated by economic interests rather than love, and to pose a threat to national security and sovereignty. When my three informants arrived in Taiwan, they had to face the challenges and the consequences of being framed as an undesired 'other.'

From Being *Some-one* to Becoming *No-one*

Chengjie and Linuo arrived in Taiwan in the early 2000s, at one of the most difficult times for PRC marriage migrants. The Democratic Progressive Party (DPP), whose pro-independence orientation did not favour the recognition of PRC marriage migrants in Taiwan, was ruling the country. Despite the party's emphasis on multicultural ideals, PRC spouses were subjected to tough treatment with strict legal restrictions, negative media coverage and social stigmatisation (Hsia 2007; Lu 2008).

The majority of marriage migrants from the PRC suffered the consequences of these structural inequalities. Deprived of the right to work, they were placed in a position of subordination to their Taiwanese spouses. This also had an impact on the entire household, and lower-class families in particular, since one of the members of the family was not allowed to engage in formal employment. It was not merely a matter of the lack of the right to work: PRC spouses were left dependent on their Taiwanese partners and families in several other spheres of their lives. For instance, they were required to provide proof of financial resources and a letter of guarantee from their partner in order to acquire Taiwanese citizenship. Also, in the case of divorce or when the partner died, the migrant was required to leave the country within a short period of time. Qualifications from most PRC universities were not recognised in Taiwan (Friedman 2010a, 2010b; Liao 2007; Yang and Lee 2009). My respondents were among those subjected to these structural constraints.

For instance, Chengjie experienced the limitations of being a PRC citizen in Taiwan. Unable to establish himself in China because of his lack of powerful networks, Chengjie realised that in Taiwan, his status had not improved. His greatest concern was that as a citizen of the PRC, he would not be able to engage in paid employment until he had obtained the status of permanent residency, which would take about six years. This restriction, which effectively limited a migrant's sphere of action to the domestic and reproductive sphere, found easy acceptance if the migrant were a woman, since she could fulfil society's expectations of herself by playing the role of mother, wife, and daughter-in-law, but would entail a series of other issues if the migrant were a male. As a matter of fact, financial stability and personal autonomy were not Chengjie's main concerns; he was more worried about his social status and recognition. As Chengjie disappointedly remarked: 'It is important for a man to earn money and be the *father* in the family. A woman can stay at home and look after the children and elders, but a man's position is outside; he should work and provide financially for the rest of the family. Being deprived of the means to meet such expectations is unfair.' The fact that he was unable to provide financial support for his wife combined with his PRC origins fuelled his in-laws' contempt for him.

Similarly, for Linuo, access to work was neither a financial issue nor a matter of economic independence. Linuo's personal and family economic situation was relatively stable, and she did not need to work. She enjoyed her husband's support and understanding, and did not need to establish further financial autonomy for herself. Her situation was quite different to that of Chengjie's: she was not expected, as a woman, to find employment. On the other hand, Linuo wanted to work: she perceived employment as a basic right that all humans should be entitled to, regardless of their gender and their reason for emigrating to another country. Above all, Linuo perceived employment as part of her identity, rather than something on which the financial situation of a family depended, since she saw it as the means for her to achieve her own personal ambitions and recognition.

Before marriage my life was dedicated completely to my career. It was very difficult for me to adapt to this new role of mother and housewife. In the first three years, I just wanted to go back to China with my daughter. I wanted to start working again, to be independent again, to have my own space and self-recognition.

In the loneliness and emptiness of her new life, her daughter became her main interest: 'I went through much bitterness and hardness. Especially the first three years. I didn't have any friends, any contacts. I only took care of my baby daughter.'

In 2004, however, the DPP granted a number of concessions in response to civil society's requests for the equal treatment of PRC marriage migrants. For instance, with regard to the right to work, PRC marriage migrants were allowed access to formal employment if they had been victims of domestic violence, if they had borne children or if the Taiwanese spouse was a low-income earner, aged over 65, disabled, or suffering from a severe disease or illness. It is clear that this concession, most likely motivated by the state's interest in reducing the burden of these families on public resources, was of little help to individuals such as Chengjie and Linuo, who despite living in relatively stable financial and family conditions still wanted their talents and skills to be acknowledged.

As a result of the shift in the political arena and the improvement in cross-Strait relations after 2008, the new party in power, the Nationalist government (Guomindang GMD), embraced a more indulgent policy towards immigrants from the PRC. For instance, the procedure for acquiring Taiwanese citizenship was curtailed from eight to six years; PRC marriage migrants obtained the right to remain in Taiwan if their Taiwanese partner died; restrictions on the right to work were lifted; educational qualifications from a number of Chinese universities were recognised (Friedman 2010a; Tseng et al. 2013). PRC marriage migrants were able to benefit from these concessions, regardless of their family's economic situation. But some of the old problems remained and new ones emerged.

Xingmei arrived in Taiwan in 2008. Previously a teacher in public institutions, she had hoped that she would be able to continue with her career. However, despite the fact that PRC marriage migrants were entitled to work, she could not compete in national examinations for positions in public schools until ten years after she had been granted Taiwanese citizenship (a total of 16 years, if we consider the average time of six years that it took to become a citizen). As she argued, she would be in her mid-forties when she would finally be able to take part in these national examinations, and at that age, it would be almost impossible to compete with other applicants, who would most likely be in their twenties. Her career as a teacher was finished. Her only chance, for the years to come, was to accept temporary jobs as a replacement for ordinary teachers or to search for an occupation in private schools. 'Such a waste of resources both for the family and for society!' Xingmei argued disappointedly.

Before marrying Yijun, Xingmei was to some extent prepared to face the challenge of being a PRC spouse in Taiwan. She also enjoyed the full support of her understanding and sensitive husband. Yet she soon realised that the problem was a strain on their good will and health of their union:

Before marrying and coming to Taiwan, my husband prepared me with regard to the various problems that mainland spouses may face in this island. We have to work hard to find a solution to these problems, both individually and as part of a family. Yet this is not sufficient. We need the support of the broader society and of the government otherwise we cannot go too far. And often we lack this broader support, we are hampered instead!

In her first months in Taiwan, without any friends other than her husband, Xingmei spent most of her time in the solitude of her home, loafing, getting bored, and waiting for Yijun to come back from work. Her hesitant personality further contributed to her unhappiness.

In circumstances in which they could not nurture their skills and talents and could not preserve the same status as that enjoyed back home, my respondents faced the dilemma of becoming 'no-one' as soon as they arrived in Taiwan. Linuo recollected a lesson she was taught during one lecture organised by a Taiwanese civil society organisation in cooperation with the National Immigration Agency as part of a multicultural activity packet:

I will never forget what my lecturer said during one of the classes I attended: 'A person is like a cup: if you don't pour out the old water you cannot refill it with new water.' I had to forget everything of myself and recognise myself in this new nation and society. I had to acquire the useful tools and knowledge to start a new life here.

Her previous life style, her privileged position as a highly educated, professional woman residing in one of the most vibrant cities in East Asia and China, did not have any value for her life in Taiwan. As she argued, 'I am from a different social level but here I am zero!'

She admitted that this had been hard to accept in the first instance since she had had to position herself at the same level as many other spouses who had had no education, belonged to lower social classes, or came from rural areas. The higher their social status before departure, the more significant the effort needed to erase their previous identity and accept the new one imposed on them. This could have serious consequences for their sense of self. As Charles Taylor (1994: 25) pointed out, '[n]on-recognition or misrecognition can inflict harm, can be a form of oppression, imprisoning someone in a false, distorted, and reduced mode of being'. To my question 'What do Chinese spouses need the most?' a young woman once said:

We need to acquire a certain degree of self-respect, self-esteem, and dignity. And to do so, others have to respect you! And we also need to be treated in an equal way! You realise that these factors are important when people discriminate against you. And you understand that this is not fair. You shift from China, where you are someone and you have a position, to here, where you are no-one, you are at the bottom! It is very difficult to accept it. (Interviewed on 22 June 2011)

As Wang (2005) explained, the culture and identity of migrant populations have been completely disregarded by the Taiwanese state in its efforts to 'educate' the migrants in local habits and culture. This analysis, centred on subjective accounts of the experiences of migration, suggests that Taiwanese government's approach towards PRC marriage migrants has produced other subtle losses that directly affect a person's dignity, identity, and self-esteem. On the other hand, the accounts of my respondents suggest that, through a patient process of acceptance, adaptation and transformation, it has been possible for them to regain the degree of recognition and acceptance that they longed for.

A Turning Point: Becoming a *New One*

In 2011, I happened to meet Linuo a second time, during a public rally in protest against the unfair legal treatment reserved for PRC marriage migrants. She was sharing her experience of frustrations with those who were attending the rally. She had turned forty-seven that year and she was carrying a young baby in her arms, her second daughter. She seemed to be very different, compared with the first time that I had met her during the summer of 2008. She was more confident and serene, comfortable in her role as a mother. She recollected how her life had gradually improved as a result of her personal struggles as well as external changes. For instance, she had succeeded in changing her neighbours' attitude towards her:

My neighbour used to call me dalumei [mainland sister]. *At the beginning I didn't know the meaning of this term, but I felt the meanness when he pronounced it. So I decided to talk to him. I told him that I didn't know what he meant by that expression, but since I am in Taiwan and I have a daughter, who actually is a Taiwanese daughter, he had to stop behaving like that with me. Gradually, he and the other neighbours learned that I am a good person, I have an education, and they accepted me.*

Nevertheless, the most important change came when she was able to put an end to her experience of 'home confinement.' With the lifting of the restrictions on the right to work in 2009, she immediately accessed the job market and was hired as a marketing designer in a local company. 'I was so happy to be granted such a basic right!' she said ironically. As soon as she learned that she was pregnant again, however, in her mid-forties, Linuo decided to leave her job and become a full-time mother, prioritising her personal health and her duties as a mother. This decision did not lead to the same frustrations as when she was compelled to stay at home the first time. The fact that she was the one in charge of her life made it easier for her to accept and even embrace the decision to become a full-time mother. Similarly, a turning point in Chengjie's life occurred when he obtained permanent residency status and, along with it, the right to formal employment in Taiwan. Since finding a stable and respectable job in a business enterprise, his life had changed for the better. Not only did he eventually gain a certain degree of respect from his in-laws, but he also acquired the economic power to consider alternative ways to increase his family's social capital beyond the context of the PRC and Taiwan. He arranged for his wife to be in the United States at the end of her pregnancy so that their daughter, born on American soil, could hold an American passport, which was more valuable to them than Chinese or Taiwanese passports. 'This was my present for her first birthday and for her future life!' announced Chengjie with a proud smile. He could not forget, however, that this was the outcome of a long process of learning and change that had lasted over ten years, during which Taiwan first took away his dignity as a man and a husband, and only then offered him new opportunities to establish his family, become a father and increase his personal and family social capital.

Xingmei, in contrast to Linuo and Chengjie, was still struggling with conditions she could not fully accept when I met her again in 2010. Since she could not continue her profession as a teacher, she had joined a civil society organisation, as a volunteer, that offered services and support for PRC marriage migrants. This decision helped her personal empowerment as well as the well-being of the couple. She had met new friends; by helping others she had regained the dignity she had lost in her first months in Taiwan; furthermore, by comparing her relatively privileged situation with that of other marriage migrants who had financial, family, or personal difficulties, she also looked at her marriage with different eyes. On the other hand, she had not fully managed to resolve her frustrations: Xingmei's voluntary work with a civil society organisation was simply a means of keeping occupied, of meeting new friends, and re-establishing a certain balance in her marriage, but it definitely did not help to nurture her self-recognition as a professional young woman who could make a contribution to both her family and society.

It cannot be disputed that broader factors, such as the relaxation of the immigration laws related to PRC migrants in Taiwan, increased economic and social exchanges between the two sides, and a pro-China government in Taiwan, have improved the legal and social status of PRC marriage migrants on the island. As the case of Xingmei shows, however, a number of problems still limited the degree of recognition that PRC individuals could obtain in Taiwan. As these accounts show, if the acquisition of citizenship rights marked a turning point in the lives of my respondents, their personal struggles and their families' support were also important factors in shaping their gradual process of adaptation and the consequent reconfiguration of their identities and social positions in the new societies. Thus, social inclusion and recognition should be interpreted as a complex and gradual process of personal change and adjustment to external conditions rather than as a top-down measure or a fixed condition shared by a whole social category.

Concluding Remarks

This paper, building on critical literature that suggests exploring migrants' experiences by looking at the different status that they are assigned during the process of migration, has assessed three PRC marriage migrants' strategies for affirming their identities in a social and political context where they were deprived of basic citizenship rights and were despised as a consequence of a mix of factors, such as their national origins and their motivation for migrating.

In exploring the process of transformation from the 'someone' they were before departure to the 'no-one' they became in Taiwan and the consequent re-definition of their new identities, this paper suggests that social inclusion and recognition should be understood as a process determined by structural factors as well as by individuals' abilities to form strategies to negotiate external structures. With regard to the majority of migrants from the PRC in Taiwan, major structural constraints shaped their social inclusion and recognition: the legal restrictions imposed on their freedom and access to citizenship rights, the stigmatisation of a society that viewed the PRC through a lens of biased assumptions and fear, the gendered expectations regarding their contributions to family and society. The literature argues that marriage migrants from the PRC were a 'second class' social group (Liao 2007), but the accounts of Chengjie, Linuo and Xingmei show that structural constraints did not affect this social group in a homogeneous way. Instead, migrants' different status would also imply different experiences of inclusion/exclusion and recognition/misrecognition. Interestingly enough, being better-off in the sending society and enjoying great recognition there did not play a positive role in the process of adaptation and achieving recognition in the receiving society, especially in the early years.

As adults with a well-defined identity in mainland China, prepared to face the challenge of starting a new life with the person they loved, none of them expected to go through a process of resetting their own identity and being associated with other spouses with inferior backgrounds back home. This was not, however, a fixed condition. Indeed, my three informants' experiences also showed that change and transformation are possible thanks to a combination of external factors, such as the gradual acquisition of citizenship rights, and personal and family struggles, that aimed to affirm their neglected identities and interests in the new environment. In the narratives of my respondents, rather than a process of downward or upward mobility as a consequence of migrating for marriage to Taiwan, a more complex condition can be identified in which different aspects of their lives, emotional and material, developed asymmetrically yet affected each other and created conditions for frustration and stress, reconfiguration and change, as well as, sometimes, even success. Above all, this paper shows that, at a time when the Taiwanese government was promoting multiculturalism, Taiwan failed to appraise the interests, identities, and voices of its migrants, and also deprived the migrants of the opportunity to enjoy the fruits of their labour, of their diverse talents and skills, as productive subjects who could make a valuable contribution to the economic and social development of Taiwan.

References

Bélanger, Daniele; Lee, Hye-Kiung and Wang, Hong-Zen (2010) 'Ethnic Diversity and Statistics in East Asia: 'Foreign Brides' Surveys in Taiwan and South Korea', *Ethnic and Racial Studies*, 33(6) 1108-1130.

Cheng, Isabelle and Fell, Dafydd (2014) 'The Change of Ruling Parties and Taiwan's Claim to Multiculturalism Before and After 2008, *Journal of Current Chinese Affairs*, 43(3) 71-103.

Friedman, Sarah (2010a) 'Marital Immigration and Graduated Citizenship: Post-Naturalization Restrictions on Mainland Chinese Spouses in Taiwan', *Pacific Affairs*, 83(1) 73-93.

Friedman, Sarah (2010b) 'Determining the "Truth" at the Border: Immigration Interviews, Chinese Marital migrants, and Taiwan's Sovereignty Silemmas', *Citizenship Studies*, 14(2) 167-183.

Friedman, Sarah (2012) 'Adjudicating the Intersection of Marital Immigration, Domestic Violence, and Spousal Murder: China-Taiwan Marriages and Competing Legal Domains', *Indiana Journal of Global Legal Studies*, 19(1) 221- 255.

Hsia, Hsiao-chuan (2007) 'Imaged and Imagined Threat to The Nation: The Media Construction of the "Foreign Brides" as Social Problems in Taiwan', *Inter-Asia Cultural Studies*, 8(1), 55-85.

Jones, Gavin (2012) 'International Marriage in Asia: What We Know, and What We Need to Know?' *Asia Research Institute Working Paper Series* No. 174, Singapore: National University of Singapore.

Jones, Gavin and Shen, Hsiu-Hua (2008) 'International Marriage in East and Southeast Asia: Trends and Research Emphases', *Citizenship Studies*, 12(1), 9-25.

Kim, Hyuk-Rae, and Oh, Ingyu (2012) 'Foreign Cometh! Paths to Multiculturalism in Japan, Korea and Taiwan', *Asian and Pacific Migration Journal*, 21(1), 105-133.

Kymlicka, Will (1995) *Multicultural Citizenship: A Liberal Theory of Minority Rights*, Oxford: Clarendon Press.

Kymlicka, Will (2007) *Multicultural Odysseys: Navigating the New International Politics of Diversity,* Oxford: Oxford University Press.

Kymlicka, Will (2012) 'Multiculturalism: Success, Failure, and the Future. Research', ommissioned by the Migration Policy Institute. Retrieved from www.migrationpolicy.org on 20 August 2015.

King, Winnie (2011) 'Taiwanese Nationalism and Cross-strait marriage. Governing and Incorporating Mainland Spouses', in: Gunter, Schubert and Damm, Jens (eds.) *Taiwanese Identity in the 21st Century: Domestic, Regional and Global Perspectives*, Abingdon: Routledge, 176-193.

Liao, Bruce Yuan-Hao (2007) 'The Exclusionary Taiwan Immigration Laws', Paper presented at the International Conference on Border Control and Empowerment of Immigrant Brides (September 29-30, 2007) Taipei: Shih Hsin University, 55-64.

Lu, Melody (2008) *Gender, Marriage and Migration. Contemporary Marriages between Mainland China and Taiwan*, doctoral dissertation, Leiden: Leiden University.

Mahler, Sarah J. and Pessar, Patricia R. (2001) 'Gendered Geographies of Power: Analysing Gender across Transnational Spaces', *Identities*, 7(4), 441-459.

Neizhengbu [内政部 Ministry of the Interior] (2015) *Ge xian shi wai yi, wai peiou renshu yu dalu (han Gang-Ao) peiou renshu an zhengjian fen* 各縣市外裔、外籍配偶人數與大陸(含港澳) 配偶人數按證件分 [Foreign and mainland Chinese (including Hong Kong and Macao) spouses in Taiwan in each city and according to their status (National Immigration Agency of the Ministry of the Interior (retrieved from http://www.immigration.gov.tw/ct.asp?xItem=1292323&ctNode=29699&mp=1 on 1 March 2015).

Momesso, Lara (2015a) 'Between Official and Concealed: Cross-Strait Marriage Migrants' Strategies of Resistance', in: Lipinsky, Astrid (ed.) *Immigration Societies - Taiwan and Beyond. Vienna Taiwan Studies Series Vol. 1*, Berlin: LIT. Publication, 171-193.

Momesso, Lara (2015b) 'Change and Permanence in Contemporary Chinese Families: A Case Study of Marriage Across the Taiwan Strait', in: Ehlers, H., Kalisch, C., Linke, G., Milewski, N., Rudlof, B., Trappe, H. (eds.) *Migration – Geschlecht – Lebenswege.* Münster: LIT Verlag, 51-76.

Parekh, Bhikhu (2000) *Rethinking Multiculturalism: Cultural Diversity and Political Theory,* New York: Palgrave Publishers.

Sandel, Todd L. and Liang, Chung-Hui (2010) 'Taiwan's Fifth Ethnic Group: A Study of the Acculturation and Cultural Fusion of Women Who Have Married into Families in Taiwan', *Journal of International and Intercultural Communication*, 3(3) 249-275.

Schachar, Ayelet (2001) *Multicultural Jurisdictions. Cultural Differences and Women's Rights,* Cambridge: Cambridge University Press.

Shih, Shu-mei (1998) 'Gender and a New Geopolitics of Desire: The Seduction of Mainland Women in Taiwan and Hong Kong Media', *Signs*, 23(2): 287-319.

Stjernfelt, Frederik (2012) 'Liberal Multiculturalism as Political Philosophy: Will Kymlicka', *The Monist*, 95, 1, 49-71.

Taipei Times (2003a) 'Editorial: A Match Made in Hell', November 5, 2003 [Retrieved from http://www.taipeitimes.com/News/editorials/archives/2003/11/05/2003074668 on February 16, 2012.

Taipei Times (2003b) 'Better National Security Net Needed', November 16, 2003 [Retrieved from http://www.taipeitimes.com/News/editorials/archives/2003/11/16/2003076077 on February 16, 2012.

Taipei Times (2003c) 'The Danger Brought by Our Guests from China', November 5, 2003 [Retrieved from http://www.taipeitimes.com/News/editorials/archives/2003/11/05/2003074670 on February 16, 2012].

Taylor, Charles (1994) 'The Politics of Recognition', in: Taylor, Charles and Gutman, Amy (eds.) *Multiculturalism and The Politics of Recognition*, Princeton: Princeton University Press, 25-74.

Tseng, Yu-chin, Cheng, Isabelle, and Fell, Dafydd (2013) 'The Politics of the Mainland Spouses' Rights' Movement in Taiwan, in: Fell, Dafydd, Chiu, Kuei-Fen and Lin, Ping (eds.) *Migration to and From Taiwan,* London: Routledge, 205-226.

Wang, Hong-Zen and Bélanger, Daniele (2008) 'Taiwanizing Female Immigrant Spouses and Materializing Differential Citizenship', *Citizenship Studies*, 12 (1): 91-106.

Wang, Li-Jung (2005) 'The Formulation of "Transnational Communities". A New Challenge to "Multicultural Taiwan"', *International Journal of Cultural Policy*, 11(2), 171-185.

Wang Minghui [Wang, Ming-huei 王明輝] (2004) 'Taiwan waiji peiou jiegouxin ruoshi qingjingzhi fenxi 臺灣外籍配偶結構性弱勢情景之分析 [The analysis of disadvantaged conditions characterizing transnational marriage in Taiwan], Shequ fazhan jikan 社區發展季刊 [Community Development Journal], 103, 320-335.

Yang Wangying [Yang Wang-ying 楊婉瑩] and Li Pinrong [Lee Pin-rong 李品蓉] (2009) '*Dalu peiou de gongminquan kunjing – guozu yu fuquan de gongmou*' 大陸配偶的公民權困境一國族與父權的共謀 [The citizenship dilemma of mainlander spouses in Taiwan: the conspiracy of nationalism and patriarchy], Taiwan minzhu jikan 臺灣民主季刊 [Taiwan Democracy Quarterly], 6(3), 47-86.

Yuval-Davis, Nira (1997) 'Women, Citizenship and Difference', *Feminist Review*, 57, 4-27.

Feng-yi Chu

Benevolent Self vs. Malignant Other: The East-West Antagonistic Narrative of Taiwanese People's Chinese Identity

According to the annual surveys conducted by the Election Study Centre (ESC),[1] almost one-third of the population in Taiwan possess dual identity - that is, they identify themselves as both Chinese and Taiwanese simultaneously.[2] This data has posed a great puzzle about Taiwanese society - particularly in the light of the recent upsurge in Taiwanese nationalism, which necessarily implies an acceptance of Taiwanese identity. Why would such a large proportion of Taiwanese people retain, if not insist upon, their Chinese identity, notwithstanding the fact that the proportion who claim Taiwanese identity (whether singly or in combination) has increased to 60 per cent in the past two decades. Furthermore, the continued embracing of Chinese identity by so many people in Taiwan does not square with the fact that only 7.4 per cent of the population are in favour of Taiwan unifying with China.[3] Clearly, there are many in Taiwan who claim Chinese identity but do not aspire to a united Chinese nation and, judging from this, it seems problematic to view their Chinese identity as a form of national identity (see Rigger 2006: 22; Wu 1993; Chang and Wang 2005; Huang 2005). Indeed, if national identity is understood to be exclusive as many theorists suggest (e.g. Smith 1983), if the concepts of 'China' and 'Taiwan' signify two different political entities (or communities, as Benedict Anderson [2006] puts it), - that is, the People's Republic of China (PRC) and Republic of China (ROC) respectively - the existence of the dual identity clearly manifests the fact that both Chinese and Taiwanese identities are not exclusive national identities (Shi 2001). Another possible explanatory framework takes into account the impact of the historical provincial-origin (ethnic) conflict - that is, the struggle between *waishengren* (外省人) and *benshengren*[4] (本省人) groups in Taiwan. Indeed, re-

---

[1] The Election Study Centre, established in 1989, is a reputed survey institution affiliated with the National Chengchi University, Taipei. The institute has periodically conducted various surveys on elections in Taiwan and the political orientations of Taiwanese people. It also contributes to scholarship by maintaining a large database of election research and publishing a journal, Election Studies. Since 1992, the institute has conducted an annual series of national surveys dealing with Taiwanese people's Chinese/Taiwanese identity as well as their preferences for Taiwan independence or unification with China. The data can be accessed at http://esc.nccu.edu.tw/course/news.php?class-201.

[2] According to the survey, 32.5 per cent of participants profess dual identity. The statistical data can be viewed on the ESC website: http://esc.nccu.edu.tw/course/news.php?Sn=166#. Chen Wen-chun's (陳文俊) research, Taiwan de zuqun zhengzhi 臺灣的族群政治 (Ethnic Politics in Taiwan) (Hong Kong: Hong Kong Social Science Press, 1997), found in 1993 that 45.5 per cent of his respondents declared that they had dual identity, and also that this dual identity tended to be correlated with higher education levels and younger age.

[3] See ESC data at: http://esc.nccu.edu.tw/app/news.php?Sn=167.

[4] The generic concept of *waishengren* (外省人; literally, 'people from other provinces') collectively refers to people who came to Taiwan after 1945 (the year the Chinese GMD government took over Taiwan from Japan) and their descendants. They mainly used Mandarin as a common language to communicate with each other, regardless of their various original provincial languages/dialects. *Benshengren* (本省人; literally, 'this province' or 'local province') refers to people whose (patrilineal) forefathers had been in Taiwan prior to 1945.

Berliner China-Hefte/Chinese History and Society 47 (2016), 37-55

search such as that of Chen Wenjun [Chen Wen-chun] has suggested that there is a correlation between people's provincial origin and their Chinese/Taiwanese identity. Nevertheless, not all *waishengren* would identify themselves as Chinese, and not all *benshengren* would reject Chinese identity.[5] In short, one's provincial origin does not determine or account for one's Chinese and Taiwanese identification.[6]

This paper responds to the challenge of this puzzle - analysing why some Taiwanese people, regardless of their preference for Taiwan's future or their provincial origin, profess Chinese identity without hesitation (some of them claiming dual identity). The paper proposes a theory of the 'ethical narrative' - a particular type of narrative depicting a primitive scenario of moral dualism, a conflict between two sides, good versus evil. The ethical narrative exercises its influence by adopting two approaches. On the one hand, it implies a moral obligation to support the good side and reject the evil side. This moral framework is constructed in two ways. The first is the arbitrary dualistic division. When introducing the narrative's heroes and villains, the narrator ascribes virtues to the former and vices to the latter. The second construction of moral values occurs by means of the narrative's storyline, which tends to be simple: it usually depicts a brutal, powerful group mercilessly oppressing a powerless, benevolent one. Clearly, the oppressors constitute the bad side, while the oppressed make up the good.

On the other hand, the ethical narrative provokes an emotional response, inspiring positive feelings - such as sympathy and a sense of justice - for the good side and, conversely, negative responses - condemnation, anger, sometimes resentment - towards the bad side. By arousing strong emotional responses, the ethical narrative demands moral action from its audience, urging them to participate in supporting good and combating evil. With this mechanism, the ethical narrative offers its audience two coordinates: one emotional, the other moral. In other words, the ethical narrative does not merely tell a story; it invites its audience to play a part in that story. And because the story is highly simplified (there are only two characters) and devoid of nuance (the good is simply good; the evil is simply evil), the audience has no choice but to identify with those designated as good and to adopt their perspective. In other words, the ethical narrative by definition presents a platform for the practice of morality by its audience and in so doing, forges and shapes the latter's identity.

This research argues that it is through this capacity to evoke emotions and instil moral obligations that identity becomes truly functional. Without the ability to shape human feelings and values, an identity is merely a name in a generic system that people use to classify the world. Only by association with emotional and value-oriented discourses can an identity acquire this capacity. The ethical narrative is one of those emotional and value-oriented discourses that adds dimension to an identity.

From the analysis of data derived from 108 interviews in my fieldwork, this paper identifies a particular type of ethical narrative--namely, East-West antagonism, which endows Chinese identity with the allurement to inspire its subjects' loyalty. This discourse has four

Today, the *benshengren* are further classified into two ethnic subgroups, Hoklo (河洛; also known as Minnanren 閩南人, i.e., people from the South of Fujian) and Hakka (客家), according to the languages they speak.

5 Lin Chia-lung (2002) claims 'although there is a high correlation between the two, one should not equate ethnic identity [provincial origin] with national identity [Chinese/Taiwanese identity]'.

6 Another approach is to explore what concepts and meanings are linked to the ideas 'Chinese' and 'Taiwanese' for Taiwanese people (see Liu 1998; Wu 2001; Huang, Liu and Chang 2004).

characteristics. First, it structures a moral dualism between Easterners and Westerners. Second, the idea of 'Easterners' is closely connected to the idea of 'Chinese', referring to those who exhibit the typical Asian phenotype, such as yellow skin, black eyes and black hair. Third, the narrative is set primarily in the late nineteenth and early twentieth centuries in China (not Taiwan), with Chinese people depicted as being bullied, oppressed and exploited by imperialists coming from the West. Thus, in the East-West antagonism, the oppressed Chinese people (i.e., Easterners) are the good guys, while the oppressing Westerners are the bad guys. This discourse offers a platform, inviting the audience to engage with its story, arousing their hostility against Westerners, obliging them to identify with and support China/the Chinese in opposition to Westerners.[7]

East-West antagonism can be traced back to the late nineteenth century when it emerged in China, which faced a constant demand for free trade and the threat of imperialism from the developed powers, and was ill-equipped to deal with the challenge.[8] Many of the concepts and discourses that appeared during that period were closely linked to East-West antagonism. The construction of the discourse on the yellow race is a good example. Frank Dikötter contends that the introduction or construction of the racial discourses on the yellow race and descent ideology of 'the offspring of the Yan Emperor and the Yellow Emperor'

7 A similar concept is Rigger's (1997) notion of 'anti-imperialism'. Stressing the cognitive aspect, Rigger uses this term to explain the mindset of some unificationists in Taiwan (people supporting unification with China). The anti-imperialist discourse suggests: (1) the 'true' borders of China include all those territories claimed by the Qing at the end of the eighteenth century; (2) Japan's claim to Taiwan was illegitimate and its occupation interrupted Taiwan's link to its mother country, bringing nothing but misery to the Chinese people residing on the island; (3) all expressions of support for Taiwan independence or continued separation are on-going imperialist interference in China's affairs. However, I argue that in terms of identity, the anti-imperialist discourse may not be a very appropriate analytical unit because, first, as illustrated, Rigger's analysis is only at the cognitive level, yet identity functions not merely on the basis of one's knowledge but also on other aspects, such as psychology, emotions, senses of morality, etc. Second, the term 'East-West antagonism' clearly shows both the form (i.e., the dualistic structure) and the content (i.e., East versus West) of this ethical narrative at once, while 'anti-imperialism' only emphasizes the content (i.e., fighting against Western imperialists). This does not therefore necessarily render 'anti-imperialism' relevant to identity. For example, a left-wing supporter in Taiwan may oppose imperialism, but this does not mean this person would claim Chinese identity.

8 In fact, 'West' as an 'Other' of China is a complex concept, conveying varied images to Chinese people in the nineteenth century. One might see the West as possessing more advanced technology, a more modern and civilised society, and a higher standard of living; another might focus instead on the West posing a threat to China. The perception of the West is not always antagonistic, and there have been numerous attempts to explain and theorise about relations between East and West. Zhang and Cheng (1990) designate several paradigms, including 'Chinese essence, Western application' (*Zhongti xiyong* 中體西用), 'Western essence, Chinese application' (*xiti Zhongyong* 西體中用), 'wholesale Westernisation' (*quanpan xihua* 全盤西化), 'Chinese exceptionalism' (*Zhongguo benwei wenhua* 中國本位文化), etc. That said, this paper intends neither to engage with these debates, nor to study the developments of these discourses. Rather, it extracts from these discussions the common theme of dualistic discourse between the two ideas, East/Easterners and West/Westerners, exercising significant influence in the society. Given the historical fact of the military threat posed by Western imperialists, it is hardly surprising that hostility and resentment emerged amongst people in China, fostering or bolstering their Chinese identity. See, also, Wang (2015) for further discussion on the theme of resentment in modern Chinese nationalism.

(*Yanhuang zisun* 炎黃子孫) can be traced back as far as the late nineteenth century (Dikötter 1997). He claims that 1898 reformers, such as Liang Qichao and Kang Youwei, 'selectively appropriated scientific knowledge from foreign discursive repertoires, actively manipulated evolutionary theories to bolster theories of pure origin; they reconfigured folk notions of patrilineal descent into a racial discourse which represented all inhabitants of China as the descendants of the Yellow Emperor (ibid. 15). These racial discourses were usually invoked in the context of resisting the Western imperialists. As discussed by Dikötter, the ideas that 'China is the yellow race', and 'only the yellow race competes with the white race' were introduced in primary school textbooks in the early 1920s (ibid. 21).

It can be argued that East-West antagonism emerged and exercised an influence in Taiwan during the same period. Wu Zhuoliu (吳濁流), an indigenous Taiwanese novelist who was born in 1900, offers an example. In his memoir, The Fig Tree, Wu wrote:

... It [mother country] was a concept, an intangible concept, but somehow my heart was pulled towards it as if by gravity, absorbed by it in some subtle process of attraction. [...] It was almost instinctive and only those who have lived under foreign domination as colonial subjects can really appreciate how I felt. People in China naturally felt it under the Manchus; people in Taiwan felt it under the Japanese, even those, like myself, who had known no other rulers (Wu 1994: 5).

Wu does not only regard China as his mother country (and thus identifies himself as a member of the Chinese nation), but apparently is also aware that his mother country has been bullied and oppressed by foreign races (Chen 2008). It can therefore be said that Wu was affected by the East-West antagonistic discourse. It is difficult now to discern how their life experiences under Japanese administration influenced such early Taiwanese 'Chinese-identifiers', or how widespread this Chinese identity was at that time in Taiwan. However, judging by the ease with which news was transmitted at the time, it is hardly surprising that the East-West antagonistic discourse infiltrated Taiwan and fashioned a Chinese identity for some Taiwanese people.

Nonetheless, the major contributor to the development of East-West antagonism in Taiwan was the national education programme promoted by the Guomindang (GMD, also: Kuomintang KMT) government when the regime took over the island after 1958. On the one hand, the primary school textbook series promoted the concept of a supra-ethnic Chinese nationality, not only by downplaying differences among the various ethnic groups residing in China (ROC), but also by stressing what they had in common - namely, a shared lineage, either because they are the offspring of the common ancestor, Huang-di, or because they have intermarried extensively. These discourses on origin and ethnic assimilation imply that all the ethnic groups in China have the same racial phenotypes. On the other hand, the textbooks frequently use the terms 'Europeans' and 'Westerners', whether drawing a contrast with Chinese culture and Chinese life styles, or referring to democratic comrades in the struggle against communist regimes, or, very broadly, denoting the predators who tried to divide China in the late nineteenth century. One unit in Volume 11 of the social studies school textbook (pre-1990 versions), entitled 'Radical Changes in Modern China', is a good example. It recounts four major changes in the world around the middle of the Ming dynasty that had a significant impact on China: (1) the discovery of the new trade route, which facilitated cultural exchanges between East and West; (2) democratic revolutions in the Western nations, which influenced the entire world; (3) Western invasions of China, both by sea and by land; and (4) the danger of being besieged and divided, which galvanised China. By using the generalised, flattened dualistic concepts of 'Chinese' and 'Westerners', and by focusing on their interactions in the imperialist period, these descriptions explicitly assist the construction of the East-West antagonistic discourse in contemporary Taiwan.

Narrative Analysis, Identity, and Research Methods

My theory of the influence of East-West antagonism is developed from and supported by the fieldwork that I conducted from 2010 to 2014 in 13 out of 21 cities/counties of Taiwan.[9] The research mainly utilises the technique of narrative analysis, which has been widely applied in various disciplines (Brockmeier and Carbaugh 2001). With this technique, the researcher is able, as Andrew, Squire, and Tamboukou (2008: 1-2) describe, 'to investigate not just how stories are structured and the ways in which they work, but also who produces them and by what means; the mechanisms by which they are consumed; and how narratives are silenced, contested or accepted' (Andrew, Squire and Tamboukou 2008: 1-2). Because its central focus is human expression and representation, narrative analysis is a very useful tool for exploring issues related to identity. In *Narrative and Identity*, Brockmeier and Carbaugh (2001: 1) describe narrative as an 'expressive embodiment of our experience, as a mode of communication, and as a form for understanding the world and ultimately ourselves'. They provide a succinct but detailed review of current developments, including: (1) the change in theoretical perspective (and materials) from narratology and narrative theory itself, towards an interdisciplinary semiotic and cultural theory of narrative texts and contexts;[10] (2) the change in perspective from seeking structures 'through formal 'clausal analysis'' to investigating them 'through cultural analyses of the forms through which, and the contexts in which stories are told;'[11] and (3) recognition of the openness of life narratives. These developments have paved the way for identity researchers to use the technique of narrative analysis not only to explore the characteristics of contemporary identity - personal self-identity or social identity - embedded in social categorisations, but also to discover the mechanism of identity formation under the influence of broader social and cultural contexts. In the Taiwanese context, Hsiau A-chin, in his remarkable book, *Return to Reality: Political and Cultural Change in 1970s Taiwan and the Post-war Generation*, has applied the technique of narrative analysis to study a cohort he calls 'the generation of returning to reality'. This generation was born during the 1950s - the post-war period - and became young adults in the 1970s. By analysing documents compiled by the elites among this cohort (biographies, diaries, articles, etc.), Hsiau details developments and changes in their national identities, perceptions of history, and political attitudes. He argues that, being acutely aware of the crises that their country faced in the 1970s, such as the sovereignty dispute over the

---

9 Since place of residence was not a significant factor for Chinese/Taiwanese identity according to past research, the case selection in my fieldwork did not place much emphasis on it. Nonetheless, interviews were conducted in all Taiwan cities/counties except Jilong [Keelung] City, Miaoli County, Xinzhu [Hsinchu] County, Nantou County, Yunlin County, Pingdong [Pingtung] County, Taidong [Taitung] County, and Penghu County, which collectively, account for a minor part of Taiwan's population.

10 This includes, as Brockmeier and Carbaugh (2001: 4) remark, 'physical activities like dance and sport events, artifacts of remembrance like memorials and museum displays, social rituals like funerals and public ceremonies, and other cultural phenomena like fashion and landscape design'.

11 Ibid. 7.

Senkaku Islands and the revocation of UN membership, this cohort longed for reforms, criticised the 'diaspora mentality' of the previous generation, and even dared to challenge the existing political system. Among Hsiau's findings concerning this cohort, what is particularly pertinent is that it possessed a strong sense of Chinese identity, which reflected the enormous power the party state (the GMD) exercised over the construction of history, collective memories and identity, especially through national education. Yet, I argue that it would be wrong to ascribe absolute power to national education. After the GMD surrendered power in the first party changeover, and the Chinese nationalism content in primary school textbooks was toned down considerably, there were still younger generations who would identify themselves as Chinese. Apparently, certain elements of Chinese identity hold an allure that transcends generations, ethnic categories, and any demographic classification in Taiwanese society, inducing one-third of the population to claim that identity.

My fieldwork research collected data from 108 interviews in Taiwan to explore what attracts people to claim Chinese identity or Taiwanese identity. The fieldwork comprised three phases. The first, conducted from October 2010 to May 2011, entailed open sampling, using the technique of snowball sampling and recruiting participants through Internet forums. In order to maximise the diversity of cases considered, the only condition applied to recruitment was place of residence (Taibei [Taipei], Tainan, or Gaoxiong [Kaohsiung]). At the same time, relational/variational sampling was achieved by setting several basic prerequisites for case selection based on past research findings, including the subject's party affiliation, provincial origin, and age. In addition, other demographic factors, such as gender, education, and career, were also carefully tracked in the sampling process. In the second phase, from December 2011 to February 2012, I continued both open sampling and relational/variational sampling, although I paid greater attention to the latter based on findings obtained in the first phase.[12] Finally, the follow-up fieldwork (highly selective sampling) was carried out mainly in the third phase, between December 2012 and February 2013. The interviews were conducted in thirteen of Taiwan's twenty cities and counties. All interviews lasted for at least 100 minutes, and the contents were all transcribed and coded according to the principles of grounded theory developed by Anselm Strauss and Juliet Corbin for further narrative analysis (Strauss and Corbin 1998). The demographic information on my interviewees is listed below in Table 1.

Apart from the conventional narrative research, which focuses more on personal self-identity, my main research target is the generic classifications constructed in the society - that is, Chinese and Taiwanese identities in Taiwan. As a consequence, my interview questions

---

12 Open sampling and relational/variational sampling are methodological concepts developed in Strauss and Corbin's (1998) Basics of Qualitative Research: Techniques and Procedures for Developing Grounded Theory. Open sampling aims to 'discover, name, and categorise phenomena according to their properties and dimensions', and thus expects that researchers '[will be] open to all possibilities during interviews, during observations, when reading documents, and so on and will want to take full advantage of every opportunity that comes up, exploring each as much as is feasible'. Relational and variational sampling is the process in which 'the researcher is looking for incidents that demonstrate dimensional range or variation of a concept and the relationships among concepts'. Both techniques are designed for qualitative researchers to, on the one hand, explore the population as thoroughly as possible and, on the other, to discover particular cases that are crucial for developing new theories.

were designed primarily to illuminate these two identities and their related discourses, including party politics, the ethnic conflict in Taiwan, and the prospect of unification or Taiwan independence, rather than autobiographical self-reporting. Finally, this specific research goal and interview design lead to a distinctive type of analytical technique - one that explores participants' narratives around the concepts of concern (Chinese and Taiwanese identities) - whether relating actual personal experiences that shed light on these identities, or fictional stories about them.

Categories	Sub-categories	Number of participants	%
Gender	Male	64	59.3
	Female	44	40.7
Chinese/Taiwanese Identity	Chinese	5	4.6
	Dual	53	49.1
	Taiwanese	47	43.5
	Other Responses	3	2.8
Year of Birth	Before 1945[13]	32	29.6
	1946-1983	47	43.5
	After 1984[14]	29	26.9
Provincial origin	Benshengren	74	68.5
	Waishengren	34	32.5
Residential region	North Taiwan[15]	44	40.7
	Central Taiwan	16	14.8
	South Taiwan[16]	38	35.2
	East Taiwan	9	8.3
Total number of participants		108	

Table 1: Demographic information for 108 cases.

[13] In this year, Japan was defeated in World War II and Taiwan was retaken by the GMD government.

[14] Subjects who were born in this year (1984) entered primary school in 2000 and used new editions of textbooks, which placed less emphasis on Chinese history and geography than had the previous editions.

[15] Cities/counties north of Miaoli County.

[16] Cities/counties south of Jiayi [Chiayi] County.

Among the total 108 participants, 53 claim Chinese identity,[17] and among these 53 Chinese identifiers, 23 manifest the effect of the East-West antagonistic narrative - expressing either their identification with the Chinese people and resentment against Western imperialists, or their fervent support for Taiwan's unification with China in order to complete a great unified Chinese nation with the capacity to compete among the modern developed Western nations and to be a world superpower. Their demographic information is listed in Table 2. Because this research is qualitative by nature, having the acquisition of new theoretical insights as its main purpose rather than seeking to present statistically descriptive data, and because data selection in this research largely relies on purposive sampling rather than random sampling, these numbers do not possess statistical significance.

All the interviews conducted with these 23 participants share several striking similarities that may be included under the theme of East-West antagonism described in the previous section, and these characteristics do not vary according to participants' gender, generation, provincial origin, or region of residence. In this paper, I firstly spotlight one benshengren interviewee, Haoping, and one *waishengren* participant, Jane, to show how an ethical narrative (the East-West antagonist narrative) exercises its influence on the identity of individuals (in this instance, the Chinese identity), and how it affects subjects' political attitudes. However, the construction of identity is a very complex process, and, theoretically, there is no single factor - including the East-West antagonistic narrative - that is the determinant of identity. By presenting one participant who subscribes to East-West antagonism but rejects Chinese identity, the paper discusses how discursive interpellation may fail, highlighting the complexity of the process of identity formation in which various factors jointly operate.

Categories	Sub-categories	Number of participants	%
Gender	Male	17	73.9
	Female	6	26.1
Chinese/Taiwanese Identity	Chinese	0	0
	Dual	17	73.9
	Taiwanese	5	22.0
	Other Responses	1	4.1
Year of Birth	Before 1945	4	17.4
	1946-1983	8	34.8
	After 1984	11	47.8
Provincial origin	Benshengren	13	56.5

[17] This includes 5 who identify themselves as Chinese only, and 48 who subscribe to a dual identity.

	Waishengren	10	43.5
Residential region	North Taiwan	12	52.2
	Central Taiwan	3	13.0
	South Taiwan	6	26.1
	East Taiwan	2	8.7
Total number of participants		23	

Table 2: Demographic information for 23 participants whose identities have been influenced by the East-West antagonistic narrative.

Chinese Identity and the East-West Antagonistic Narrative

Haoping is a 32-year-old military officer in Taibei City who was born in 1982 in Yilan county [I-lan 宜蘭縣], a relatively rural area on the northeast side of Taiwan, as the first child in a *benshengren* family with a younger sister. His father once worked in construction in the county, and his mother was an insurance broker. Both resigned from their previous jobs and now are brokers of agricultural products. Haoping studied in a primary school and a junior high school in Yilan and went to a vocational school after that because of his low academic achievements. Probably for that reason, as well as out of economic considerations, he joined the army after graduation. Now he is a captain in the military; he married a nurse in his hometown, and they had a baby boy in 2012.

I first interviewed Haoping in 2010 in Taibei. I began by offering five options for him to describe his identity: (1) Chinese only; (2) Taiwanese only; (3) both Chinese and Taiwanese; (4) both Chinese and Taiwanese, but primarily Taiwanese; (5) both Chinese and Taiwanese, but primarily Chinese. This exchange followed:

HAOPING: I would choose 'both Chinese and Taiwanese, but Taiwanese primarily.' But, speaking of Chinese, I'm not sure if you are referring to mainlanders [daluren 大陸人; or the PRC citizens].

Q: No, I have no such intention. It is what you think that matters.

HAOPING: Then, I think it (Chinese) refers to daluren.

Q: If so, do you still think of yourself as Chinese? Do you see yourself as daluren*?*

*HAOPING: No… When I think of myself as Chinese, the term actually refers to, eh, the whole… It should mean the supra-ethnic Chinese nationality (*Zhonghua minzu 中華民族*) not only* daluren. *It should be… Well, shouldn't all Asian people be Chinese?*

Q: Asian? All Asians?

HAOPING: Yes. It is just like… 'I am Taiwanese, and I am also Yilanren [a person from Ilan]. *'*

Q: Is it? So, a 'Chinese-Taiwanese' person is just like a 'Taiwanese Yilanren*'?*

HAOPING: Yes. That's what I'm thinking; that's my metaphor… My [definition of] Chinese refers to all… all Asians. Okay, all Asians... That is, amongst all Chinese people in Asia, I am Taiwanese. I am one of them [Chinese people].

Q: So, to you, the idea 'Chinese'…

HAOPING: It does not only refer to [people in] a specific country. It is not only a country. It is like Easterners [dongfangren 東方人] *and Westerners* [xifangren 西方人], *a* [concept of] *race.*

This is the basic profile of Haoping's identity pattern. Clearly to Haoping, the term 'Chinese' can be at once very exclusive (mainlanders) and very inclusive (the supra-ethnic Chinese nationality, Asian, or Easterners). When he identifies himself as Chinese, he is adapting its inclusive meanings, regarding himself as a member of the supra-ethnic Chinese nationality, Asian, or Easterners.

In fact, this terminological confusion sometimes bothers Haoping. For instance, Haoping would not indicate that he is Chinese when meeting foreigners, because he thinks he would be mis-perceived as being from the PRC:

Q: Would you say you are Chinese or Taiwanese in front of foreigners?
HAOPING: I would say that I am Taiwanese.
Q: Why not say you are Chinese?
HAOPING: Because... if I say I am Chinese, they might mistake me for a mainlander [daluren].
Q: So, why don't you want to be mistaken for daluren?
HAOPING: Because I am a Taiwanese
Q: Not Chinese?
HAOPING: Not daluren. They (foreigners) would think 'China' is 'mainland' [dalu 大陸].

In everyday life, Haoping is actually reluctant to claim Chinese identity. The meaning that he ascribes to 'Chinese' refers exclusively to '*daluren*', and he prefers to be called 'Taiwanese' when travelling abroad because he worries about being misunderstood as 'daluren' by foreigners.

Nevertheless, Haoping still insists on his Chinese identity despite lacking occasions to invoke it. The opportunity for him to claim Chinese identity is a scenario that is purely hypothetical, one that is farfetched in today's world - a scenario harking back to the age of imperialism, when the West wielded its superior power over the late Qing Dynasty and early Republican China (i.e., the 'Eight-Nation Alliance' period, as Haoping specifies):

Q: Is there any occasion on which you will claim that you are Chinese?
HAOPING: At present? Eh... When... [we are] 'invaded' by foreigners? How should I describe that? Let me think for a moment...
Q: You mean, when being bullied?
HAOPING: When we have to defend ourselves from outside enemies.
Q: Why don't you say you are Taiwanese then?
HAOPING: The feelings are different. We should 'develop' a 'Chinese solidarity' [Zhongguoren de tuanjie 中國人的團結].
Q: You mean that Taiwanese are not united?
HAOPING: It might be a little bit strange, but it should be that... when Mainland China and we, together, are against enemies from outside, I would be proud of being Chinese, not Taiwanese. That is, we are together holding certain Chinese characteristics and the spirit to fight against foreigners' invasions.
Q: Are we being invaded now?
HAOPING: No. It was a long time ago... the 'Eight-Nation Alliance' period (in 1990).
Q: Then, currently, there seems to be no such occasion for you to say that you are Chinese?
HAOPING: No. There is none at present.

According to Haoping, he identifies himself as Chinese only in a fictional situation - a narrative with its background set in China during the late nineteenth and early twentieth centuries, when the Qing Empire was suffering from the depredations of Western imperialists (such as the 'Eight-Nation Alliance'). He formulates his Chinese identity only when he senses the threat of outside enemies, and these enemies are fictionally imagined to be Western imperialists. More clearly, Haoping claims Chinese identity only when he wishes to contrast himself to Westerners - his Chinese identity is based on the conceptual dichotomy between Easterners and Westerners, or more precisely, on the moral dualism of an 'East-West antagonistic narrative' in which Chinese people (Easterners) are benevolent, whilst the Western imperialist powers are the opposite.

Influence of the East-West Antagonistic Narrative on Political Attitudes and Identities

Moral dualism - the core structure of ethical narrative - induces various strong affections, basically, positive feelings for the benevolent and negative feelings for the vicious. Only with this capacity for the inducement of feelings can a particular narrative ethic truly enmesh people in specific attitudes and actions, and thus identities. My reporter, Jane, a 33 years-old *waishengren*, can serve as a fitting case to explore the tangled connections between feelings, moral dualism and narrative ethics as well as their mechanisms for affecting political attitudes, actions and identities. She was born in the US in 1977, and her parents decided to take her back to Taiwan for her early education.[18] She spent most of her childhood in Taibei. At the age of 18, she returned to the US to go to college, and she came back Taiwan to work after graduation. She is married to a *benshengren* who was her classmate in primary school in Taiwan.

When asked to describe her identity, Jane claimed that she is both Chinese and Taiwanese without prioritising either. Like Haoping, Jane's Chinese identity is associated with the idea of Easterners, formed in contrast to the concept of Westerners. The influence of East-West antagonism on her identity formation can be discerned in her reply to the question, 'do you feel proud of being Chinese?':

JANE: I feel pretty proud [of being Chinese]. We can't choose the colour of our skin or our race. Since you belong to this race, you have to be proud of your race [...] We have five thousand years of history. We invented many things: the compass, gunpowder, etc. We invented these, and should feel proud. We Chinese people are preeminent in many aspects, because we are pretty smart. Why not be proud of being Chinese? If there is anyone reluctant to be Chinese, I think it is because he or she is under great pressure from racial discrimination. This discrimination results from white people's arrogance and self-conceit. After all, China was so weak in the period of the Qing Dynasty. The Eight-Nation Alliance bullied and embarrassed us excruciatingly. Because opium use was prevalent at that time, China and the Chinese people fell apart. Then white people arose, so they had self-conceit and pride in their race. If China had not been so weak and so miserable, if China had been very powerful and unrestrained, China would not be the China that exists today; China would be a superpower, and we would not be discriminated against anywhere.

[18] The decision, according to Jane, was made because of her parents' strong Chinese identity: 'It is obvious due to the fact that my mother sent me back to Taiwan [for my early education]. She said to me that I'm Chinese and I cannot change that fact. Since I'm Chinese, I should have certain standards of listening, speaking, reading, and writing Mandarin'; she said in the interview.

Here we can see how the East-West antagonism preoccupies Jane. When explaining why people should be proud of China and identify themselves as Chinese, she points to the nation's long history and its celebrated inventions and technological achievements - elements commonly used to contrast China with Western civilisation. When explaining why some people reject Chinese identity, she said they are influenced by the sense of discrimination directed at them by Westerners or, more precisely, by a sense of inferiority in the face of the superior white race. Apparently, Jane's Chinese identity (as well as her struggle within this identity) is formed by the contrast between concepts of East and West.

Not only Jane's identity pattern but also her various political attitudes and perceptions are forged and shaped by this East-West antagonism. Her views on the three subjects cited below offer good examples. The first is the movement in China to boycott some foreign commodities, on which she has this to say:

JANE: [...] When dealing with problems with other countries, such as Korea, for instance, they (the Chinese) might boycott the goods of Korea, or Japan. They (the Chinese) would use this method. It is because we have too much historical feeling (love, hatred, amity, and enmity [aihen qingchou 愛恨情仇]), and that's why they use the term 'China' as an excuse (a tool) to mobilise people and to provoke nationalist sentiments. Well, it's not an excuse... I think it is necessary, because we are Chinese. [...] We know about the painful events of history, like the Nanjing Massacre. I think a nation is made by its history, by what it has passed through, and we certainly should maintain and support our national characteristics. Otherwise, why should we be Chinese? Today, you are Chinese, and you should have a sense of belongingness. Therefore, when people say that we have to boycott Japanese goods because the Japanese have bullied us Chinese for too long, I think it is okay.

The second subject is Tibetan independence, Jane's opinion of which also reflects the influence of East-West antagonism:

Q: Do you support Tibet's independence?

JANE: Of course not! Because, I think, if they are independent...Well, take Taiwan as an example... How many ethnic groups are there in Taiwan? Are you going to allow all of them to be independent? If so, Taiwan will be divided! How should you divide the land? Drawing boundaries according to some mountains? [...] It's impossible. I think supporting independence just because of ethnic differences is irrational.

Q: But, isn't the situation of Tibet different from that of Taiwanese aboriginals?

JANE: Yes... the culture of Tibet is quite historic... The ethnicity and culture of Tibet are quite different from Taiwan's. [...] They have many 'pure' Tibetans; their ancestors were not hybridised with Han. And they preserve their culture quite well... [...]

Q: Even so, you would not support their independence?

JANE: No, I would not. Because, I think if Han, Manchu, Mongol, Hui, Tibetan, Miao, and Yao all seek independence, then China will be divided. How can you distinguish who is Tibetan and who is Han, nowadays? We have gone through five thousand-years [of Chinese] history, and there can't be 'pure' Han blood running through anyone's veins. If you seek independence just because of certain political reasons, China will collapse! China's collapse won't benefit anyone.

The third subject is the current state of international affairs:

JANE: [...] If China divides, you will have no resources and become separate countries. It will be very difficult to feed 1.3 billion people then. Pursuing separatism and making all

miserable will benefit no one. Uniting together is the only solution. China has suffered for too long. It has been an oppressed nation. It is still being bullied in international society.
Q: For instance?
JANE: America. Yes, American has been bad to China. The US does not want to see China get strong, so it poses many obstacles for China and provokes many conflicts between Taiwan and China.
Q: Did you feel this oppression when in the US?
JANE: I only felt racism in the US. I didn't experience conflict with the Chinese (Mainlanders), no.
Q: I mean... you said that Chinese were being bullied ...
JANE: Yes, that is; in the form of racism.

Each of these three conversations shows the operation of the ethical narrative of East-West antagonism. The villains in her narratives are Westerners, Americans and Japanese - the notorious advocates of imperialism in modern East Asian history, and they keep trying to satisfy their greed by exercising their influence on contemporary world issues.

In addition, these interviews with Jane reveal how the East-West antagonistic narrative informs her strong feelings about the concepts of Chinese, Easterners, and Westerners. These feelings can be roughly classified into two categories, corresponding to the dichotomy of good and evil: on the one hand, feelings for the benevolent are apparent in her pride in being Chinese, her anxieties about China's potential division and collapse, and her great concern for its territorial integrity (as shown in her discussion of Tibetan independence). On the other hand, her feelings for the malignant emerge in her antagonism towards and resentment of racist foreigners and imperialist invaders. Moreover, the East-West antagonistic narrative also suggests moral actions corresponding to the moral dualism. These can be boycotting Japanese commodities, uniting all the Chinese people (including all ethnic minorities), making the Chinese nation stronger and alive (keep it from collapse), and fighting against global racist discrimination.

Yet what best illustrates the influence of East-West antagonism on Jane's political views would be her attitudes on Taiwan's future:

JANE: I think unification with China is a necessary route, because, from the point of view of China, they will certainly not allow Taiwan to be independent ...
Q: Why not?
JANE: Why should they? China has claimed that they would rather let one hundred million people die than surrender one inch of territory. Now they have retrieved Macau and Hong Kong, and the last [lost territory] is Taiwan.
Q: Territory ...
JANE: Territory is very important to every country. Otherwise, why does everybody fight for the Senkaku [Diaoyutai 釣魚臺] *Islands? They are only little islands. But they are territory, and territory concerns national dignity, which does not allow compromise. If they (China) allow Taiwan to be independent today, and then Tibet is independent, Xinjiang is independent, Yunnan is independent, every province is independent; then the mainland (China) is divided! A divided mainland does not benefit mainlanders.*

When discussing Taiwan's future, Jane does not take the viewpoint of Taiwan or its people but that of China (mainland) or Chinese people (mainlanders). However, it is not because Jane traitorously rejects being Taiwanese when reflecting on this issue. It is because her strong emotions are dictated by the East-West antagonistic narrative. More precisely, Jane does not reject Taiwanese identity; it is her worries and fears for the division and collapse of the Chinese nation that prompt her to take such a position. Her reason for opposing Taiwan independence once again supports the East-West antagonism analysis and manifests the potency of her feelings:

Q: If, in very ideal circumstances, China would allow Taiwan to be independent and would maintain all forms of economic interaction and not oppress Taiwan, would you support Taiwan independence?

JANE: It depends ... People say that the twenty-first century is the century of the Chinese ... I think it depends on whether Taiwan can have its share ... If China treats Taiwan as it treats the US - that is, there might be some preferential treatment for some firms, but generally taxes are high - Taiwan would not be able to sell goods to China, or the goods would be too expensive (because of the taxes), and then what should Taiwan do?

Even in the most ideal situation - one that favours Taiwan independence - Jane still opposes this option. Her opposition does not derive entirely from the standpoint of China, longing for the integrity of a greater Chinese nation. Rather, she takes Taiwan's benefit into consideration, expecting that Taiwan will receive its fair share when China turns into a world superpower. Therefore, what is important in Jane's case is not which position she takes or whose benefit she attaches greater weight to, but the particular feelings that lead her to take up her standpoints - that is, the feelings that are generated by the East-West antagonistic narrative. When Jane explains her support for unification, the East-West antagonistic narrative is operating, inducing her feelings of worry and fear for China's collapse. When she states her opposition to Taiwan independence, that discourse is at work again, provoking a feeling of excitement at the prospect of China and Taiwan, together, achieving a supreme status over all other countries of the world in the new century.

The influence of the East-West antagonistic discourse can also be found in Haoping's views on Taiwan's future. Here he explains why he supports Taiwan's unification with China:

HAOPING: Because... the population of daluren *is very large; if properly utilised, it is possible for us Chinese people to dominate the world.* [Laugh]

Q: But why is dominating the world important?

HAOPING: If we dominated the world, we wouldn't have to depend on foreign countries. Right now, we follow the Americans in many aspects, such as technology and weapons. Usually, they develop something first, and then we copy or purchase these from them. They are foreigners after all; we might become a puppet, if they control many things. [...] The other thing is that I hate learning English. I want the whole world to learn Mandarin! [Laugh]

Haoping's vision of unification is not based on careful and thorough deliberation on the future political or economic benefits that might accrue to Taiwan, but on the yearning to dominate the world; it is a backlash against the sense of backwardness and incompetence that has developed as a result of comparisons being drawn with Western countries. In other words, what dictates Haoping's attitude towards Taiwan's future is not rational calculation but, once again, the feelings induced by the East-West antagonistic narrative.

Resisting the East-West Antagonistic Narrative

Both Haoping's and Jane's interviews demonstrate the power of the East-West antagonistic narrative to forge and shape their identity patterns and political orientations. However, the operation of the discourse does not guarantee the successful construction of Chinese identity. Some people in Taiwan, while familiar with this narrative, do not claim Chinese identity. Yuxin, a 22-year-old (born in 1992) female college student in Taibei, is one such example. She is the youngest child in her family and has an older brother. Her father is a *waishengren* who works as a processor in a factory owned by a large food company and her mother is a low-level clerk at a medium-sized firm in Taibei County. Yuxin was a diligent student who attended a top high school. At the time of interview, she had just entered college, pursuing a bachelor's degree in statistics at a private university.

Yuxin firmly rejects Chinese identity and claims Taiwanese identity only. Indeed, she perceives the idea of 'Chinese', as something highly obnoxious and says in her interview that she will never ever relate to this concept. Nonetheless, she has internalised certain elements in the East-West antagonistic narrative. For instance, she tends to associate the concept of the supra-ethnic Chinese nationality with Easterners - as Haoping does - and she is aware of China's miserable history in the late nineteenth century. In our discussion about kung-fu movies (such as Ip Man) that depict the era of the late Qing Dynasty and early Republican China, Yuxin cannot resist expressing her resentful feelings towards foreign imperialists (such as Japan) - a sign that the East-West antagonistic narrative is operating.

Q: Do you like Ip Man?
YUXIN: It's not bad. His [the main character's] kung-fu is great. Donnie Yen is awesome!
Q: How about the story?
YUXIN: It's once again about Japan.
Q: So?
YUXIN: It makes me dislike the Japanese. I especially detest the Japanese in that period.
Q: In that period? So, you don't detest the Japanese now?
YUXIN: I just don't want to argue about that (the brutal deeds of the Japanese in World War II) [now], but when watching this kind of movie, I still feel averse to them.
Q: Why?
YUXIN: Because the Japanese at that time were oppressing the Chinese people. Not only the Chinese people but also us Taiwanese people. That's objectionable.
Q: For instance? What do you mean by oppress?
YUXIN: The Nanjing Massacre! They (Japanese) were so inhumane then.
Q: How about the Taiwanese?
YUXIN: Occupation. They occupied Taiwan. I really dislike that. But now, it is all in the past, after all. I don't belong to that generation; the generation of that period would probably hate them.

Ip Man (Yewen 葉問) was filmed in 2008 and featured the famous kung-fu star, Donnie Yen. The story is set in the 1930s when the Japanese invaded and occupied Foshan (佛山), the hometown of the kung-fu master, Ip Man. Not surprisingly, the main villains in the story are Japanese soldiers. Yuxin indeed acknowledges this ethical narrative and, as she reports, experiences a sense of resentment against Japanese when watching the film. However, she does not respond to its identity appeals. Even in the interview above, Yuxin does not regard herself as Chinese - she differentiates between Chinese and Taiwanese and says that both were oppressed by Japan at that time.

Thus, Yuxin only partially follows the emotional and moral coordinates set by East-West antagonism: when watching movies based on this narrative, she can recognise who are the good guys and who are the bad, sympathising with the former and resenting the latter. However, she does not link the narrative with her own reality; she sees the story as being about some historical period decades ago, one which does not relate to her present surroundings. In the interview, Yuxin emphasises this difference many times, qualifying her negative feelings towards the Japanese with expressions such as 'in that period', 'at that time', and 'all in the past.' She explains that she does not belong to 'that generation' that would be expected to hate the Japanese. By defining a distance between the story and contemporary reality, Yuxin can only partially engage with the movie. What she experiences while watching Ip Man or similar movies is the ethical narrative operating at the most elementary level - she relates to the morality in the narrative, but does not translate her response to the story into feelings about real life in the present day. More precisely, the positive feelings and the moral obligation evoked by Ip Man are exactly the same as those she feels for Superman, James Bond, Harry Potter, or any other hero in Western movies. They are feelings provoked by the story of moral dualism - arguably, natural human responses to morality - and she finds it silly to associate these feelings with vague concepts of Eastern and Western identity. Yuxin's account illustrates the fact that it is possible to elude the influence of the East-West antagonistic discourse: she may identify herself as an Easterner (as she reports in the interview, she would regard herself as Asian and as an Easterner), but she does not view Westerners as her enemies. In other words, her identification with Easterners exists only at a conceptual level, without affectional investment; the identity (and thus the East-West antagonistic discourse) does not provoke her feelings nor compel her political/moral actions. The terms of East and Easterner are merely generic ideas, words, to her, to designate specific concepts that stand in contrast to the ideas of West and Westerner. These terms lack the capacity to provoke a strong emotional response from her or any moral or political actions. The question is this: how is it that Yuxin is free from the identity interpellation of the East-West antagonistic discourse despite the fact that she is so familiar with the narrative? There seem to be two possible explanations. Firstly, it could be that Yuxin perceives a gap between the discourse and reality - a disparity akin to the difference between a fictional movie and reality. Secondly, it might be that she is attracted to another ethical narrative, one that I call 'China-Taiwan antagonism.' Unsurprisingly, the role of the benevolent actor in this equation is played by the Taiwanese people, while the malignant counterpart is played by the Chinese people or, more precisely, the people of the PRC. Aside from the fact that Yuxin claims Taiwanese identity and rejects Chinese identity, she even uses the word 'hatred' to describe her feelings towards China. From her perspective, China (the Chinese Communists) has been an enemy threatening Taiwan since the late 1940s, when the Chinese Communist Party (CCP, representing China in this discourse) drove the Nationalists (GMD, possessing the capacity to represent Taiwan in this discourse) off the mainland, and continued to fight them in skirmishes across the Strait for several years afterwards. Even now, there are still conflicts between the two states: she sees China oppressing Taiwan and trying to exclude Taiwan from international politics. Being forced to use the name 'Chinese Taibei' in international forums is a case in point that bothers her. Such injustice and oppression imposed on Taiwan are apparently more real and immediate to Yuxin than the shared problems of the Easterners described in the East-West antagonistic discourse.

Why does the China-Taiwan antagonistic discourse hold a greater attraction for Yuxin than East-West antagonism? Why do kung-fu movies such as Ip Man arouse stronger emotions in Haoping and Jane than in Yuxin? The answer seems to lie in each individual's past experiences. On the one hand, Yuxin, born after 1991,[19] was exposed to the newer editions of history textbooks, and this probably contributed to her conviction that China and Taiwan are two different and rival countries. Furthermore, she had been hearing from the Taiwan media how China throws its weight around, oppressing Taiwan on the international stage. Meanwhile, Haoping, ten years older than Yuxin, was taught from an older GMD textbook, one which placed more emphasis on the promotion of Chinese nationalism and the construction of the collective concept of the supra-ethnic 'Chinese.' Jane, of the same generation as Haoping, also received this nationalist education, but its influence has been significantly tempered by her stay in the US, where she experienced racial discrimination from white Westerners, which caused her to embrace the East-West antagonism.

Conclusion

This paper offers a theoretical framework for explaining how an individual's identity is formed - more precisely, for the deliberate selection of Chinese identity by some Taiwanese people. The key element in this theory is the ethical narrative - a particular type of narrative structured in moral dualism, featuring the mythical, fundamental struggle between good and evil. This moral dualism does not only inform the audience's emotions - evoking positive feelings for the good characters and negative ones for the villains - but also motivates their moral and political action, demanding that they support the good side and oppose the bad. In short, the ethical narrative creates a structured platform for its audience to release their feelings, fulfil their fantasies, and practice morality. This is the charm of the ethical narrative, and this is why people are willing to take part in it. The empirical reports of fieldwork participants illustrate the operation of a particular type of ethical narrative, namely, East-West antagonism. With the moral dualistic structure in which the Chinese people (the good) fight against Western imperialists (the evil), the East-West antagonist narrative forges, shapes, and fortifies a Chinese identity.

This paper does not suggest that East-West antagonism is 'purely' fictional. The construction of the discourse is in fact based on historical facts. More precisely, this discourse is created by selectively emphasising certain historical events, and by purposefully interpreting and directing the events to the rivalry between the two collective ideas, Easterners and Westerners. This is not to suggest that East-West antagonism is wholly determinative of identity, either. In fact, any claim that there is a single determinant of identity formation is problematic and cannot pass scientific examination. Yuxin's case, the counter-example, shows that the East-West antagonistic narrative might fail when competing for influence on one's identity and political orientations with other discourses. Indeed, multiple narratives and discourses exist in society, that are competing to dominate a person's identity formation (for instance, the East-West antagonism and the China-Taiwan antagonism compete for Yuxin's interpretation and conceptualisation of the idea 'Chinese'). The task of researchers is to explore the various factors and discourses behind identity formation, while recognising that these factors may not exert an equal influence on all members of the society in question.

---

[19] After 2000, school textbooks were published in multiple versions and allowed to be edited by private publishers, which suggests that the content was subject to fewer controls by the government than it had been before. Generally, all students in Taiwan who were born after 1991 would have been taught with the newly edited textbooks.

Yuxin's case also explicitly manifests the operation of identity - in the absence of a discourse capable of provoking emotions and mobilising action, an identity is merely a generic label. Yuxin knows she is an Easterner but, for her, this is merely a term of classification; without the operation of the East-West antagonistic discourse, she does not identify herself as Chinese. The East-West antagonism presented in this paper is one type of ethical narrative - and thus one of the many forms of emotional and value-oriented discourses capable of arousing emotions and stimulate actions. By examining the operation of the ethical narrative, this paper offers a useful analytical lens for investigating the complex mechanisms of identity formation - as well as the tangled relationships among emotion, identity, and morality.

References

Anderson, Benedict (2006) *Imagined Communities: Reflections on the Origin and Spread of Nationalism*, London: Verso Books.

Andrews, Molly (2007) *Shaping History: Narratives of Political Change*, Cambridge: Cambridge University Press.

Andrews, Molly, Corinne Squire and Tamboukou, Maria (eds.) (2013) *Doing Narrative Research*. Thousand Oaks: Sage.

Brockmeier, Jens and Carbaugh, Donald A. (eds.) (2001) *Narrative and Identity: Studies in Autobiography, Self and Culture*, Amsterdam: John Benjamins Publishing.

Chang, G. Andy, and Wang, T. Y. (2005) 'Taiwanese or Chinese? Independence or Unification? An Analysis of Generational Differences in Taiwan', *Journal of Asian and African Studies* 40(1-2), 22-49.

Chen Cui-lian 陳翠蓮 (2008) Resistance and the Identity of the Taiwanese People: 1920-1950, Taibei [Taipei]: Yuan-Liou Publishing Co., Ltd. [遠流出版社]

Chen Muming [Chen, Mu-ming 陳牧民] (2006) 'Taiwan guojia ren tong yanjiu de xiankuang yu zhanwang' 臺灣國家認同研究的現況與發展 [National identity studies in Taiwan: the present and the future], Taiwan International Studies Association, http://www.tisanet.org/Activity/20060610/conference/1-2.pdf, accessed 15 Nov. 2015.

Chen Wenjun [Chen Wen-chun 陳文俊] (1997) *Taiwan de zuqun zhengzhi* 臺灣的族群政治 [Ethnic politics in Taiwan], Hong Kong: Hong Kong Social Science Press.

Dikötter, Frank (1997) 'Racial Discourse in China: Continuities and Permutations', in id. (ed.) *In The Construction of Racial Identities in China and Japan: Historical and Contemporary Perspectives*, London: Hurst & Company, 12-33.

Gellner, Ernest (1983) *Nations and Nationalism*, Malden, Mass.: Blackwell.

Hsiau, A-chin [Xiao Aqin 蕭阿勤] (2008) *Return to Reality: Political and Cultural Change in 1970s Taiwan and the Post-war Generation*, Taibei [Taipei]: Institute of Sociology, Academia Sinica.

Huang Chi [Huang Ji 黃紀] (2005) 'Dimensions of Taiwanese/Chinese Identity and National Identity in Taiwan', *Journal of Asian and African Studies* 40(1-2), 51-70.

Huang Li-li [Huang Lili 黃囇莉], Liu, James H. and Chang, Maanling [Zhang Manling 張滿玲] (2004) 'The 'Double Identity' of Taiwanese Chinese: A Dilemma of Politics and Culture Rooted in History', *Asian Journal of Social Psychology* 7(2), 149-68.

Lin, Chia-lung [Lin Jialong 林佳龍] (2002) 'The Political Formation of Taiwanese Nationalism', in Corcuff, Stéphane (ed.) *Memories of the Future*, London and New York: M.E. Sharpe.

Liu Yizhou [Liu, I-chou 劉義周] (1998) 'Taiwan minzhong de guojia rentong - yige xin de celiang fangshi' 臺灣民眾的國家認同：一個新的測量方式 [National identity of

Taiwanese people - a new study method), paper presented to the Annual Conference of the ROC Political Science Association.

Marsh, Robert (2005) 'National Identity and Ethnic Identity in Taiwan: Some Trends in the 1990s', in Corcuff, Stéphane (ed.) *Memories of the Future: National Identity Issues and the Search for a New Taiwan*, London and New York: M.E. Sharpe, 144-59.

Rigger, Shelley (1997) 'Competing Conceptions of Taiwan's Identity: The Irresolvable Conflict in Cross-strait Relations', *Journal of Contemporary China*, 6(15): 307-317.

Rigger, Shelley (2006) *Taiwan's Rising Rationalism: Generations, Politics, and 'Taiwanese Nationalism',* Washington D.C.: East-West Center Washington.

Shi Zhengfeng [Shih Cheng-feng 施正鋒] (2001) 'Taiwanren de guojia rentong' 臺灣人的國家認同 [Taiwanese people's national identity] in: Taiwan Historical Association (ed.) *Guojia rentong lunwenji* 國家認同論文集 [Collected papers on national identity], Taipei: Daoxiang [Dawshiang] Publishing.

Smith, Anthony D. (2010) *Nationalism: Theory, Ideology, History*, Cambridge: Polity Press.

Strauss, Anselm and Corbin, Juliet (1998) *Basics of Qualitative Research: Techniques and Procedures for Developing Grounded Theory*, Thousand Oaks; London: Sage.

Wang, Horng-luen [Wang Honglun 汪宏倫] (2015) 'Comparison for Compassion: Exploring the Structures of Feeling in East Asia', in Shih, Shu-mei and Liao, Ping-hui (eds.) *Comparatizing Taiwan*, London: Routledge, 59-89.

Wu, Nai-teh [Wu Naide 吳乃德] (1993) 'Shengji yishi, zhengzhi jichi he quojia renting' 省籍意識，政治支持和國家認同 [The provincial conscience, political support, and national identity), in: Chang, Mau-kuei [Zhang Maogui 張茂桂] (ed.) *Zuquan guanxi yu guojia rentong* 族群關係與國家認同 [Ethnic relations and national identity], Taibei [Taipei]: Yeqiang, 27-51.

Wu, Zhuo-liu [Wu Zhuoliu 吳濁流] (1994) *The Fig Tree: Memoirs of a Taiwanese Patriot 1900-1947*, New York: Sharpe.

Wu Yushan [Wu, Yu-shan 吳玉山] (2001) 'Liang'an guanxi zhong de Zhongguo yishi yu Taiwan yishi' 兩岸關係中的中國意識與臺灣意識 [Chinese and Taiwanese consciousness in cross-strait relations], *Zhongguo Shiwu* 中國事務 [China Affairs Quarterly] 4, 71-89.

Zhang, Dainian 张岱年 and Cheng Yishan 程宜山 (1990) *Zhongguo wenhua yu wenhua zhenglun* 中國文化與文化論爭 [Chinese culture and cultural debates], Beijing: Renmin University of China Press.

.

Ek-hong Ljavakaw Sia

Crafting the Taiwanese Nation: Exclusivist and Inclusivist Theses of the Post-war Taiwanese Nationalism

The post-war Taiwanese nationalism is ambiguous, because in the early stage of its ideological embryogenesis, two logics of subject formation emerged under highly-constrained historical conditions in resistance to the two rationales of the dominant Chinese nationalism. The first was the logic of differentiating the self from the other; the second was the logic of integrating the intruding other into the self. The former, which is referred to as the exclusivist thesis in this study, rejected the rationale of the China-based ROC's re-orientating *nationalist engineering, which had sought to tear Taiwan apart from its Japanese matrix and to merge it to the Chinese nation-state. Instead, it sought to build a Taiwanese nation-state by* excluding *the émigré state and population in Taiwan. The latter, which is referred to as the inclusivist thesis in this paper, advocated the reconstruction of the ROC-in-exile's reconstructive nation-building project that had sought to forge the native and émigré populations into an 'authentic' Chinese nation in accordance with three principles, i.e., irredentism, authoritarianism, and assimilation. By reconstructing the ROC-in-exile's nation-building, the* inclusivist *thesis sought to build a Taiwanese nation-state with the* transformative inclusion *of the émigré state and population.*

A Nationalism Unpositionable

The national question of Taiwan is often reduced to the bickering between China, a giant continental country represented by the People's Republic of China (PRC) and Taiwan, a small island republic represented by the Republic of China (ROC). This framing in terms of binary opposition, although it seems to make the situation easier to comprehend, is an oversimplification, if not outright misleading. In particular, the national subject – which is supposed to be the core of the national question – is entirely overlooked in this binary frame. What is the national subject of Taiwan? Who belongs to the Taiwanese nation and who does not? How did, or should, the Taiwanese nation be formed? The formation of the national subject is at the core of the national question in Taiwan, yet it is obscured in the binary frame.

Taiwanese nationalism as an ideology that addresses the national question is probably one of the most complicated and confusing nationalisms in the world. As a belated nationalism, it was first brought into being during the 1920s and 1930s in resistance against Japanese colonial rule. Japan, a newly-formed modern nation-state which had risen rapidly in the late 19th century, resisted real and perceived Western threats by means of sustained imperialist expansion into adjacent territories and by the differential incorporation of these adjacent colonies. Wu Ruiren [Wu Rwei-ren] (2003), a leading scholar on Taiwanese nationalism, refers to this ideology as a paradoxical anti-colonial and nationalizing colonialism. Ideologically, Taiwanese nationalists, during the 1920s and the 1930s, were compelled to form a discursive alliance with the enemy of the enemy (that is, with the Western countries which were deemed to be the origins of modernity/civilization) in order to resist their oriental colonizer, Japan, by criticizing its modernity/civilization as incomplete (ibid.). While the dis-

cursive strategies were delicate and roundabout, their ultimate goal was quite straightforward – like most anti-colonial nationalisms in the twentieth century, the pre-war Taiwanese nationalism sought to build a Taiwanese nation-state by expelling the Japanese colonizer.
There was obviously a gap between the pre-war and the post-war Taiwanese nationalism. Temporally and geographically, pre-war Taiwanese nationalism can be properly classified in the category of Asian and African anti-colonial nationalisms that was formulated by Benedict Anderson (2006 [1983]) as the fourth wave in the historical development of nationalism. However, after the national question of Taiwan was 'shunted' off the track of Japanese-Taiwanese nexus onto the track of Chinese-Taiwanese nexus in the aftermath of WWII, the post-war Taiwanese nationalism has seemed much more vague and ambiguous than its pre-war counterpart in terms of the formation of the national subject, making it distinct from any of the historical variants of nationalism.
In his classic work, Anderson historically formulates four types of nationalism that emerged between the late 18th and the 20th century. The post-war Taiwanese nationalism was hardly analogous to the first-wave creole nationalism, because it was an ideology in resistance not against the *colonial metropole* but against the *émigré state* which was expelled from its motherland, China, despite the fact that it was indeed first articulated by the Taiwanese nationalists who have been typically considered as a creolized population – that is, the descendants of earlier immigrants from Southern China one or two hundred years previously. Neither was it the second-wave mass linguistic nationalism which attempted to integrate peoples with a variety of fragmented local/regional/feudal identities into a larger scale nation through linguistic standardization and assimilation. In fact, post-war Taiwanese nationalism was a *converting* nationalism that sought to *convert* a populace, which had been indoctrinated to regard itself as a homogeneous, 'authentic' Chinese nation, into a multicultural Taiwanese nation. Furthermore, it was of course not analogous to the third-wave top-down official nationalism; on the contrary, it was a bottom-up reaction to the official Chinese nationalism. Finally, although some people, including many Taiwanese nationalists themselves, tended to identify post-war Taiwanese nationalism with the fourth wave of anti-colonial nationalism, even if we regard Taiwan's status as 'colonial', this was not a typical colonialism imposed by an *alien* power but a unique status that combined a system of domination established by an *émigré* state under constant threat from a *neighbouring* state which was willing to back up its claim to sovereignty over the island by force if necessary.
Moreover, John Breuilly (1982), perceiving nationalism as a kind of political movement closely related to state power, articulates a trichotomy which categorizes nationalisms into separatist, unificationist, and reformist types according to their intended relations with the existing state. However, post-war Taiwanese nationalism cannot be classified as any of these types. First of all, it is not separatist nationalism because it has never sought to secede any part of the island's territory from the jurisdiction of the current state, let alone from the PRC which has never ruled Taiwan. Secondly, Taiwanese nationalism is not an unificationist ideology, because it has no intention of unifying Taiwan with any other state. Finally, it is stretching the point too far to claim that the ultimate goal of Taiwanese nationalism is to reform the existing state. Of course, the goals of Taiwanese nationalists have varied, ranging from expelling the émigré ROC entirely or asking it to become 'naturalized' as a state belonging to the envisaged Taiwanese nation. However, the goal of Taiwanese nationalism has never consisted only of the reform of the émigré state.

Although the rise of Taiwanese nationalism over the last three decades has coincided with the ethnic/regional revivals that appeared in the course of the disintegration of former communist confederations in Eastern Europe (Brubaker 1996, Beissinger 2002) and secessionisms/sub-state nationalisms that have appeared in the established states in Western Europe and North America, such as the United Kingdom (Scotland and Wales), Spain (Catalonia and Basque), Belgium (Flanders), and Canada (Quebec)[1] as well as in East Asia, including Japan (Okinawa), China (Tibet and East Turkestan), and the Philippines (Mindanao)[2], it is difficult to form an analogy between Taiwanese nationalism and these other nationalisms. Obviously, these other nationalisms emerged in very different contexts to Taiwanese nationalism. More importantly, Taiwanese nationalism aims to dismantle the ethnic hierarchy imposed by the émigré state and to mould a multicultural nation bonded by civic solidarity rather than to secede from an existing state or to found a new ethnically-based nation state following the breakup of a confederation.

This lack of compatibility suggests that we should not start by drawing an analogy between the post-war Taiwanese nationalism and nationalisms elsewhere in the world. On the contrary, we are compelled to look squarely at the very conditions under which post-war Taiwanese nationalism emerged. For this reason, this study examines the embryogenesis of post-war Taiwanese nationalism at its early development stage (from the late 1940s to the 1970s) with a focus on its *ideological* development. We do not intend to describe the various nationalist organizations and their actions and individual discourses in detail as previous studies have done[3]; instead, we focus our attention on the very core of nationalist ideology — in other words, how post-war Taiwanese nationalism constructed the national subject as a Taiwanese nation.

The main argument of this study can be summarized as follows. Post-war Taiwanese nationalism is ambiguous, because in the early stage of its ideological embryogenesis two logics of subject formation were brought into being in resistance against the two rationales of the dominant Chinese nationalism under highly-constrained historical conditions. The first is the logic of differentiating the self from the other; the second is the logic that seeks to integrate the intruding other into the self. The former, which is referred to as the exclusivist thesis in this study, rejected the rationale of the China-based ROC's *re-orientating* nationalist engineering which undertook to tear Taiwan apart from its Japanese matrix and to merge it to Chinese nation-state. Instead, it sought to build a Taiwanese nation-state by *excluding* the émigré state and population in Taiwan. The latter, which is referred to as the inclusivist thesis in this study, advocated the reconstruction of the ROC-in-exile's *reconstructive* nation-building, which had aimed to forge the native and émigré populations into an 'authentic' Chinese nation in accordance with three principles, i.e., irredentism, authoritarianism, and assimilationism, with the aim of building a Taiwanese nation-state with the *transformative inclusion* of the émigré state and population.

---

1 See Guerina and Pelletiera (2000) (Spain); Billiet, Maddens, and Frognier (2006) (Belgium); Paquin (2002) (Scotland). For a comparison between the U.K, Belgium, and Canada, see Béland and Lecours (2005); for a comparison between Quebec, Scotland and Wales, see Hamilton (2004); for a comparison between Scotland, Wales, Catalonia, and Quebec, see McCrone (1998).

2 See Wu (2014) and Wang (2015) (Okinawa); Wang (2009) (Tibet); Wang (2007) and Chen (2014) (East Turkestan), and Vitug and Gloria (2000) (Mindanao).

3 See, for example, Mendel (1970), Chen (1998, 2006), and Geoffroy (1997).

In the following two sections, the ROC's re-orientating nation-building and the birth of the exclusivist thesis of Taiwanese nationalism as well as the ROC's reconstructive nation-building and the circuitous development of the inclusivist thesis are examined. In the conclusion, the political consequences of the two theses of post-war Taiwanese nationalism are briefly discussed.

The Re-Orientating Nation-Building and the Exclusivist Thesis

The ROC's Re-Orientating Nation-Building: 1945-49

In the aftermath of WWII, the national question of Taiwan was 'shunted' off the track of the Japanese-Taiwanese nexus onto the track of the Chinese-Taiwanese nexus in a way that was largely beyond the control or expectations of the Taiwanese. Following the surrender of Japan, Japanese forces within Taiwan and French Indo-China north of the sixteenth parallel were ordered, in accordance with the General Order No. 1 issued by the U.S. General Douglas MacArthur, to surrender to one of the designated Allied commanders, Generalissimo Jiang Jieshi [Chiang Kai-shek]. On 25 October, 1945, Chen Yi as Jiang's delegate began to enforce the military occupation of Taiwan. Although the military occupation was not supposed to effect any transfer of sovereignty, the Chinese nationalist leadership did not see it this way. The *retrocession* of Taiwan had been upheld as a major appeal to mobilize mass sentiment against Japan after the ROC formally declared war on Japan in 1941. This appeal was affirmed by the Cairo Declaration, a statement of intent made by the leaders of the U.S., the U.K., and the ROC. The Chinese nationalist leadership were confident that they would reclaim sovereignty over Taiwan, and at the outset perceived the military occupation as an interim stage before the full resumption of sovereignty (Su n.d.; Yun 2007).

Jiang's representative started the re-orientating blueprint of nationalist engineering which attempted to tear Taiwan apart from its Japanese matrix and then merge it into Chinese nation-state. This re-orientating nation-building had concrete political, economic, and cultural manifestations. In terms of politics, the highest occupational authority at the earliest stage was established in the name of the Governor Administration *of Taiwan Province*, exercising its powers through the integration of administrative, legislative, and judicial functions in exactly the same manner as the Japanese Governor-General of Taiwan. Furthermore, the Governor himself served concurrently as the Garrison Commander. This high centralization of power was designed as a special interim arrangement in the hope of ultimately incorporating Taiwan as a formal province of China (Su n.d.). Although the Chinese occupational authority inherited the well-developed Japanese colonial state apparatus with only minor changes, the Japanese monopoly on middle- and high-level occupations was replaced with a Chinese monopoly. Moreover, due to the reductions in the number of staff , a large number of low-level civil servants who were mainly Taiwanese were laid off. This transitional arrangement obviously contradicted the anticipation of Taiwanese local elites who were looking forward to playing a greater political role following the end of Japanese rule and to making Taiwan join the Chinese state system as an island-wide autonomous regional entity (Zheng Zi 1992: 263; Chen Mingtong 2001: chapter 2; Chen Cuilian 1995: 71-80).

In economic terms, the Chinese occupational authority re-directed economic core-periphery relations from a Japan-Taiwan to a China-Taiwan pattern. In the eyes of Chinese officials,

Taiwan was not expected to be re-built as a self-sufficient economy, but rather as a periphery supplying resources needed by the core, this time, mainland China. To fulfil this goal, all the industries left by the Japanese were nationalized and made subordinate to the central government based in Nanking or the Governor Administration of Taiwan Province. The Monopoly Bureau and Trade Bureau were retained to control the production, domestic trade, import and export of various products, functioning as a machine to tirelessly extract profitable agricultural products and mineral resources, such as rice, sugar, salt, coal, timber, and so on, and transfer them to China in order to supply the wartime needs of the Chinese Nationalist Party (also known as Guomindang [Kuomintang]; hereafter, abbreviated as GMD [KMT]) in the Chinese Civil War. As a consequence, domestic inflation caused by the shortage of materials and the ill-disciplined printing of money as well as imported inflation induced by the policy of deliberately devaluing the Taiwanese currency against the Chinese and a large number of arbitrage transactions erupted concurrently. The shortage of materials, inefficient production, corrupt distribution of resources, a high unemployment rate, and out-of-control inflation pushed the island-wide economy to the edge of breakdown (Chen Cuilian 1995: 81-104; Chen Mingtong 2001: 56-64).

In terms of culture, aggressive Sinicization, which could be encapsulated as 'uprooting Japan, implanting China' was carried out soon after the Chinese takeover (Huang Yingzhe 2007). Following their bitter eight-year struggle, Chinese officials deemed the Japanese to be the arch-enemy and viewed the Japanized Taiwanese as an 'enslaved' people. The legacies of Japanese assimilation, including language, costumes, and customs, and even the by-products of colonial rule, such as 'modern' behavioural habits like observing the law and being punctual were all considered to be proofs of the 'enslaved state' of the Taiwanese. The Taiwanese were denied the right to serve as civil servants and teachers because of their lack of proficiency in the Chinese language. Taiwanese intellectuals who wrote in Japanese suddenly lost their livelihoods since publications were legally required to be published in Chinese. Ordinary 'domesticated' Taiwanese, who had long been used to the law-abiding, generally incorrupt, and efficient Japanese colonial rule were distressed when faced with the illegal, corrupt and uncivilized behaviour of civil officials and soldiers sent from mainland China (Kerr 1991; 2014).

The view held by the Chinese nationalist leadership on the retrocession of Taiwan is obviously based on the reasoning of ethnic nationalism. Taiwan as a whole was deemed to be the 'lost son' of the Chinese fatherland/national family. Since the Taiwanese had been 'corrupted' by Japan, they required 're-education' in order to readapt themselves to their family of origin. The re-education – that is, Sinicization – was to be conducted by a highly-centralized state dominated by the Chinese coming from the fatherland. The Taiwanese could be deemed to be qualified and equal members of the big national family when, and only when, the re-education was completed.

The re-orientating nationalist project caused strong dissatisfaction among almost all classes of society, which eventually exploded into an outright revolt known as the February 28 uprising in 1947. During the seven-day island-wide mass uprising, most native elites still retained a *reformist* position, hoping to improve the failed Chinese administration of the past two years by reconstructing it through a policy of democratic self-rule (Su 2004; Chen Cuilian 1995). However, the bloody military crackdown carried out by reinforcements sent from mainland China effectively eliminated the resistance. The subsequent purge of local elites in the name of rooting out communism ended the hopes of reformist-minded elites. Many of the elites were killed in the crackdown and subsequent purge, others managed to flee abroad, while those who remained withdrew from politics (Chen Cuilian 1995: 81-104; Zhang Yanxian 1992, 2000, 2006: Chapter 2). In short, the bloody military crackdown and subsequent purge after the 228 incident brutally eradicated the Taiwanese resistance against the ROC's re-orientating nation-building.

The elites who managed to flee abroad before or after the 228 incident became the earliest post-war Taiwanese nationalists. Their decisive attitude toward taking 'China/Chinese' as the other in opposition to the Taiwanese nation revealed the main difference between them and their predecessors under Japanese rule, who had regarded 'Japan/Japanese', rather than 'China/Chinese', as the other which was suppressing the Taiwanese nation. This was the birth of the exclusive line of post-war Taiwanese nationalism.

Exclusivist Thesis: Rejection of the Re-Orientating Nation-Building

Two unintended political legacies of Japanese rule, a politicized territorial-regional identity and a widely held belief in the legitimacy of democratic self-rule, still retained legitimacy in the minds of Taiwanese (Wu 2007a: 11). To some extent, these two legacies can psychologically explain the reaction of the Taiwanese to the Chinese takeover, which changed quickly from initial acceptance to resistance in the space of just two years (Chen Cuilian 2008; Li Xiaofeng 1994, 1995). The exclusivist thesis of the post-war Taiwanese nationalism was undoubtedly triggered by the failed nationalist project of re-orientating Taiwan towards China. The exclusivist thesis was characterized by the decisive repudiation of ties with the Chinese, and the insistence that the native population of Taiwan alone was qualified to be a distinct nation.[4] The logic of the exclusivist thesis was therefore to exclude all Chinese influences in order to build a Taiwanese nation-state. It was, to use a biological metaphor, the normal response of an organism suffering the intrusion of foreign body, that is, a natural impulse to directly exclude the foreign body from the organism.

In terms of *territory*, the idea of territorially attaching island Taiwan to mainland China had soon become regarded as undesirable. The illusionary pre-war attachments to the so-called 'mother country' and the post-war opportunism linked with becoming one of the major world powers by being incorporated into China were both extinguished in the minds of Taiwanese elites (Chen Zuilian 2008: 333-86; Li Xiaofeng 1994, 1995). The former illusion was extinguished by the actual experience of Chinese rule; the latter opportunism was

4 The main proponents of the exclusivist thesis of Taiwanese nationalism had served as leaders of nationalist organizations, for example, Joshua Liao (1950), Liao Wenyi [Liao Bun-gi] (1956), Su Beng (1980), Wang Yude [Ong Iok-tek] (1979; 2002), Li Tianfu [Li Tian-hok] (1958), and Chen Longzhi [Chen Lung-chu] (with Harold Lasswell 1967). The main points of the exclusivist thesis presented here are basically the crystallization of their augmentations. By categorizing their theses together as an exclusivist thesis of Taiwanese nationalism, I neither deny the subtle differences among their theses, nor claim that the embryogenesis of the exclusivist thesis should be reduced to the mental activities of these individuals. Instead, I would contend that, despite some minor differences in their arguments, strategies, and theoretical orientations, the main motivations and aims of the exclusivist thesis were shared among those theorists who found themselves situated within the same structural conflict. In this sense, the birth of the exclusivist thesis should not be reduced to a product of the internal mental activities of nationalist thinkers. In this study, the works of these writers are perceived as a clear expression of the existing structural conflict.

stamped out by a series of historical contingencies, namely, the GMD's failure in the Chinese Civil War and its retreat to Taiwan in 1949, the breaking out of the Korean War in 1950 and the subsequent American interventions which congealed the *de facto* territorial separation between island Taiwan and mainland China. It was not surprising, given the subjective and objective conditions mentioned above, that the exclusive-line Taiwanese nationalists rekindled the idea of their predecessors in the 1920s to support the founding of an island-wide Taiwanese nation-state without being territorially attached to mainland China.

In terms of *nation*, the exclusive line attempted to prove that the native population on Taiwan alone was qualified to form a Taiwanese nation distinct from and comparable with any other nation in the world. Despite their different theoretical orientations, theorists of the exclusivist thesis interpreted the genesis of the Taiwanese nation through an evolutionary perspective of historical socio-biology which can be summarized as follows: a distinct nation called Taiwanese has been historically forged out of a variety of human groups which, although ethno-culturally different from one another, had lived and interacted together within a defined geographical space, that is, the island of Taiwan, for a long period of time.[5] Based on this thesis, the exclusive line simultaneously claimed that the native inhabitants of Taiwan alone were qualified to be a Taiwanese nation and denied the right of the one million more Chinese in total, who had come to Taiwan after WWII, to form a constituent part of the Taiwanese nation because they had been absent from the historical process during which the Taiwanese nation had been forged. Therefore, in the exclusivist thesis, the Chinese émigrés in Taiwan were entirely excluded from the historically-formed Taiwanese nation. It was notable, nevertheless, that the socio-biological evolutionary thesis was not, in any sense, a sort of static, closed essentialism. In fact, it was an 'open-ended' historical discourse which implied the future possibility of incorporating the Chinese émigrés in Taiwan in the Taiwanese nation providing various subjective and objective conditions were met.

In terms of the *state*, the exclusive line argued that the rule of the GMD-dominated ROC over Taiwan was illegitimate in both international and domestic terms and that therefore the émigré ROC should be expelled. According to international laws, the rule of the émigré ROC over Taiwan, which based its legitimacy on a statement of intent in wartime – that is, the Cairo Declaration - rather than on the San Francisco Peace Treaty between Japan and the victorious Allied Powers which was officially signed by forty-eight nations in 1951, was illegal and illegitimate. Domestically, the ROC's rule over Taiwan was no different from internal colonialism. On the basis of these two points, the exclusive line argued that the ROC should be expelled from Taiwan, and that the native inhabitants of Taiwan were as much entitled as those of other ex-colonies to the right of national self-determination (Chen and Lasswell 1967).

To sum up, the exclusivist thesis of the post-war Taiwanese nationalism maintained that the given historically-formed Taiwanese nation based on a defined island territory of high consensus among its inhabitants was entitled to a state established by the native population. From this point of view, the émigré state and population should be excluded from the formation of the envisaged Taiwanese nation-state. The proponents of the exclusivist thesis

[5] In fact, similar views had already prevailed under Japanese colonial rule at least among Taiwanese intellectuals in the 1930s. See Wu (2003: Chapter 4) for a comprehensive examination of the thoughts of Taiwanese intellectuals in various academic fields.

did not probe into the different implications of the military occupation since 1945 and the transplantation of the ROC and the migration of one million more Chinese émigrés into Taiwan after 1949. The ROC and the emigres, in the eyes of exclusive-line nationalists, were nothing but more 'intruding foreign bodies' to be excluded. Politically speaking, the exclusive-line theory met with limited success during the first thirty years after WWII; nevertheless, as the post-war archetype of anti-colonial nationalism in Taiwan, it has had ideological and political consequences for nationalist politics in the eras of democratization and post-democratization.

The Reconstructive Nation-Building and Inclusivist Thesis

The ROC's Reconstructive Nation-Building after 1949

In the early post-war period, the U.S. as the principal occupying power did not express explicit objections to the project of re-orienting Taiwan away from Japan toward China that was implemented by the Chinese nationalist leadership in the course of the military occupation. However, Taiwan's seemingly inevitable incorporation into China was abruptly disrupted by two historical contingencies: first, the overthrow and retreat to Taiwan of the GMD-dominated ROC by Chinese communists in 1949 and, second, the outbreak of the Korean War in 1950.

These two earth-shaking changes led to a 'reversal of hostilities' (*dixing fan zhuan* 敵性反轉) in post-war East Asia (Yun 2007). The U.S., the Soviet Union and China were wartime allies; now they became post-war enemies. Furthermore, the wartime enemy, Japan, became the primary ally of the U.S. in reconstructing the post-war East Asian order. As a result, the 'neutralization' policy directed toward the Taiwan Strait that was put forward by the U.S. in the hope of preserving the moribund ROC in order to contain communist 'New China' in fact precluded the ROC-in-exile from recapturing China and the newly-established PRC from taking over Taiwan. This new situation meant two things. First, the ROC's unwilling detention in Taiwan would be lengthened indefinitely. Second, to the native population of Taiwan, although the newly-established PRC was at most an external threat that had no direct influence on their everyday lives, the émigré ROC was a close and real 'China factor'[6] that they were forced to deal with on an everyday basis.

The émigré ROC on Taiwan was therefore situated within historical conditions entirely different to those between 1945 and 1949. First, after the GMD-dominated ROC fled to Taiwan, the newly established CCP-dominated PRC claimed to be the sole representative of China. This was an ironic situation – while Taiwan was indeed torn apart from its Japanese matrix, the ROC was also torn apart from its Chinese matrix. In the view of the ROC, the status of Taiwan had shifted from a 'lost piece to be reattached the fatherland' to the 'last fortress for recovering the fatherland'. Second, after experiencing the 228 massacre and the subsequent purge, the Taiwanese were generally hostile to the regime, despite the fact that they were powerless to resist and therefore forced to remain silent. At the same time, while not all émigrés showed unconditional allegiance to the émigré state, in reality most of them relied on it heavily, both materially and emotionally. Third, the émigré population, at that

---

6 The now widely used term 'China factors' was coined by Wu Jiemin [Wu Jieh-min] (2009, 2012). Wu mainly refers to the PRC when using this term, but 'China factor', in my view, should be further divided into the ROC and PRC factors when it comes to the analyses of Taiwanese nationalism and the national question of Taiwan.

time, was numerically in a minority in relation to the native population of Taiwan (with a population of approx. one million compared to a native population of approx. six million). Some scholars, such as Ronald Weitzer (1990), Wu Ruiren [Wu Rwei-ren] (2002), and Gung Yijun [Kung I-chun] [Gung and Wu (2010)], have referred to the ROC on Taiwan as a 'settler state'. Following this concept, the ROC's rule over Taiwan is qualified as a sort of *minority rule model* of settler colonialism, as was the case in South Africa, where a dominant minority consolidated their authoritarian rule over a native majority through a full complement of coercive and non-coercive means. Nevertheless, although the post-1949 ROC rule over Taiwan indeed had many features that were similar to those found in settler colonialism, it is best considered a *mutation* due to one fundamental difference that distinguished it from the typical form of settler colonialism.

Since the nationalist blueprint the Chinese émigrés had in mind was very different, their actions were also distinctive from those of the settlers. First, they did not view Taiwan as a new world or as a promised land in the way that ordinary settlers often do, but rather as a temporary shelter, which they would leave when the national emergency came to an end. Second, they believed that the *de facto* separation between Taiwan and China was temporary and they did not have any intention of seeking *de jure* separation from their mother country. Third, the Chinese émigrés, who were leaders or admirers of the former state, did not build a new state in the territory in which they arrived; instead, they *rebuilt* the ROC, a state that had previously been in existence before it was overthrown by the Chinese communists, in the hope of *recovering their motherland.*

Based on the distinctive historical conditions and the particular émigré mentality, the post-1949 motif of nation-building was entirely different to that of pre-1949. The émigré elites carried out a feat of aggressive nationalist engineering that, in the hope of recovering mainland China, aimed to *reconstruct* the émigré and native populations into an 'authentic' Chinese nation which was in reality territorially confined to Taiwan in accordance with three principles, namely, irredentism, authoritarianism, and assimilationism. In following paragraphs, I will illustrate how the three principles articulated and legitimized the fundamental arrangement of the envisioned realities of the nation – that is, the 'authentic' Chinese nation which in reality existed in Taiwan alone.

The first and primary principle was *irredentism*, which *prescribed* that the territory of the 'authentic' Chinese nation included both mainland China and island Taiwan. However, since mainland China was 'illegally' occupied by an insurrectionist group, i.e., the CCP, the primary task of the 'authentic' Chinese nation, which provisionally retained sovereignty over a small corner of Chinese territory, was to recover mainland China. Under the rationale of irredentism, the 'National Mobilization for the Suppression of the Communist Rebellion' regime established in mainland China in 1948 remained in force in Taiwan for over 40 years. Moreover, since the territorial separation was viewed as the temporary result of the internal struggles of the Chinese nation, a polity designed to rule the whole of China as well as an overdeveloped wartime military-administrative apparatus were preserved and transplanted in Taiwan. It should be noted that this irredentism also had international implications crucial for the survival of the émigré state in Taiwan. The irredentism was framed in the guise of anti-communist ideology in order to remain in line with the U.S.-led Western Camp in the Cold War. In so doing, the émigré ROC gained considerable political, military, and economic support from the U.S. and was able to maintain its international status as the sole representative of China at the United Nations (UN). This is the bedrock on which the émigré ROC's foreign minority rule rested.

The second principle, *authoritarianism*, was a derivative of irredentism. To maintain the 'whole China' polity in preparation for a future return to mainland China, the re-election of the parliamentary representatives as well as most constitutional rights were simultaneously suspended through a continuation of the temporary wartime regime and the imposition of martial law in 1949. As a result, the excessive under-representation of the native population and the over-representation of the émigré elites, who did not have a social base in Taiwan, in the legislature and central governmental offices created extremely favourable conditions for Jiang's dictatorship and the omnipresent power of the party-state (Chen Mingtong 2001: chapter 3; Cheng 1989). By 1954, Jiang Jieshi had reorganized the highly factionalized GMD into a centralized Leninist party under his personal dictatorship. The party set up numerous parasitical party cells to control the state apparatus as well as almost all important social groups, nationalized industries, media organizations, and even schools and universities (Gong 1998). With the suspension of elections at central level, the émigré state managed to connect with, or to put it more precisely, *to unilaterally penetrate* the receiving society by bringing socio-economically important groups under control through state corporatism and local political factions through clientelism (Wu 1987; Chen Mingtong 2001; Cheng 1989; Wakabayashi 1994).

The third principle, *assimilationism*, was meant to integrate natives and émigrés into the 'authentic' Chinese nation. This principle was typically varnished over in official propaganda: it was described as a melting pot mode of ethnic integration (*zuqun ronghe* 族群融合) which implied that a natural, bi-/multi-lateral, socio-economically-driven process of fusion between natives and émigrés would take place. However, as Wang Fuzhang [Wang Fuchang] (1993), a leading scholar on ethnic politics in Taiwan, insightfully pointed out, the nature of the so-called ethnic integration in post-war Taiwan was in fact quite different; it took the form of forced, unilateral, politically-driven, and institutionalized assimilationism that deliberately promoted the natives' assimilation with the émigré minority in terms of identity and culture, but prevented the émigrés from becoming socially fused with the native majority through occupational and residential segregation (Gates 1981).

Since the late 19th century, Chinese nation-builders had adopted an assertive view of ethnic nationalism (Shen 1997), perceiving 'the nation' as a community founded upon homogenous culture, ethnicity, blood, and common ancestral origins (Smith 1986: 129-152). After 1949, the Chinese nation-builders transplanted this belief to Taiwan (Chen Peifeng 2006: 479-86). As a result, the task of consolidating natives and émigrés into an 'authentic' Chinese nation had a high priority in the 'basic national policy' of recovering mainland China. However, Chinese nation-builders encountered two problems that collided with their assertive ethnic nationalism. First, after experiencing the 228 massacre and the following purge and white terror, the natives generally identified themselves with the notion of a 'Chinese nation' in a very passive manner. Second, due to their absence from the process of modern Chinese nation-building and their experience of Japanese assimilation, the natives lacked sound 'Chineseness' and adherence to the contemporary highly-politicized Chinese national culture (Chun 1994). What a misfortune it was, in the eyes of the Chinese nation-builders, that when an 'authentic' Chinese nation was reconstructing itself in Taiwan, the natives as the main constituent part of the envisaged nation had been contaminated by Japanese assimilation and were suffering from a lack of familiarity with modern Chinese culture, in particular a lack of proficiency in Mandarin and an absence of the anti-imperialist, most importantly, anti-Japanese Chinese identity. Assimilationism was therefore developed in order to resolve the discrepancy between the realities and the official ideology of constructing an 'authentic' Chinese nation.

This assimilationism can be regarded as a reinforced extension of the aggressive Sinicization policy directed towards 'uprooting Japan, implanting China' that was adopted between 1945 and 1949. Language policy was chosen as the main instrument of assimilationism. In ideological terms, the émigré state upheld Mandarin as the 'national language' (*guoyu* 國語) and dismissed native languages as 'local dialects' that did not deserve any cultural prestige or official resources such as those enjoyed by Mandarin (Huang 1995). Needless to say, émigrés played a major role in implementing the compulsory Mandarin-centric policy of converting natives into 'qualified' members of the 'authentic' Chinese nation by serving as agents of assimilationism.

Not surprisingly, assimilationism defaulted on its self-proclaimed promissory note of ethnic integration and built an *ethnic hierarchy*. When the predominance of Chinese émigrés was created, justified, and sustained on the basis of blaming the *insufficient Chineseness* of the native, a 'two-tier dual system' of social classification was officially formulated. The first tier was the classification of *waishengren* (外省人, literally, people of non-Taiwan provincial origins) which referred to the émigrés with a variety of Chinese provincial origins and *benshengren* (本省人, literally, people of Taiwan provincial origins) which signified the native inhabitants who were considered to be ethnically Han, including the Hoklo- and Hakka-speaking populations. The second tier was to differentiate the *shandi tongbao* (山地同胞, literally, fellow countrymen of mountainous areas) who were Austronesian aborigines from both *benshengren* and *waishengren* as a whole and to place aborigines on the lowest rung of the ethnic hierarchy on the basis of their incorrigible lack of Chineseness. The ethnic hierarchy was therefore composed of an advantaged minority – *waishengren*, a disadvantaged majority – *benshengren*, and the most disadvantaged extreme minority – *shandi tongbao*. In a word, a paradoxical 'nationalizing ethnic hierarchism' emerged from the policy of assimilation. On the one hand, it attempted to homogenize various ethnic groups as members of an 'authentic' Chinese nation, while on the other, the policy of assimilation produced an ethnic hierarchy rather than ethnic integration. This was the origin of the ethnic resurgence during democratization (Wang 1989) and ethnic tensions in the nationalist struggles (Zhang Maogui 1993) during the 1980s and 1990s.

To sum up, by inculcating irredentist, authoritarian, and assimilationist ethnic Chinese nationalism, the émigré ruling elites articulated and justified the nationalist project that aimed to reconstruct natives and émigrés into an 'authentic' Chinese nation.

Inclusivist Thesis: Reconstruction of the Reconstructive Nation-Building

Compared with the lucid, straightforward, and eloquent discourses of the exclusivist thesis, the inclusivist thesis of post-war Taiwanese nationalism that emerged under the oppressive rule of the émigré state seemed to develop much more circuitously than its overseas counterpart, taking almost thirty years to reach theoretical maturity. Given the fact that Taiwanese nationalists had insufficient power to expel the émigré ROC and that the PRC was casting covetous eyes on Taiwan, the inclusivist thesis that advocated building a Taiwanese nation-state with the transformative inclusion of the émigré state and population was an *involuntary* strategy, indeed a reluctant concession. To use a biological metaphor once more, it displayed the alternative response of an organism suffering the intrusion of foreign body, so to speak, a self-restrained determination to patiently integrate the foreign body into itself within an extremely constrained context.

In this section, I have selected three important incidents, the Free China incident in the 1950s, the Peng Mingmin [Peng Ming-min] incident in the 1960s, and the Presbyterian Church in Taiwan (PCT) incident in the 1970s, each of which signified an ideological leap that contributed to the theoretical maturity of the inclusivist thesis. In a theoretical sense, the three incidents did not only directly challenge the three interlocking principles underlying the 'authentic' Chinese nation, but also led to new principles being put forward that became guidelines in the following formation of an inclusive Taiwanese nation.

Free China

Given the effective 'neutralization', to borrow a concept from Charles Tilly (1985), of any resistance within Taiwanese society by means of the 228 massacre and the subsequent white terror, the pre-war political movement in pursuit of island-wide self-rule soon withered to fragmented and constrained electoral mobilization within a framework established up by the émigré ruling elites (Wu 1995: 70). In this situation, a small group of liberal-minded émigré elites who were marginalized in the regime gathered around the *Free China* periodical, forming the only meaningful opposition from *the inside*.

Ideologically speaking, the *Free China* group represented what Wu Ruiren (2007b: 94) insightfully called a sort of 'Chinese liberalism on Taiwan' that represented a historical archetype of 'negative liberty' in Taiwan, accentuating freedom from interference (of the state). The gist of their appeal was expressed by Yin Haiguang [Yin Hai-guang], one of the leading philosophers in the group, as '...the fortune of *individuals* who are in the mouth of such a *Leviathan* is always at stake. Thus, in this situation, the core of politics is *to secure each individual from the mouth of Leviathan*' (author's italics, cited from Wu 2007b). By highlighting liberalism and constitutionalism, they criticized the monopolization of political power by the supreme leader, Jiang Jieshi, and a small circle of elites and opposed the unreasonable expansion of state power.

This 'Chinese liberalism on Taiwan' directly challenged the authoritarian rule of the émigré state. It should be noted, however, that although the *Free China* group argued for constitutional constraints to be placed on state power and for the protection of individual rights, they did not address the legitimacy problem of the émigré state (Xue 1996). More precisely, as émigré insiders, they did not consider the ROC's foreign and minority rule over Taiwan, which lacked the consent of the ruled in the sense of liberal democracy, as problematic at all. Therefore, while the *Free China* group opposed the authoritarian state and Jiang's dictatorship, they basically shared the officially-inculcated Chinese identity as an 'authentic' Chinese nation. They argued that the 'authentic' Chinese nation which was comprised of the populations of the territory including both mainland China and island Taiwan must be politically founded on the basis of liberalism and constitutionalism, instead of on the basis of authoritarianism or personal dictatorship. For this reason, they opposed Jiang's policy of suspending elections and supported the re-election of the representatives of all the provinces of China in Taiwan. That is to say, the *Free China* group only challenged one of the three principles, i.e., authoritarianism, and shared with the ruling elites the same irredentist attachments; they were also completely unperturbed by the ethnic hierarchy shaped by assimilationism.

However, this fact did not diminish the ideological significance of *Free China* in the development of inclusivist Taiwanese nationalism. The ideological thrusts of this 'Chinese liberalism on Taiwan', i.e., liberalism and constitutionalism, were inherited by the succeeding Taiwanese nationalists, of course, after the elements of Chinese nationalism had been weeded out. What is more, although their discourses directly challenged the authoritarianism of the regime, they were tolerated until they tried to align with the native politicians in the late 1950s. While the political alignment eventually ended in failure, it highlighted potential opportunities for cooperation between the émigré and the native and triggered 'the fusion of two horizons' (Wu 2007b: 101-5), bringing together the negative liberty of the émigré Chinese elites and the positive liberty of the native Taiwanese elites.

Ironically enough, the suppression of *Free China* exposed the Achilles' heel of the émigré state, in the form of the vulnerability of the émigré state when faced with the challenge arising from the cooperation between natives and émigrés. This vulnerability inspired the succeeding Taiwanese nationalists. The Peng Mingmin incident served to illustrate, both theoretically and politically, the successive development of the inclusivist thesis. During the 1960s, Peng boldly challenged the founding principle of the regime, irredentism, and articulated a new thesis on nation-building.

Peng Mingmin [Peng Ming-min]

While the émigré state was consolidating authoritarian minority rule over Taiwan during the 1950s, its international status as the sole representative of China had been gradually eroding away. Ordinary people in Taiwan remained unaware of the ROC's gradual loss of support at the UN during the 1950s and the early 1960s, but Peng Mingmin, a native elite who was appointed as a representative on behalf of the ROC to secure its status as the representative of China in the UN, fully recognized the difficulty of the ROC's position. By the early 1960s, Peng had foreseen the possibility of the ROC being expelled from the UN and deserted by its allies, especially the U.S. While Peng as a member of the native elite whose father had suffered in the 228 massacre did not wholeheartedly lament the weakening international status of the ROC, he did fear that the U.S. might eventually acquiesce in a deal to hand Taiwan over to the PRC, which went foul of the Soviet Union at that time, in exchange for the PRC's cooperation in containing the Soviet Union (Peng 1995; 2009).

'A Declaration of Formosan Self-Salvation' came from Peng's privileged knowledge of the ROC's precarious international position, in which the keenly-felt pain of 'being besieged' was manifested, as Wu (1995: 73) puts it, rather than any patriotism towards the ROC. The core of the declaration was expressed through its three goals, which are cited here:

1. Realize that *the "re-conquest of China" is impossible. Overthrow the Chiang Kai-shek regime*. Gather the strength of *the 12 million people, regardless of their origins*, to build *a new nation* and establish *a new government*.
2. Adopt a *new constitution* to protect the basic *human rights*. Establish an effective government that is *responsible to the Parliament*. Realize *true democracy*.

3. As a member of *the free world*, *rejoin the United Nations* and *establish diplomatic ties with all peace-loving countries*, and work together towards world peace. (Emphasis added.)

The Declaration, as Wu Ruiren (1995: 57) points out, heralded a new native-born 'civic-territorial Taiwanese nationalism' inspired by the French historian, Ernest Renan (1882), and articulated the first post-war appeal to a 'community of destiny' comprising the native population and the ordinary Chinese émigrés. As a member of the native elite who was besieged within Taiwan but promoted by the émigré state to a political position to secure its international status, Peng was more keenly aware than ordinary citizens of the ROC's political weakness and its excessive dependence on the U.S. as well as than overseas elites of the gradual settling down of the Chinese émigrés in Taiwan.[7] As a result, Peng made two revolutionary propositions, incorporating the ordinary Chinese émigrés and overthrowing the émigré state.

Peng sharply denounced irredentism by analysing the unfeasibility of the irredentist policies from military, political, and economic perspectives and exposing its undesirability for both natives and émigrés as 'a decoy for maintaining Jiang's illegitimate regime and suppressing the people of Taiwan'. Within his eloquent critique of irredentism, Peng made a delicate distinction between the émigré ruling elites and the ordinary émigrés in a dichotomous way: the former were self-serving, suppressive, corruptive, and incompetent rulers; the latter, that is, the ruled, were deceived, powerless, and suffering. By making this dichotomy, the fate of the ordinary émigrés was strategically linked to that of the natives, since the 12 million people of Taiwan, including both natives and émigrés, were all 'unwilling to be governed by the Chinese Communist Party or destroyed by Chiang Kai-shek [Jiang Jieshi]'. In other words, Peng contended that the natives and the ordinary émigrés who shared the common ground of putting up resistance to a potential invasion by the PRC and suffering under repression from the ROC should pull together to form a new nation-state territorially confined to the island. This common suffering constituted the basis for the envisaged nation that replaced the 'authentic' Chinese nation claimed by the émigré ruling elites. In the declaration, Peng specifically mentioned the arrest of Lei Chen, the leading figure of the *Free China* group, and asserted that 'Chiang (Kai-shek) [Jiang Jieshi] fully knows that the day when the Taiwanese and the mainlanders cooperate would also be the day that his regime collapses'. This discourse could be seen as an attempt by Peng to facilitate the unfulfilled task of the *Free China* group.

Furthermore, compared with the exclusivist thesis that demanded the expulsion of the émigré state, Peng placed equal weight on both the expulsion of the ROC and establishing a new state. The exclusivist Taiwanese nationalists seemed to concern themselves less with the existence of the émigré population and did not feel compelled to develop a political solution that was attractive to them. On the contrary, Peng was more concerned about the gradual settling down of the ordinary émigrés and the difficulties involved in building a new state. Thus, a feasible solution, at least in Peng's view, was to invite the ordinary émigrés to join the native population in establishing a new state on Taiwan. As to the character of

7 Stefan Fleischauer (2007) points out that some overseas student nationalists in the U.S. started to articulate a stance that favoured incorporating ordinary Chinese émigrés on both *strategic* and *humanitarian* grounds during the 1970s. This argument closely resembled Peng's argument in the Declaration. Two reasonable explanations for this coincidence are: first, the students were also aware of the gradual settling down of the Chinese émigrés before they went to study abroad; second, Peng's exile in the U.S. since 1970 had been conducive to disseminating his ideas among overseas nationalist organizations. For Peng's interactions with these overseas organizations, see Chen (2007).

the envisaged state, Peng was largely in agreement with the émigré dissidents on the ideal polity, which was conceived as an anti-communist, Western-style, and constitution-abiding liberal democracy. It should be noted, however, that while Peng's vision of a constitution-abiding liberal democracy resembled the liberalism and constitutionalism articulated by the Free China group, this was in fact 'Taiwan-based liberalism' rather than 'Chinese liberalism on Taiwan'. As Margaret Canovan (1998) reminds us, all important modern political theories, including liberalism, are based on nationhood or a political community. In contrast to the émigré dissidents, Peng's liberalism was confined to Taiwan territorially and based on a citizenry that only included the native population and the ordinary émigrés on the island. In other words, the inclusivist form of Taiwanese nationalism inherited liberalism and constitutionalism from the Free China group while the assumption of a Chinese nation including the population in mainland China was filtered out. Following this course, it was very natural for Peng to envision that one Taiwan and one China coexisted in the world and that therefore the envisaged Taiwanese nation was entitled to *join* the UN, instead of *staying within* the UN under the name of the ROC that was seeking by all possible means to represent the 'whole of China'.

It should be noted that Peng mentioned almost nothing about the issue of ethnic inequality. It is fair to say that he presumed an *equal partnership* between the native and the émigré in a very roundabout way when calling for the cooperation of both to overthrow the émigré state and to form a new nation. He deliberately avoided this issue, probably to prevent misgivings from being raised among the émigrés, especially the émigré dissidents who were his most likely partners. In addition, Peng failed to mention the second-tier inequality within the 'two-tier dual system'. A reasonable conjecture was that Peng, as a Hoklo-speaking *benshengren* who enjoyed advantages within the second-tier ethnical hierarchy, might have been 'completely unperturbed' by the suffering of the Austronesian aborigines. Or perhaps, even if he understood their sufferings, Peng did not feel under any imperative to refer to this in the Declaration. This limitation of Peng's nationalist thesis was addressed by the succeeding PCT thesis in the 1970s.

The Presbyterian Church in Taiwan

The PCT in the 1970s was a most distinctive civil organization, characterized by its island-wide governing bodies, indigenous leadership, and organizational autonomy. It was the first native organization to make political statements that diverged from the official nationalism without being immediately suppressed by the authoritarian state.[8] During the 1970s, the PCT made three successive political statements: *Public Statement on Our National Fate* (1971), *Our Appeal* (1975), and *A Declaration on Hunan Rights* (1977)[9]. These three documents could be read together as a complete nationalist thesis which signified the birth of a mature inclusivist thesis on post-war Taiwanese nationalism, pursuing a Taiwanese nation-state with the transformative inclusion of the émigré state and population. Ideologically

---

[8] The question of why the PCT started to challenge the foreign rule of the ROC in the 1970s, after being submissive to the two previous foreign ruling powers (the Qing Empire and the Japanese Empire), even to the point of cooperating with them, and passive during the 1950s and the 1960s, is still a historical puzzle. Amae (2010) mentions the above-mentioned three organizational features, providing us with some clues to assist in resolving this puzzle.

[9] The three statements can be found on the website of The Presbyterian Church in Taiwan (2014).

speaking, this mature inclusivist thesis inherited liberalism and constitutionalism from its two forerunners and was in agreement with Peng's idea of incorporating the ordinary émigrés. What made the PCT's thesis so significant was that it articulated new principles for the *transformative inclusion* of the émigré state and population into the envisaged Taiwanese nation-state.[10]

In the 1970s, the ordinary people in Taiwan were well aware of the diplomatic crises faced by the ROC.[11] The ROC's deteriorating diplomatic situation made the ruling elites' irredentist claims appear increasingly fanciful. The most urgent task of the émigré ruling elites was no longer 'recovering China' but securing their rule over Taiwan and saving the ROC from losing its seat at the UN and disturbing its diplomatic relations with friendly countries. That is to say, *irredentism*, the founding principle of the regime, had self-dissolved in the external crises without being challenged by the native population. More seriously for the émigré ruling elites, the external crises were appropriated by domestic dissidents, including the PCT, as political leverage to force them to abandon the other two principles, authoritarianism and assimilationism. The rationale of the PCT's nationalist thesis was simple: it was a

---

[10] The PCT's role in the development of Taiwanese nationalism is widely recognized and documented. This study does not draw heavily on previous works as a basis to interpret the PCT's three declarations as a complete nationalist discourse. First, some of these studies do not move far beyond recounting the actual content of the PCT's three declarations. These studies are descriptive, repetitive, and, most regrettably, lack theoretical self-consciousness an *analysis* of church ideology (see, for example, Zhang Zhaolin 2005; Xu Minhong 2008; Wang 2003; Lin 1990; Rubinstein 1991, 2001; Xue 2007). In other words, these works do not offer convincing interpretations of the content of the nationalist ideology.

Second, other works indeed attempt to *explain*, rather than merely describe, the emergence of nationalist ideology in the Church. They start from the assumption that the PCT's three declarations are an *unquestioned* discourse of Taiwanese nationalism and then explain the genesis of this ideology by attributing it to the Church's theological and biblical views (, Chen Nanzhou 1991), or by highlighting the Church's organizational, institutional, or ideological characteristics (Chen Jialun 1985; Kuo 2008; Zheng 2005; Li Weicheng 2009). These studies have stronger theoretical self-consciousness, enabling them to explore the conditions under which nationalist ideas emerged in a minority and 'foreign' religious group. Although this question is important and intriguing, it does not fall within the scope of this study.

The above-mentioned studies are concerned with how nationalist ideology came into being within the PCT, while the concern of this study is the ideological development of post-war Taiwanese nationalism, especially its early stage of ideological embryogenesis. Therefore, the former tries to demonstrate some causal relationship or mechanisms that may exist between certain factors and the emergence of the nationalist ideology, while the latter probes into the very *content* of the ideology. In short, previous studies explain what causes the ideology, while this study interprets the ideology itself.

This study, instead, examines the PCT from the perspective of the development of nationalism by interpreting the discourse articulated by the PCT – that is, the mature inclusivist thesis – as an important link in the course of the formation of post-war Taiwanese nationalism. The aim of the study is to demonstrate a dialectical way of understanding the emergence of the nationalist theses and antitheses within the distinctive historical conditions and ideological structure in post-war Taiwan.

[11] The major crises included the shift of China's representation in the UN from the ROC to the PRC (1971), the normalization of U.S.-PRC relations (1970s), and the transfer of the U.S.'s diplomatic recognition from Taibei [Taipei] to Beijing (1979), all of which seriously undermined the legitimacy of the ROC's rule over Taiwan and produced anxiety in Taiwanese society.

conditional offer proposed by the PCT, which claimed to speak for not only 200,000 Christians but for all compatriots in Taiwan, to include the émigré state and population in the envisaged Taiwanese nation on the strength of two premises: the émigré state must be transformed democratically and the suffering caused by the ethnic hierarchy must be resolved.

Transformative Inclusion of the Chinese Émigrés

The PCT's nationalist thesis was very distinctive in terms of justification and content. Unlike the exclusive-line nationalists who justified the right of the Taiwanese to self-determination by means of either international laws or historical narratives, the PCT developed a more potent justification, but one that was reserved for people with a religious consciousness, i.e., *sanctification*. By asserting that these were all bestowed by God, the PCT 'sanctified' three elements deemed relevant in the post-war Taiwanese national genesis, the right to self-determination (in *National Fate*)[12], native languages (in *Our Appeal*)[13], and homeland (in *Human Rights*)[14]. In doing so, the PCT did not only justify the foundations of its nationalist thesis but also *empowered* the subjects of the forthcoming nation, especially the native majority who had been psychologically wounded by the discrimination practised against them within the ethnic hierarchy. Only when the human dignity and the cultural value of the native majority were restored and justified through affirmative sanctifications could the ethnic hierarchy upon which the 'authentic' Chinese nation was built be replaced with genuine ethnic equality.

Founded upon the affirmative sanctifications, the PCT's nationalist thesis could be properly described as a 'multiculturalist civic Taiwanese nationalism', which was well-expressed in the down-to-earth prose of the first two declarations:

"To All Nations Concerned: *We, the people on Taiwan, love this island which, either by birth or chance, is our home. Some of us have roots here going back a thousand years; the majority counts a residence of two or three centuries, while some have come [here] since the Second World War*. We are all well aware of our *different backgrounds* and *even conflicts*, but at present we are more aware 33of a *common certainty* and *shared conviction. We long to live here in peace, freedom and justice*. And *we do not wish to be governed by Peiping."* (National Fate, emphasis added.)

"To Help toward the *Reconciliation and Working Together of All People Living in Taiwan*: At this time and in this place we should not permit differences, arising out of [the question

[12] 'We oppose any powerful nation disregarding the rights and wishes of fifteen million people and making unilateral decisions to their own advantage, *because God ordained*, and the United Nations Charter has affirmed, that *every people has the right to determine its own destiny'*. (National Fate, emphasis added).

[13] 'The people in every nation in the free world enjoy full religious liberty. Thus *every person should be able to enjoy the freedom to use his own language to worship God and to express his own religious faith*....The authorities concerned regard the printing of the Bible in local languages as a contravention of the policy to promote the use of the national language and this is their reason for suppressing it. However, one such decision can never contravene the basic spirit of the constitution.... but *most important of all we urge that the freedom to continue to publish and distribute the Bible in any language be guaranteed*'. (Our Appeal, emphasis added).

[14] 'Our church confesses that Jesus Christ is Lord of all mankind and believes that *human rights and a land in which each one of us has a stake are gifts bestowed by God*.... As we face the possibility of an invasion by Communist China, we *hold firmly to our faith* and to the principles underlying the United Nations Declaration of Human Rights. We insist that *the future of Taiwan shall be determined by the 17 million people who live there*'. (Human Rights, emphasis added.)

of] *one's place of origin* and [the question of] whether one is *a member of a Party* or not, to create *unfortunate divisions* which would *ruin our living and working together*. Immediately before us is a very difficult situation, and it is only [when] we realize that *we are all in the same boat* that we [will be able to] weather the crisis. In order to eliminate *discrimination* based on *provincial origin* or *party membership* we should not countenance any feeling that *one person is superior to another*. Everybody should enjoy *the opportunities of equal privilege and responsibility*. Basically, *we are all brothers and sisters living together in Taiwan* and *we ought to treat each other in a [way that shows] understanding, help and acceptance*." (Our Appeal, emphasis added.)

Reading how the PCT defined 'we' – that is, the envisioned nation – at the beginning of the first document, two points are particularly noteworthy. First, the Austronesian aborigines were recognized as a constituent part of the nation. This was the first Taiwanese nationalist thesis which highlighted the existence of the Austronesian aborigines and recognized their equal position in the nation. The best of the pre-war Taiwanese nationalists, who generally shared with the Japanese colonizers the racial bias against the Austronesian aborigines, reluctantly counted them as eligible members of the Taiwanese nation; Peng did not mention the Austronesian aborigines at all in his declaration; the Austronesian aborigines in the exclusive-line nationalist discourses were confined to a subordinate position.

Secondly, the highly politicized gauge of 'Chineseness' was replaced by 'the order of arrival (in Taiwan)' to define ethnic relations within the envisaged nation. According to this new gauge, ethnic groups in Taiwan should no longer be classified as superior and inferior according to the respective degrees of Chineseness they contained, but would be defined as long-time residents and newcomers according to how long they had been in Taiwan. These two points were theoretically revolutionary, since they subverted the core ethic of the official assimilationist ethnic Chinese nationalism, which created, justified, and sustained the predominance of Chinese émigrés by blaming the natives for their insufficient Chineseness, and articulated a new ethical foundation for a multicultural nation based on ethnic equality. The PCT admitted that it was well aware of the existence of the ethnic differences. It also pointed out that the established ethnic hierarchy was the result of political manipulation, and specifically highlighted 'the discrimination based on *provincial origin* or *party membership*'. However, the PCT's attitude toward ethnic differences was neither to 'erase' them by assimilationist policies nor to create an alternative pattern of ethnic hierarchy favourable to natives. Instead, it put forward a sort of multiculturalism defined by ethnic equalitarianism and anti-assimilationism.

The ethnic equalitarianism was well-expressed in *Our Appeal*, including: '...we should not countenance any feeling that *one person is superior to another*. Everybody should enjoy *the opportunities of equal privilege and responsibility*...'. This ethnic equalitarianism was diametrically opposed to the ethnic hierarchism that lurked in the building of the 'authentic' Chinese nation.

The anti-assimilationist stance was clearly manifested in the PCT's protests against the confiscation of the Bibles printed in native languages. In the context of aggressive Sinicization, the meaning of the PCT's protests went far beyond religious liberty. The PCT stated that it was fully aware that these Bibles had been confiscated because 'the authorities concerned regarded the printing of the Bible in local languages as a contravention of the policy to promote the use of the national language'. Initially, out of pragmatic evangelism, the PCT simply perceived native languages as effective instruments for evangelization in Taiwan. Nevertheless, the language assimilation policy *politicized* the usage of languages by subjugating native languages to the supremacy of Mandarin. What the PCT had done was to challenge the ethnic hierarchy at its roots, namely, the language assimilation policy, by *re-politicizing* languages in a different way, that is, sanctifying native languages by regarding them as part of the inalienable freedom to worship God. This was not meant to imply an alternative ethnic hierarchism, but to proclaim that all mother tongues used in Taiwan were intrinsically equal before God and were thus entitled to equal political status and cultural prestige.

Within the political context of aggressive Sinicization, the PCT was the first civil organization which dared to express the view that cultural differences among ethnic groups were something valuable and to be preserved. The PCT's positive and egalitarian view of cultural differences was the first *salad bowl thesis* in Taiwanese political history. Although the PCT presumed the inclusion of the Chinese émigrés into the envisaged nation, it did not envisage a nation composed of a homogenous population nor did it argue that the native population should be assimilated into an 'authentic' Chinese culture or that the Austronesian aborigines should be assimilated into the mainstream, majority culture. Instead, the PCT launched an appeal urging the people 'to treat each other in a way that showed of *understanding, help and acceptance*', because 'we are all *brothers and sisters living together in Taiwan*'. Brothers and sisters merely *live together*, without becoming assimilated into one another. Brothers and sisters should show mutual *understanding* and *accept* their differences, rather than becoming the same.

Transformative Inclusion of the Émigré State

In addition to putting forward a thesis to forge a multicultural civic nation founded on ethnic equalitarianism and anti-assimilationism, the PCT also proposed a conditional offer to the émigré state for its transformative inclusion. The PCT proposed a blueprint entirely different from those of the above-mentioned parties: it was neither to retain the ROC intact, as the ruling Chinese elites insisted, nor to re-elect the parliamentary representatives of all the provinces of China in Taiwan as the Free China group wished, nor to overthrow or expel the émigré state as Peng and the exclusive-line nationalists were demanding. The blueprint required the émigré state to become 'naturalized' to the envisaged nation; the method of achieving this 'naturalization' was democratization, by which means the 'Republic of China' would in reality be transformed into the 'ROC *of Taiwan*'. Had the ROC accepted the deal proposed by the PCT in the 1970s, it is indeed possible that the ROC would no longer have been an émigré regime, but instead a newly-formed democratic state that belonged to the envisaged nation. The core of the blueprint was expressed in its usual simple and unadorned fashion in the three declarations, which are cited in order:

"*To the Leaders of the Republic of China:…Our nation* has recently become the victim of international political bargaining in world affairs. If this trend is not soon reversed, some day in the near future the people on Taiwan may share the tragic fate of people in countries of Eastern Europe which have been oppressed by communism. In order to maintain *our position and reputation* in the international community, we therefore request that *our government* and people *grasp the opportunities available to raise our demand for justice and freedom, and for thorough internal renewal….*

...Recently *the government* has stressed *the use of new people in official positions*. Therefore we earnestly request that, *within the Taiwan area, elections should be held for all representatives to the highest government bodies to succeed the present representatives who were elected 25 years ago on the mainland*. The Federal Republic of Germany is not yet unified with East Germany, but its people have been able to *elect a new representative government under a temporary constitution*. This is an example which our government might consider. Such a political system has enabled the Federal Republic of Germany to find an honourable place among the world nations, even though so far it is not a member of the United Nations..." (National Fate, emphasis added.)

"Our church has not moved from this original purpose, and firmly believes that only if *all the rights which are guaranteed under the constitution are actually observed* - which would mean a *political reformation* - can we have a really *democratic government*. Our church has not been negligent in its efforts to achieve this goal." (Our Appeal, emphasis added.)"In order to achieve our goal of *independence and freedom* for *the people of Taiwan* in this critical international situation, we urge *our government* to *face reality* and to take *effective measures* whereby *Taiwan may become a new and independent country*." (Human Rights, emphasis added.)

It was obvious that the PCT formulated its proposal in a very diplomatic manner; it did not begin by questioning the legitimacy of the ROC's rule over Taiwan as did the exclusive-line nationalists and Peng; on the contrary, the PCT *presumed* the accommodation of the émigré state in all three declarations. However, the PCT skilfully appropriated the diplomatic crises as leverage to 'earnestly request' the authoritarian state to hold a general election. This proposed 'deal' required concessions to be made by both the rulers and the ruled. The PCT's deal might have been idealistic, but it was not preposterous. Since dramatic geopolitical changes had caused a crisis for the ROC in the 1970s, a rare overlapping consensus between the native population and some émigré elites on a practical solution for the national question had emerged. In reality, when the ROC was expelled from the UN in the early 1970s, at least two insiders within the small ruling group[15] had secretly suggested that Jiang Jieshi transform the ROC in a way that resembled the PCT's appeal to establish a new and democratic state independent of China, territorially confined to Taiwan, and representing only the native and émigré populations currently residing in Taiwan. It is fair to say that the PCT's 'transformative inclusion' deal was not a wishful fantasy, but was in fact a political expediency with which both the native and émigré elites might agree.

We all know, in retrospect, that the supreme rulers, Jiang Jieshi and his son, did not choose to accept the deal. The armed ruler did not make a deal with the unarmed prophet. The PCT's proposal remained an unrealized historical possibility. Nevertheless, the PCT infused the ideas from this mature inclusivist thesis of Taiwanese nationalism into the opposition camp through its public alignment with political dissidents after the General Secretary of

---

[15] In 1971, Yang Xikun [Yang His-kun 楊西崑], who was vice-minister of foreign affairs at the time, advised Jiang Jieshi to establish a new state called 'The Chinese Republic of Taiwan' (*Zhonghua Taiwan gongheguo* 中華台灣共和國) in Taiwan, to set up an assembly to draft a new constitution, and to hold an island-wide referendum and a general election. Almost at the same time, Lei Zhen [Lei Chen], who had just been released after serving a ten-year prison sentence for organizing an opposition party in 1960, also advised Jiang to establish 'The Sino-Democratic Republic of Taiwan' (*Zhonghua Taiwan minzhuguo* 中華台灣民主國). See Li Xiaofeng (2013).

the PCT was imprisoned in 1980 for sheltering one of the leaders of the Meilidao Incident.[16] The dissemination arguably contributed, as Wang Fuzhang (1996) points out, to the shift from 'democratic reform' to 'Taiwanese nationalism' in the ideology of 'consensus mobilization' deployed by the opposition camp in the 1980s.

Conclusion

Over subsequent decades, different nationalist movements combined exclusivist and inclusivist theses in varying proportions. During the 1980s, as the ROC's rule began to show signs of political liberation, which Edwin Winckler (1984) called 'a shift from hard to soft authoritarianism', the exclusivist and inclusivist theses were further elaborated on by intellectuals, writers, and political dissidents, domestic and overseas, through the continuing dialogue and conflict. While neither the exclusivists or the inclusivists ever succeeded in holding the field unchallenged, two prominent directions emerged. One was the development of the overseas exclusivist thesis, which was introduced into Taiwan and merged with the inclusivist ideas, becoming an eclectic thesis that advocated replacing the ROC with a newly-established state through *nonviolent* means, such as plebiscite, while also including the émigré population on a voluntary basis (Geoffroy 1997).[17] The other was to culturally substantiate the Taiwanese identity as suggested by the mature inclusivist thesis by redefining the national literature, reviving the suppressed native languages, and rewriting national history from Taiwan-centric perspectives, as well as highlighting the cultural particularity of Taiwanese by portraying it as a cultural community which was internally heterogeneous yet collectively distinct from other nations, especially from the Chinese (Hsiau 2003). While these trends were theoretically important for nurturing a full-fledged nationalist ideology, not one of them was politically potent enough to impose its own nationalist blueprint on state and society in the 1980s.

The reification of the national subject as a Taiwanese nation, in the way suggested by the inclusivist thesis, was actually accelerated in the 1990s as one outcome of the evolving struggle in the course of democratization between political forces with diverse nationalist visions. During the 1990s, as a result of electoral mechanisms, two major political forces, Li Denghui's [Lee Teng-hui] GMD (the so-called 'the mainstream faction' or 'the native GMD') and the mainstream of the Democratic Progressive Party (DPP) surpassed intra-party radical factions, which split into the Chinese New Party in 1993 and the Taiwan Independence Party in 1996 respectively, and then converged on a point akin to multiculturalist civic Taiwanese nationalism. This moderate and inclusive nationalist ideology, which Wu Ruiren (2002: 213) called 'pragmatic nationalism', had 'gained a status of 'moral and intellectual leadership' from which almost no serious political contender can afford to deviate'.

The inclusivist thesis, which has prevailed over the exclusivist thesis in domestic nationalist politics, foretold and guided the incremental nationalist conversion from an 'authentic' Chinese nation into a multicultural Taiwanese nation during the last three decades, although

[16] Amae (2007) offers a detailed examination of the process within which the PCT disseminated its ideas to the opposition camp.

[17] This stance was written into the party constitution of the first opposition party, the DPP, in 1991, and is commonly known as the 'Taiwan Independence Clause' (*Taidu danggang* 台獨黨綱).

certain goals remain unfulfilled. At the same time, a revised exclusivist thesis, which accepts the idea of including émigrés and their descendants in the envisaged nation but insists on non-violently replacing the ROC with a new state, has slowly but steadily gained greater social support over the same period.[18] The nearly-completed Taiwanese nation growing within the façade of the ROC is something like 'a new wine put in an old wineskin'. No one can tell whether or not, when, or in which way the old wineskin will burst from the pressure, which may carry forward its own momentum and crash into the tectonic power plates between the US and the PRC.

The history of the subject formation of a Taiwanese nation continues along the same thorny path where it has been threatened by the second wave of China factors that have emerged since the 1990s, namely, military threats, political blockades, and economic inducements from the PRC. These antagonistic PRC factors present a constant challenge to the people of Taiwan, making urgent demands on their will, wisdom, and ideological creativity to continue the unfinished journey of subject formation as the Taiwanese.

References

Amae, Yoshihisa (2007) *Taiwan's Exodus: Presbyterian Church in Taiwanese Nationalism, 1945-1992*. Ph.D. Dissertation. Department of Political Science, University of Hawaii.

Amae, Yoshihisa (2010) 'Europeans and the Formation of a Presbyterian Enterprise: A Prototype of a Civic Taiwanese Nation?' in Damm, Jens and Lim, Paul Lim (eds.), *European Perspectives on Taiwan*, London: Routledge, 46-65.

Anderson, Benedict (2006 [1983]) *Imagined Communities: Reflections on the Origins and Spread of Nationalism*, Revised Version. New York: Verso.

Beissinger, Mark R. (2002) *Nationalist Mobilization and the Collapse of the Soviet State*. Cambridge: Cambjridge University Press.

Béland, Daniel and Lecours, André (2005) 'The Politics of Territorial Solidarity: Nationalism and Social Policy Reform in Canada, the United Kingdom, and Belgium', *Comparative Political Studies* 38 (6), 676-703.

Billiet, Jaak; Maddens, Bart and Frognier, André-Paul (2006) 'Does Belgium (Still) Exist? Differences in Political Culture between Flemings and Walloons,' *West European Politics* 29 (5), 912-32.

Breuilly, John (1982) *Nationalism and the State*, Manchester: Manchester University Press.

Breuilly, John (1996) 'Approaches to Nationalism,' in Balakrishnan, Gopal (ed.) *Mapping the Nation*, London: Verso, 146-74.

---

[18] According to the latest survey of June 2014, 60.4% of inhabitants in Taiwan recognized themselves as 'Taiwanese', 32.7% 'both Taiwanese and Chinese', and only 3.5% 'Chinese'; in terms of unification/independence stances, 60.8% of inhabitants in Taiwan preferred 'maintaining status quo', 20.8% 'Taiwan independence', and 10.2% 'unification with the PRC'. Please see the Election Study Center, National Chengchi University (2014a, b). A study using conditional questionnaires revealed that, if the risk of Chinese invasion and the difficulty of cross-Strait integration were excluded, 59.2% of citizens would support Taiwan independence, 16.2% would support maintaining the status quo, and 24.6% would support unification with China (Keng, Liu and Chen 2009). In addition, as a latest poll of October 2014 conducted by a media revealed, provided the questionnaires with only two options between Taiwanese and Chinese and between unification and independence, 78% of inhabitants in Taiwan recognized themselves as 'Taiwanese' and only 13% 'Chinese'; 71% preferred 'Taiwan independence' and only 18% 'unification with the PRC'. Please refer to The Liberty Times (2014).

Brubaker, Rogers (1996) *Nationalism Reframed: Nationhood and the National Question in the New Europe*, Cambridge: Cambridge University Press.

Canovan, Margaret (1996) *Nationhood and Political Theory*, Cheltenham, United Kingdom: Edward Elgar.

Chen Cuilian [Chen Tsui-lien 陳翠蓮] *(1995) Paixi douzheng yu quanmou zhengzhi: 228* beiju de ling yi mianxiang 派系鬥爭與權謀政治： 二二八悲劇的另一面向 [Faction conflicts and political conspiracies: another aspect of the February 28 tragedy], Taibei [Taipei]: China Times Publishing.

Chen Cuilian [Chen Tsui-lien 陳翠蓮] (2008) *Taiwanren de dikang yu rentong 1920-1950* 台灣人的抵抗與認同 1920-1950 [Taiwanese people's resistance and self-identity 1920-1950], Taibei [Taipei]: Yuanliu [Yuanliou] Publishing.

Chen Jiahong [Chen Jia-hong 陳佳宏] (1998) *Haiwai taidu yundong shi: Meiguo 'Taidu' tuanti zhi fazhan yu tiaozhan, wushi niandai zhong zhi jiushi niandai zhong* 海外臺獨運動史： 美國「臺獨」團體之發展與挑戰-50 年代中至 90 年代中 [The history of overseas Taiwan independence movement: the development and challenges of 'Taiwan independence' groups in the United States from mid-50's to mid-90's], Taibei [Taipei]: Qianwei [Avanguard] Publishing.

Chen Jiahong [Chen Jia-hong 陳佳宏] (2006) *Taiwan duli yundong shi* 台灣獨立運動史 [The history of Taiwan independence movement], Taibei [Taipei]: Taiwan Shan she [Interminds] Publishing.

Chen Jialun [Chen Jia-lun 陳家倫] (1985) *Taiwan shehui zhi zongjiao yu zhengzhi guanxi de yanbian: yige zongjiao tuanti de shehuixue fenxi* 臺灣社會之宗教與政治關係的演變：一個宗教團體的社會學分析 [The evolution of church-state relations in Taiwan: a sociological analysis of a religious group], Master Dissertation, Graduate Institute of Sociology, National Taiwan University.

Chen Longzhi [Chen Lung-chu 陳隆志] and Harold D. Lasswell (1967) *Formosa, China, and the United Nations: Formosa in the World Community*, New York: St. Martin's Press.

Chen Mingtong [Chen Ming-tong 陳明通] (2001) *Paixi zhengzhi yu Taiwan zhengzhi bianqian* 派系政治與台灣政治變遷 [Factional politics and political transition in Taiwan], Taibei [Taipei]: Xin ziran zhuyi [Third Nature] Publishing.

Chen Nanzhou 陳南州 (1991) *Taiwan jidu zhanglao jiaohui de shehui, zhengzhi lunli* 台灣基督長老教會的社會、政治倫理 [The social and political ethics of the Presbyterian Church in Taiwan], Taibei [Taipei]: Yong Wang Culture Co.

Chen Peifeng [Chen Pei-feng 陳培豐] (2006) *Tonghua de tongchuang yimeng: rizhi shiqi taiwan de yuyan zhengce jindaihua yu rentong* 同化の同床異夢： 日治時期台灣的語言政策、近代化與認同 [The different intentions behind the semblance of 'Douka': the language policy, modernization and identity in Taiwan during the Japan-ruling period], Taibei [Taipei]: Maitian [Rye Field] Publishing.

Chen Yishen [Chen Yi-shen 陳儀深] (2007) 'Peng Ming-min yu haiwai taidu yundong (1964-1972): cong Waijiaobu dangan kandao de mianxiang' 彭明敏與海外台獨運(1964-1972): 從外交部檔案看到的面向 [Peng Ming-min and overseas Taiwan independence movement (1964-1972): a perspective from the Foreign Ministry's archives] in *Guoshiguan xueshu jikan* 國史館學術集刊 [Bulletin of Academia Historica] 10, 189-219.

Chen Yu-wen (2014) *The Uyghur Lobby: Global Networks, Coalitions and Strategies of the World Uyghur Congress,* London: Routledge.

Cheng Tung-jen (1989) 'Democratizing the Quasi-Leninist Regime in Taiwan,' *World Politics* 41 (4), 475-477.

Chun, Allen (1994) 'From Nationalism to Nationalizing: Cultural Imagination and State Formation in Postwar Taiwan,' *The Australian Journal of Chinese Affairs* 31, 49-69.

Election Study Center, National Chengchi University (2014a) *Taiwanese/Chinese Identification Trend Distribution in Taiwan (1992/06-2014/06)*. <http://esc.nccu.edu.tw/course/news.php?Sn=166#http://esc.nccu.edu.tw/course/news.php?Sn=166#>, accessed 25 September 2014.

Fleischauer, Stefan (2007) 'The 228 Incident and the Taiwan Independence Movement's Construction of a Taiwanese Identity,' *China Information* 21 (3), 373-401.

Gates, Hill (1981) 'Ethnicity and Social Class,' in Emily Martin Ahern and Hill Gates (eds.) *The Anthropology of Taiwanese Society*, CA: Stanford University Press, 241-81.

Geoffroy, Claude (1997) *Taiwan duli yundong: qiyuan ji* 1945 *nian yihou de fazhan* 台灣獨立運動： 起源及 1945 年以後的發展 [Taiwan independence movement: origins and the development after 1945] (Huang Fatian [Huang Fa-tien trans. 黃發典譯, trans.), Taibei [Taipei]: Qianwei [Avanguard] Publishing.

Gong Yijun [Kung I-chun 龔宜君] (1998) *'Wailai zhengquan' yu bentu shehui: gaizao hou Guomindang zhengquan shehui jichu de xingcheng(1950-1969)*「外來政權」與本土社會: 改造後國民黨政權社會基礎的形成（1950-1969） ['Foreign regime' and local society: the formation of the reformed KMT's social bases], Taibei [Taipei]: Daoxiang [Dawshiang] Publishing.

Gong Yijun [Kung I-chun 龔宜君 and Wu Kunlu [吳鯤魯] (2010) 'Wairen? Guoren? Guomindang yiru zheng quan de zuqun zhengzhi' 外人？國人？國民黨移入政權的族群政治 [Foreigner? nationals? the ethnic politics of the immigrant KMT GMD regime] in Taiwan jiaoshou xiehui 台灣教授協會編 [Taiwan association of university professors (ed)] *Zhonghuaminguo liuwang taiwan 60i nian ji zhanhou taiwan guoji chujing* 中華民國流亡台灣 60 年暨戰後台灣國際處境 [The 60th year of the ROC's exile in Taiwan and the postwar international status of Taiwan], Taibei [Taipei]: Qianwei [Avanguard] Publishing.

Guérina, Daniel and Rejean Pelletiera, Rejean (2000) 'Cultural Nationalism and Political Tolerance in Advanced Industrial Societies: The Basque Country and Catalonia,' in *Nationalism and Ethnic Politics* 6 (4), 1-22.

Hamilton, Paul (2004) 'Converging Nationalisms: Québec, Scotland, and Wales in Comparative Perspective,' in *Nationalism and Ethnic Politics* 10 (4), 657-85.

Hsiau, A-chin (2003) *Contemporary Taiwanese Cultural Nationalism*. London, New York: Routledge.

Huang Xuanfan [Huang Hsuan-fan 黃宣範] (1993) *Yuyan, shehui yu zuqun yishi: taiwan yuyan shehuixue de yanjiu* 語言、社會與族群意識： 台灣語言社會學的研究 [Languages, society, and ethnic consciousness: a sociological study on languages in Taiwan], Taibei [Taipei]: Wenhe Publishing.

Huang Yingzhe [Huang Ying-che 黃英哲] (2007) *Qu Riben hua, zai Zhongguo hua: zhan hou Taiwan wenhua chongjian 1945-1947* 去日本化、再中國化： 戰後台灣文化重建 1945-1947 [Uprooting Japan, implanting China: cultural reconstruction in postwar Taiwan 1945-1947], Taibei [Taipei]: Maitian [Rye Field] Publishing.

Keng Shu 耿曙, Liu Jiawei [Liu Jia-wei 劉嘉薇], and Chen Luhui [Chen Lu-huei 陳陸輝] (2009) 'Dapo weichi xianzhuang de misi: Taiwan minzhong tongdu jueze zhong linian yu wushi de liangnan' 打破維持現狀的迷思：台灣民眾統獨抉擇中理念與務實的兩難 [Between principle and pragmatism: the unification-independence choice of the Taiwanese people] in *Taiwan zhengzhi xuekan* 臺灣政治學刊 [Taiwanese Political Science Review] 13 (2), 3-56.

Kerr, George H. (1991) *Bei chumai de Taiwan* 被出賣的台灣 [Formosa Betrayed] (Chen Rongcheng [Chen Jung-Chen trans. 陳榮成]譯, trans), Taibei [Taipei]: Qianwei [Avanguard] Publishing.

Kerr, George H. (2014) *Bei chumai de taiwan* 被出賣的台灣 [Formosa Betrayed] (Zhan Li-ru and Ke Cui-yuan tans. 詹麗茹、 and and Ke Cuiyuan 柯翠園譯), Taibei [Taipei]: Qianwei [Avanguard] Publishing.

Kuo Cheng-tian (2008) *Religion and Democracy in Taiwan.* Albany, N.Y.: State University of New York Press.

Li Tianfu [Li Thian-hok 李天福] (1958) 'The China Impasse: A Formosan View,' in *Foreign Affairs* 36 (3), 437-448.

Li Weicheng [Li Wei-cheng 李偉誠] (2009) *Taiwan jidu zhanglao jiaohui* yu zhanhou taiwan minzu zhuyi A Tale of Two World: 台灣基督長老教會與戰後台灣民族主義 [A tale of two world: the Presbyterian Church in Taiwan and postwar nationalism in Taiwan], Master Dissertation, Graduate Institute of Sociology, National Tsinghua University.

Li Xiaofeng [Lee Shiao-feng 李筱峰] (1994) 'Guojia rentong de zhuanxiang: yi zhanhou Taiwan fandui renshi de shi ge gean weili' 國家認同的轉向： 以戰後台灣反對人士的十個個案為例 [The change of national identity: ten dissenters in postwar Taiwan] in Zhongyang yanjiuyuan jindai shi yanjiusuo 中央研究院近代史研究所編 [Institue of Modern History, Academia Sinica (ed)] *Rentong yu guojia: jindai zhong xi lishi de bijiao* 認同與國家： 近代中西歷史的比較 [Identity and the state: a comparison of China and the West in modern period], Taibei [Taipei]: Institue of Modern History, Academia Sinica, 323-362.

Li Xiaofeng [Lee Shiao-feng 李筱峰] (1995) 'Yibainian lai taiwan zhengzhi yundong zhong de guojia rentong' 一百年來台灣政治運動中的國家認同 [National identity in the political movements in Taiwan in the latest century] in *Taiwan: wo de xuanze!* 台灣，我的選擇！[Taiwan, my choice!], Taibei [Taipei]: Taiwan Shan she [Interminds] Publishing.

Li Xiaofeng [Lee Shiao-feng 李筱峰] (2013) Taiwanshi 101 wen 台灣史 101 問 [101 questions about the history of Taiwan], Taibei [Taipei]: Taiwan Shan she [Interminds] Publishing.

Liao Joshua (1950) *Formosa Speaks*, Hong Kong: Formosan League for Re-emancipation.

Liao Wenyi [Liao Bun-gi 廖文毅] (1956) *Taiwan minben zhuyi* 台灣民本主義 [Taiwanese Nativism], Tokyo: Taiwan Minpo.

Lin Benxuan [Lin Ben-xuan 林本炫] (1990) *Taiwan de zhengjiao chongtu* 台灣的政教衝突 [The conflicts between politics and religions in Taiwan], Taibei [Taipei]: Daoxiang [Dawshiang] Publishing.

McCrone, David (1998) *The Sociology of Nationalism: Tomorrow's Ancestors.* London: Routledge.

Mendel, Douglas (1970) *The Politics of Formosan Nationalism*, Berkeley and Los Angeles: University of California Press.

Paquin, Stéphane (2002) 'Globalization, European Integration and the Rise of Neo-Nationalism in Scotland,' in *Nationalism and Ethnic Politics* 8 (1): 55-80.

Peng Mingmin [Peng Ming-min 彭明敏] (1995) *Ziyou de ziwei: Peng Ming-min huiyilu* 自由的滋味: 彭明敏回憶錄 [A taste of freedom: the memoir of a Formosan independence leader Peng Ming-min], Taibei [Taipei]: Qianwei [Avanguard] Publishing.

Peng Mingmin [Peng Ming-min 彭明敏] (2009) *Taowang* 逃亡 [A perfect escape], Taibei [Taipei]: Taiwan Shan she [Interminds] Publishing.

Renan, Ernest (1882) 'Qu'est-ce qu'une nation? (What is a Nation?)' (Martin Thom trans.), in Conférence faite en Sorbonne, le 11 mars 1882.

Rubinstein, Murray A. (1991) *The Protestant Community on Modern Taiwan: Mission, Seminary, and Church*. Armonk, N.Y.: M. E. Sharpe.

Rubinstein, Murray A. (2001) 'The Presbyterian Church in the Formation of Taiwan's Democratic Society, 1945-2001,' in *American Asian Review* 19 (4), 63-96.

Shen Songqiao [Shen Sung-chiao 沈松僑] (1997) 'Wo yi woxie jian xuanyuan: huangdi shenhua yu wanqing de guozu jiangou' 我以我血薦軒轅-黃帝神話與晚清的國族建構 [The myth of Huang-ti (the Yellow Emperor) and the construction of Chinese nationhood in late Qing] in *Taiwan shehui yanjiu jikan* 臺灣社會研究季刊 [Taiwan: A Radical Quarterly in Social Studies] 28, 1-77.

Smith, Anthony (1986) *The Ethnic Origins of Nations*, Oxford: Basil Blackwell.

Su Beng 史明 (1980) *Taiwanren sibainian shi* 台灣人四百年史 [Taiwanese people's 400 year history], San Jose, CA: Pengdao Wenhua.

Su Yaochong [Su Yao-tsung 蘇瑤崇] (2004) 'Ge Chao-zhi, tuoguanlun yu 228 shijian zhi guanxi' 葛超智、託管論與二二八事件之關係 [George H. Kerr, trusteeship, and the 228 incident] in *Guoshiguan xueshu jikan* 國史館學術集刊 [Bulletin of Academia Historica] 4, 135-188.

Su Yaochong [Su Yao-tsung 蘇瑤崇] (n.d.) 'Taiwansheng xingzheng zhangguan gongshu yu taiwan zongdufu tizhi zhi bijiao yanjiu 台灣省行政長官公署與台灣總督府體制之比較研究' [A comparative study of the Governor Administration of Taiwan Province and the Governor-General of Taiwan], unpublished paper.

The Liberty Times (2014) TVBS mindiao 71% xiwang taiwan duli. [TVBS Poll: 71% prefer Taiwan Independence] <http://news.ltn.com.tw/news/politics/paper/726553http://news.ltn.com.tw/news/politics/paper/726553>, accessed 13 December 2014.

The Presbyterian Church in Taiwan (2014) *Public Statements* <http://english.pct.org.tw/enArticle_public_main.htmhttp://english.pct.org.tw/enArticle_public_main.htm>, accessed 25 September 2014.

Tilly, Charles (1985) 'War-making and State Making as Organized Crime,' in Peter B. Evans, Dietrich Rueschemeyer, and Theda Skocpol (eds), *Bringing the State Back In*, Cambridge: Cambridge University Press.

Vitug, Marites D. and Glenda M. Gloria (2000) *Under the Crescent Moon: Rebellion in Mindanao*. Manila: Ateneo Center for Social Policy and Public Affairs Institute for Popular Democracy.

Wakabayashi Masahiro 若林正丈 (1994) *Taiwan: fenlie guojia yu minzhuhua* 台灣：分裂國家與民主化 [Taiwan: divided nations and democratization], Taibei [Taipei]: Xin ziren [Third Nature] Publishing.

Wang Fu-chang (1989) *The Unexpected Resurgence: Ethnic Assimilation and Competition in Taiwan, 1945-1988.* Ph.D. Dissertation, Department of Sociology, University of Arizona.

Wang Fuzhang [Wang Fu-chang 王甫昌] (1993) 'Shengji ronghe de benzhi: yige lilun yu jingyan de tantao' 省籍融合的本質：一個理論與經驗的探討 [The nature of provincial integration: a theoretical and empirical discussion] in Zhang Maogui [Chang Mau-kuei 張茂桂] (ed) *Zu qun guan xi yu guojia rentong* 族群關係與國家認同 [Ethnic Relations and National Identity], Taibei [Taipei]: Yeqiang Publishing, 42-100.

Wang Fuzhang [Wang Fu-chang 王甫昌] (1996) 'Taiwan fandui yundong de gongshi dongyuan: 1979-1989 nian liangci tiaozhan gaofeng de bijiao 台灣反對運動的共識動員：一九七九～一九八九年兩次挑戰高峰的比較' [Consensus mobilization of the political opposition in Taiwan: comparing two waves of challenges, 1979-1989] in *Taiwan zhengzhi xuekan* 台灣政治學刊 [Taiwanese Political Science Review] 1, 129-210.

Wang Fuzhang [Wang, Fu-chang 王甫昌] (1996) "Taiwan fandui yundong de gongshi dongyuan: 1979-1989 nian liangci tiaozhan gaofeng de bijiao 台灣反對運動的共識動員：一九七九～一九八九年兩次挑戰高峰的比較" [Consensus mobilization of the political opposition in Taiwan: comparing two waves of challenges, 1979-1989] in *Taiwan zhengzhi xuekan* 台灣政治學刊 [Taiwanese Political Science Review] 1, 129-210.

Wang Lixiong [Wang Li-xiong 王力雄] (2007) *Wode xiyu, nide dongtu* 我的西域，你的東土 [My west land, your east country], Taibei [Taipei]: Da kuai wenhua [Locus] publishing.

Wang Lixiong [Wang Li-xiong 王力雄] (2009) *Tianzang: xicang de mingyun* 天葬：西藏的命運 [Sky burial: the destiny of Tibet], Taibei [Taipei]: Da kuai wenhua [Locus] publishing.

Wang Weirui [Wang Wei-ruei 汪偉瑞] (2003) *Taiwan jidu* zhanglao jiaohui zhi zhengzhi canyu: yi tainan diqu zhanglao jiaohui weili 台灣基督長老教會之政治參與：以台南地區長老教會為例 [The political participation of the Presbyterian Church in Taiwan: a case study on Tainan area], Master Dissertation, Department of Public Affairs, Ming Chuan University.

Wang Wenyue [Wang James W.Y. 王文岳] (2015) 'Chongsheng ciguojia minzu zhengzhi zhi fazhan yu zhuanxing' 沖繩次國家民族政治之發展與轉型 [The development and transformation of Okinawan sub-state national politics] in *Dongwu zhengzhi xuebao* 東吳政治學報 [Soochow Journal of Political Science] 33 (1), 109-72.

Wang Yude [Ong Iok-tek 王育德] (1979) *Taiwan: kumen de lishi* 臺灣： 苦悶的歷史 [Taiwan: a depressed history] (Huang Guo-yan, trans. 黃國彥譯), Tokyo: Taiwan Youth.

Wang Yude [Ong Iok-tek 王育德] Ong Iok-tek 王育德 (2002) 'Taiwan minzu lun' 台灣民族論 [On Taiwanese Nation] in *Taiwan duli de lishi bodong* 台灣獨立的歷史波動 [The historical fluctuations of Taiwan independence] (Hou Rong-bang et al. trans. 侯榮邦等譯), Taibei [Taipei]: Qianwei [Avanguard] Publishing, 75-131.

Weitzer, Ronald (1990) *Transforming Settler State*, Berkeley: University of California Press.

Winckler, Edwin A. (1984) 'Institutionalization and Participation on Taiwan: from Hard to Soft Authoritarianism?' *The China Quarterly* 99, 481-99.

Wu Jiemin [Wu Jieh-min 吳介民] (2009) 'Zhongguo yinsu yu Taiwan minzhu' 中國因素與台灣民主 [China factor and Taiwan's democracy] in *Sixiang* 思想 [*Reflexion*] 11, 141-157.

Wu Jiemin [Wu Jieh-min 吳介民] (2012) *Di san zhong zhongguo xi ǎ ngxian* 第三種中國想像 [The third view on China], Taibei [Taipei]: Zuo'an wenhua [Rive Gauche].

Wu Naide [Wu Nai-the 吳乃德] (1987) *The Politics of a Regime Patronage System: Mobilization and Control within an Authoritarian Regime*, Ph.D. Dissertation. Department of Political Science, University of Chicago.

Wu Naide [Wu Nai-the 吳乃德] and Chen Mingtong [Chen Ming-tong 陳明通] (1993) 'Zhengquan zhuanyi han jingying liudong: Taiwan difang zhengzhi jingying de lishi xingcheng' 政權轉移和菁英流動： 台灣地方政治菁英的歷史形成 [Regime change and elites' mobility: the historical formation of the local political elites in Taiwan.], in Lai Jeh-hang (ed) 賴澤涵編 *Taiwan guangfu chuqi lishi lunwenji* 台灣光復初期歷史

論文集 [Collections on the history of the early postwar Taiwan], Taibei [Taipei]: Sun Yat-sen Institute for Social Sciences and Philosophy, Academia Sinica, 303-334.

Wu Ruiren [Wu Rwei-ren 吳叡人] (2007b) 'Ziyou de liangge gainian: Zha qian taiwan minzu yundong yu zhanhou 'ziyou zhongguo' jituan zhengzhi lunshu zhong guanyu 'ziyou' zhi gainian de chubu bijiao' 自由的兩個概念：戰前臺灣民族運動與戰後『自由中國』集團政治論述中關於『自由』之概念的初步比較 [Two concepts of liberty: a preliminary comparison on the concepts of liberty of the prewar Taiwanese nationalist movement and of the postwar 'Free China' group] in Yin Hai-guang jijinhui 殷海光基金會編 [Yin Hai-guang Foundation (ed)] *Ziyou zhuyi yu xin shiji taiwan* 自由主義與新世紀臺灣 [Liberalism and Taiwan in the new century], Taibei [Taipei]: Yunchen Culture, 55-105.

Wu Ruiren [Wu Rwei-ren 吳叡人] (1995) 'Mingyun gongtongti de xi ǎ ng xiun gongtongti de xiTaitaiwan Taiwan zhan hou de taiwan Taiwan gongmin minzu zhuyi' 命運共同體的想像：自救宣言與台灣戰後的台灣公民民族主義 [The imagination of 'community of destiny': 'A Declaration of Formosan Self-salvation' and Taiwanese civic nationalism in postwar Taiwan] in Peng Ming-min wenjiao jijinhui 彭明敏文教基金會編 [Peng Ming-min Cultural and Educational Foundation (ed)] *Taiwan ziyouzhuyi de chuantong yu chuancheng: jinian 'taiwan Taiwan zijiu xuanyan' 30 zhounian yantaohui lunwenji* 台灣自由主義的傳統與傳承：紀念「台灣自救宣言」三十週年研討會論文集 [The tradition and inheritance of liberalism in Taiwan: collections on commemorating the 30th anniversary of 'A Declaration of Formosan Self-salvation'], Taibei [Taipei]: Peng Ming-min Cultural and Educational Foundation, 51-86.

Wu Ruiren [Wu Rwei-ren 吳叡人] (2002) 'Toward a Pragmatic Nationalism: Democratization and Taiwan' Passive Revolution' in Stephane Corcuff (ed.) *Memories of the Future: National Identity Issues and the Search for a New Taiwan,* Armonk, London: M.E. Sharpe, 196-218.

Wu Ruiren [Wu Rwei-ren 吳叡人] (2003) *The Formosan Ideology: Oriental Colonialism and the Rise of Taiwanese Nationalism, 1895-1945*. Ph.D. Dissertation. Department of Political Science, University of Chicago.

Wu Ruiren [Wu Rwei-ren 吳叡人] (2004) 'Fragments of/f Empires: The Peripheral Formation of Taiwanese Nationalism,' in *Social Science Japan* 30 (December), 16-18.

Wu Ruiren [Wu Rwei-ren 吳叡人] (2007a) 'Discountinuous and Cumulative Nation-State Formation: A Political-Historical Interpretations of Democracy in Taiwan.' Paper presented at the *International Conference on After the Third Wave Problems and Challenges for the New Democracies*. 13-14 August, Taibei [Taipei]: Taiwan Think Tank.

Wu Ruiren [Wu Rwei-ren 吳叡人] (2014) 'Meiyou minzu zhuyi de minzu? Yipopuyou de riliu tongzulun chutan' 沒有民族主義的民族？伊波普猷的日琉同祖論初探 [A nation without nationalism?: a preliminary inquiry into Iha Fuyu's nichiryu dosoron] in *Kaogu renlei xuekan* 考古人類學刊 [Journal of Archaeology and Anthropology] 81, 111-135.

Xu Minhong [Hsu Ming-hong 許銘閎] (2008) Taiwan jidu zhanglao jiaohui zhengjiao guanxi zhi yanjiu 台灣基督長老教會政教關係之研究 [A study on church-state relations: the case of the Presbyterian Church in Taiwan], Master Dissertation, Department of Political Science, Soochow University.

Xue Huayuan [Hsueh Hua-yuan 薛化元] (1996) *Ziyou Zhongguo yu minzhu xianzheng: 1950 nian dai taiwan si xiang shi de yi ge kaocha* 自由中國與民主憲政： 1950年代台灣思想史的一個考察 [Free China and constitutional democracy: a study on the history of thoughts in Taiwan of 1950s], Taibei [Taipei]: Daoxiang [Dawshiang] Publishing.

Xue Huyuan [Hsueh Hua-yuan 薛化元] (2007) "Zhanglao jiaohui yu taiwan zhutixing de zhuiqiu: yi yijiuqiling niandai wei zhongxin 長老教會與台灣主體性的追求：以 1970 年代為中心" [Presbyterian Church and the quest of Taiwan subjectivity in 1970s] in *Dangdai* 當代 [Contemporary Monthly] 237: 64-79.

Yun Cheng 雲程 (2007) *Fangyan guoji: lingtu diwei bianqian yu taiwan* 放眼國際 領土地位變遷與台灣 [Territorial status and Formosa: a global perspective], New Taibei [Taipei]: Jingyi Enterprise.

Zhang Maogui [Chang Mau-kuei 張茂桂] (1993) 'Shengji wenti yu minzu zhuyi' 省籍問題與民族主義 [Provincial problem and nationalism] in id. (ed) *Zu qun guan xi yu guojia rentong* 族群關係與國家認同 [Ethnic relations and national identity], Taibei [Taipei]: Yeqiang Publishing, 233-278.

Zhang Yanxian [Chang Yan-hsian 張炎憲] (1992) "Zhanhou chuqi taidu zhuzhang chansheng yuanyin de tantao: yi Liaojia xiongdi weili" 戰後初期台獨主張產生原因的探討： 以廖家兄弟為例 [On the early postwar claims for Taiwan independence: the case of Liao brothers], in Chen Yanyu [Chen Yan-yu 陳琰玉] and Hu Huiling][Hu Hui-ling 胡慧玲] (eds), E*rerba xueshu taolunhui lunwenji* 二二八學術討論會論文集 (1991) [Conference on the 28th February Incident], Taibei [Taipei]: Independence Evening Post, 279-304.

Zhang Yanxian [Chang Yan-hsian 張炎憲] (2000) "Liao Wenyi, Taiwan gongheguo yu daonei huodong" 廖文毅、台灣共和國與島內活動 [Liao Wen-i, Republic of Taiwan and inside-island activities], in Zhang Yanxian [Chang Yan-hsian 張炎憲], Hu Huiling [Hu Hui-ling 胡慧玲] and Zeng Qiumei [Tseng Chiu-mei 曾秋美] (eds), *Taiwan duli yundong de xiansheng: taiwan gongheguo (shangce)* 台灣獨立運動的先聲： 台灣共和國 (上冊) [The herald of Taiwan independence movement: Republic of Taiwan (volume 1)], Taibei [Taipei]: Wu San-lian Taiwan History Foundation, 1-18.

Zhang Yanxian [Chang Yan-hsian 張炎憲編] (ed) (2006) *228 shijian zeren guishu yanjiu baogao* 二二八事件責任歸屬研究報告 [Research report on the responsibility of 228 Incident], Taibei [Taipei]: 228 Memorial Foundation.

Zhang Zhaoling [Chang Zhao-lin 張兆林] (2005) *Taiwan jidu zhanglao jiaohui zhengjiao guanxi zhi yanbia* 台灣基督長老教會政教關係之演變 [The evolution of church-state relations: the case of the Presbyterian Church in Taiwan], Master Dissertation, Department of Religious Studies, Aletheia University.

Zheng Yangen [Tin Giong-un 鄭仰恩] (2005) *Dinggen bentu de taiwan jidujiao* 定根本土的台灣基督 [The Christianity rooted in Taiwan], Tainan: Ren Guang Press.

Zheng Zi [Cheng Woody 鄭梓] (1992) 'Shitan zhanhou chuqi guofu zhi zhitai celue' 試探戰後初期國府之治臺策略 [On the early postwar strategy of the ROC for governing Taiwan] in Chen Yanyu [Chen Yan-yu 陳琰玉 and Hu Huiling [Hu Hui-ling 胡慧玲] (eds), *228 xueshu taolunhui lunwenji* 二二八學術討論會論文集 [Conference on the February 28th Incident], Taibei [Taipei]: Independence Evening Post, 229-278.

Jens Sejrup

One or the Other: Synecdoche and Representation in Taiwan-Japan Controversies

This paper investigates the rhetorical interconnections between synecdoche and representation in debates, controversies and political protest initiatives following the introduction into Taiwan of two Taiwan-related Japanese publications, one historical revisionist manga *cartoon and one Japanese guidebook to prostitution in Taiwan. Doing so, this paper argues that these controversies revolved around discursive representations of exclusionary collective self-making and othering through specific techniques and deployments of the rhetorical figure of synecdoche. The aim here is to show how key political and mass-media agents have shaped their positions through the strategic deployment of synecdoche as a rhetorical catalyst for ascribing representative functions to ideological opponents, for engaging in explanation and speculation over motives, and for passing moral judgments on specific acts and utterances. At the same time, this paper shows how opponents have deployed a corresponding defensive strategy for diffusing synecdochical logic to order to escape such representative functions and to avoid the suggested large-scale responsibility.*

Discursive strategies for national self-making and othering are highly prevalent in the public discourse in Taiwan, and they play a major role for the way in which political positions are construed and communicated offensively, not least in cases and controversies involving Taiwan's current relations with its former colonial overlord, Japan. Indeed, as Yih-Jye Hwang (2010: 75-76) has argued, Japan 'plays a considerable and indispensable role as a very important ingredient of identity formation among people in Taiwan'. Although Taiwanese society is generally very favourably disposed toward Japan, this phenomenon tends to become directly and acutely articulated especially in mass-mediated controversies between the two societies, when efforts to politicize current events take on a postcolonial hue of strategic self-making, exclusion, and othering. Such discursive processes follow a distinct rhetorical logic, which this paper proposes to analyse through the classical concept of synecdoche.

In order to establish a solid temporal and thematic foundation for this investigation and to avoid decontextualizing the studied examples of rhetorical practice, statements, and actions from the debates and circumstances in which they emerged, I have chosen to structure this paper as an in-depth analysis of two particularly illustrative cases. This paper investigates the political and media rhetoric that emerged in Taiwan as a result of two mass-mediated news events involving Taiwan and Japan, each consisting of various responses to the publication of controversial Taiwan-related Japanese publications. The two cases are:

1) The *On Taiwan* (台湾論) controversy of 2001 which involved political responses to controversial statements in a Japanese nationalist *manga* by two Japan-friendly Taiwanese entrepreneurs, and

2) The *Paradise Taiwan* (極楽台湾) controversy of 2002 which involved political responses to the publication of a Japanese guidebook to the prostitution scene in Taibei (Taipei) and Gaoxiong (Kaohsiung).

As my main analytical concern is with the use of synecdoche in public discourse and its various forms and consequences, a preliminary discussion and definition of the concept is in order. Synecdoche is a rhetorical trope, a figure of speech that makes up one of the three master tropes of classical European rhetoric, the two others being the more well-known and theoretically elaborated categories of metaphor and metonymy. While the former primarily transfers meaning through analogies and imagery, and the latter operates according to relations of association and contiguity, synecdoche is concerned with conceptual transfer between part and whole (*pars pro toto* and *totum pro parte*) or through genus-species relations. Traditionally, synecdoche has stood in the shadow of the other tropes – even to the point of being sometimes considered merely a subform of metonymy – but in recent decades, substantial efforts have been made to rediscover and distinguish it clearly as an independent rhetorical device, a development that Nerlich (2010) discusses in detail. Ken-ichi Seto (1999) defines synecdoche as 'a conceptual transfer phenomenon based on the semantic inclusion between a more comprehensive and a less comprehensive category' (ibid. 92), stressing that synecdoche involves a meaning transfer pattern 'from a general to a specific sense' (ibid. 115). Thus, following Seto's definition, synecdoche essentially involves relations of taxonomy, a rhetorical transfer featuring 'general nouns used to convey more specific senses than they literally mean' (ibid. 115). This paper confronts a lacuna in the study of uses of synecdoche in the East Asian public discourse by introducing and analysing specific key deployments of the trope in mass-mediated statements and political activist behaviour in Taiwan. In this way, it specifically pinpoints the semi-arbitrary ascription of representative functions to individual agents that such deployments imply, and questions the underlying representative logic inherent in much Taiwanese ideological discourse on 'self' and 'other' by introducing an analytical perspective based on formal rhetorical categories. As Hamilton (2003: 1570) notes in a study of synecdoche in employment relations, focusing on this trope enables the analyst 'to highlight its significance to a speaker's rhetorical strategies and attempts at generating movement or identification with an audience.' It is precisely the mobilizing aspects of synecdoche, its ability to conjure grounds for explanation and judgment through a logic of ascribed representation that is the focus of this inquiry, as well as the corresponding defensive counterstrategy of trying to dissolve synecdochical logic in order to escape the ascribed representational function. This paper reveals the way in which synecdoche and representation intersect in forming strategic notions of inclusivity or exclusivity, group formation, and social identification, noting that the operational resilience of specific instances of synecdochical representation in the public discourse defines the involved agents as either an unrepresentative 'one' or as a representative 'other'.

For the purpose of examining mass-media narratives and rhetorical features, this paper will primarily draw on the coverage of the two selected cases in the major Taiwanese national dailies, *China Times* (*Zhongguo shibao* 中國時報) and *United Daily News* (*Lianhe bao* 聯合報), newspapers that are generally more friendly to the Guomindang (GMD, also: Kuomintang, KMT 國民黨) and pan-blue bloc than to the Democratic Progressive Party (*Minzhu jinbu dang* 民主進步黨, DPP) and fellow pan-greens.[1] In my analysis of these sources, I will employ a critical qualitative method and derive my insights from close and careful textual interpretation of direct statements and propositions, questioning the logic and implications of the use of synecdochical motifs and reasoning. The paper is structured as follows:

[1] For a brief discussion on how the more DPP-friendly news media covered the *On Taiwan* controversy, see Hwang (2010: 85).

the first part exemplifies and investigates rhetorical strategies of group ascription and representative attribution in the sources in the theoretical context of Foucault's concept of 'subtext', the second part draws theoretically on Ricoeur's distinction between motive and intention in order to disentangle motive ascriptions, defensive strategies, and the central question of representative skill, while the third part examines aspects of misrepresentation and self-judgment as well as the limits of synecdochical logic and offensive strategies in the mass-mediated public discourse. Finally, the conclusion provides a summary of my findings and overall argument, specifies the theoretical and practical contributions made by this paper and also suggests the broader implications and possible avenues for further research into the functions and uses of synecdoche and ascribed representation in the East Asian public discourse. All the sources for this paper have been studied in the original Chinese language, although quotes and passages will be provided here in English translation (my own) only. Names, key phrases, and main concepts will also be given in the original Chinese script, however, as will Chinese-language titles in the list of references.

Synecdoche and Representative Attribution

In late 2000, the heavily media-exposed Japanese cartoonist and prominent nationalist, Kobayashi Yoshinori (小林よしのり), released *On Taiwan*, a cartoon narrative of Taiwanese history of a strongly apologist and historical revisionist nature. The book featured depictions of Kobayashi's interviews with a number of very prominent and outspoken Japan-friendly advocates of Taiwanese independence, including the business tycoons, Cai Kuncan (Tsai Kun-chan 蔡焜燦) and Xu Wenlong (Hsu Wen-lung 許文龍), the latter being the founder and chairman of the major industrial conglomerate, Chi Mei Corporation (Jimei shiye 奇美實業), who served as senior advisor to the President of the Republic of China (Zhonghua minguo 中華民國, ROC), at that time, President Chen Shuibian (Chen Shui-bian 陳水扁) of the pan-green or Taiwan-nationalist DPP. In early 2001, the Taiwanese publisher, Avanguard (Qianwei chubanshe 前衛出版社), released a Chinese translation of the book in Taiwan. Before long, politicians from the oppositional pan-blue or pro-reunification bloc along with a Taiwanese women's rights NGO stirred up a major controversy in the Taiwanese mass media (Hwang 2010, Sejrup 2014, Suzuki 2011) that was fuelled especially by their indignation over some unsavoury comments that Xu had made in Kobayashi's book (Kobayashi 2000, 231-232), to the effect that the Japanese Imperial Army had not coerced women into becoming 'comfort women' during World War II; instead, Xu claimed, the women had freely chosen to perform this task.

For the three pan-blue parties, the GMD, the People First Party (Qinmin dang 親民黨, PFP), and the New Party (Xin dang 新黨, NP), the controversy essentially revolved around Xu's controversial remarks and the Taiwan-nationalist and historical revisionist discourse of Xu, Cai, and other informants in *On Taiwan*, including Kobayashi himself. Founded in 1993 and like the younger PFP, a political formation of break-away GMD notabilities, the NP, 'continually regarded as an uncompromising unification party without the slightest concern for a separate Taiwanese national identity' (Schubert 2004: 545), soon developed into the most active of the pan-blue parties in campaigning against Kobayashi's book and staging public protests. Just after the controversy had broken, the NP legislator, Xie Qida (Hsieh Chi-ta 謝啟大), denounced Xu and Cai in the following statement to the media:

The Koreans were humiliated by the Japanese, and to this day nobody in that country speaks Japanese. Taiwanese entrepreneurs, in contrast, have remained pro-Japanese all along.

How can our government and our people continue to tolerate this kind of behaviour that has lost all sense of nation and people? Is it possible that entrepreneurs can just do whatever they want? (China Times, 22 Feb. 2001a)

Xie framed her criticism of Xu and Cai not as individuals but as part of a generic group of 'Taiwanese entrepreneurs.' She then contrasted such 'entrepreneurs' with the 'people' and with the ROC government who were portrayed as having to decide whether or not to 'tolerate' the behaviour of that particular professional group. The group had remained 'pro-Japanese' since colonial times and, without any 'sense of nation and people', appeared to be somehow at odds with the rest of society. Xie then contrasted this deplorable situation with that of the Koreans who were apparently united in their shared disdain of Japan. The idea seemed to be that Taiwanese businessmen had somehow sold their souls to Japan, and that they should not be allowed 'to do whatever they want', implying, it appears, that they *as a group* allowed themselves 'behaviour' that was intolerable to the 'people.' An underlying rhetorical motif of morals corrupted by greed (or wealth) was clearly at play, but Xie's main point was that Xu and Cai represented a professional group and were prime examples of the alleged lack of proper national sentiment that characterized the group.

Later the same day, an editorial in *China Times*' evening edition joined in and chided Xu and Cai for their lack of national spirit:

However much these people consider themselves 'former Japanese' or harbour hostility against China, one wonders what they're trying to achieve by being this ignorant of the historical facts and this blind to the inhuman humiliation that their compatriots suffered; they are simply a disgrace to the Taiwanese (China Times, 22 Feb. 2001b).

Here, the criticism is logically opposed to Xie's remark: Xu and Cai were now perceived to be an integral part of society, as having 'compatriots' whom they failed by disregarding 'historical facts' and 'inhuman humiliation.' Xu and Cai neglected their obligation to acknowledge and identify with the historical misfortunes of other Taiwanese, a failure that made them 'a disgrace' to their fellow countrymen. As one must conceivably belong to a society before one can disgrace it, they appeared to remain Taiwanese, although *bad* Taiwanese. As a consequence of their nationality, the two men seemed to be under an obligation, when expressing opinions in public, to reiterate orthodox views of Taiwan's history, their offense being that they acted as if they could step outside their native society and speak only for themselves. In speaking, they must repeat the 'facts' of their silent 'compatriots.'[2]

Thus, Xu and Cai were attacked by their critics and political opponents for having desecrated a certain quality of 'Taiwaneseness' by not acknowledging certain innate representative obligations and therefore perversely *misrepresenting* their own people in Kobayashi's book. In many ways, as Shogo Suzuki (2011: 242) has noted, the entire debate quickly became structured so that 'concerns for the welfare of the former 'comfort women' were effectively hijacked by the highly divisive issue of identity politics.' Some of Xu and Cai's opponents went further than the *China Times* editorial writer quoted above by suggesting that the statements in *On Taiwan* had actually disqualified the two from genuine membership of the nation. This line of argument found particularly clear expression at another press conference convened jointly by all three pan-blue parties on 26 February. Here, the parties

[2] Note that a clear preoccupation with motive is at play in the quoted passage ('one wonders what they're trying to achieve'). A detailed discussion of the function and distribution of motive and intention within synecdochical representation follows later in this paper.

demanded that the comfort women issue be included in history textbooks, that Xu be fired as presidential adviser, and that Kobayashi be denied entry to Taiwan.[3]During the conference, two GMD legislators characterized Xu as follows:

*(...) Guo Suchun said that Xu Wenlong 'isn't qualified to be a Taiwanese', and Xiao Jinlan then criticized Xu Wenlong for being a trader 'without any national character, personal integrity, conscience, or compassion', and she encouraged everybody to boycott Chi Mei (*China Times*, 26 Feb. 2001).*

Xiao Jinlan's (Hsiao Chin-lan 蕭金蘭) impressive list of qualities lacking in Xu's personal character connects directly to his profession as Chi Mei chairman, implying, it would appear, that a 'trader' is somehow likely to have lost such qualities but could be persuaded to reacquire them if his company became the target of a 'boycott'.[4] In addition, it seems odd that Guo Suchun (Kuo Su-chun 郭素春) would chide Xu for lacking, of all things, 'national character' (國格) and for not living up to whatever criteria it suited her to apply when judging someone as 'qualified to be a Taiwanese' (*zige dang Taiwanren* 資格當台灣人). However exclusive and distinguished a category Guo apparently wanted 'being Taiwanese' to be, Guo and Xiao's intervention effectively argued for an understanding of 'Taiwanese' that follows precisely Seto's (1999) definition of synecdoche as 'nouns used to convey more specific senses that they literally mean' (115). Guo and Xiao's contention was essentially that 'being Taiwanese' means 'being Taiwanese' *in a special way*, their statements revealing underlying patterns of exclusionary, collective self-making operationalized through a rhetoric of synecdochical representation. It should be remembered also that these characterizations emanated from two GMD lawmakers, members of a party that, like its fellow pan-blue allies, is essentially in favour of unification with China and is by no means a proponent of a uniquely Taiwanese 'national character.' It was therefore quite unclear in Xiao and Guo whether Xu's supposed lack of 'national character' was to be understood as symptomatic of his disavowal of Greater China (which he has never claimed to support), or, paradoxically, if his disqualification from 'being Taiwanese' was a product of his disregard for certain elements of Taiwanese national suffering in all his eagerness for full Taiwanese national independence.

These examples show how synecdochical representation can function in political and mass-mediated speech: first, opponents assign speaking agents representative membership in one of various large groups and then pass judgment on them by either condemning that group altogether or by criticizing them for disloyalty to the group to which they have been typologically assigned. As we have seen, that group can at times be defined broadly (Taiwanese society) or at other times more narrowly (a profession). It can also be structured in terms of age or generation, as a *United Daily News* (聯合報) editorial showed by taking yet a third approach:

The hard time people are having with understanding why Xu Wenlong and Cai Kuncan made those remarks has to do with those two actually standing unmoved before an extremely dark side of human nature, and even going to the point of defending it; from the

[3] This event marks the first time that imposing an entry ban on Kobayashi was suggested in public, but the fact that it originated here did not prevent the pan-blue bloc from vigorously opposing the pan-green government when it actually went ahead and declared Kobayashi *persona non grata* just a few days later.

[4] I will return to the idea of targeting Hsu through a consumer boycott against the Chi Mei Corporation and discuss its implications at some length later in this paper.

perspective of universal human rights this is of course unbelievable, but it represents certain Taiwanese people's memory and interpretation of the history of Japan's colonization of Taiwan back then (United Daily News, 23 Feb. 2001).

In this line of criticism, the two Japan-friendly businessmen are taken as representatives of a 'certain' group of elderly people who remember the Japanese period in Taiwan. That is, the GMD-friendly *United Daily News* must be referring to people raised in Taiwan during the colonial era, to the so-called Japanese-language or *duo-sang* (多桑) generation.[5] Apparently, that group remained 'unmoved' by, and even supportive of, the 'extremely dark side of human nature' underlying the comfort women system, a fact that placed the group as represented by Kobayashi's informants at odds with 'universal human rights.' Again, there is something paradoxical here because if the group actually 'remembers' the colonial period, it is unclear why their members should be supportive of the Japanese at all, given, as the argument goes, that the period featured horrors and humiliations generally recognized today. Unless, of course, imperialist Japan so chronically influenced the group that its members simply came to identify with their oppressors and developed a functional blindness to the misery of their fellows, an assumption that seems to underlie the editorial. As such, Xu and Cai come to 'represent' (*daibiao* 代表) the 'memory and interpretation' of a group in the same synecdochical fashion as in the other examples given above: they function as an integral part of a larger whole for which they speak, just as that whole speaks through them as its representatives. The same editorial later granted Kobayashi a similarly structured representative role, stating that 'Kobayashi Yoshinori represents Japanese people with a certain view, denying the fact that Japanese militarism did harm to the comfort women and others.' Thus all controversial agents could be turned into representatives of two different groups that were, however, similar in their wrongful thinking: they interpreted things the wrong way, they denied facts, and they lacked compassion. Xu and Cai represented their group through statements in Kobayashi's book, which was in its own right an instance of his representing his group.

This tendency in the sources to treat particular statements made by individual agents as representative expressions of the collective identity of a larger group (without those agents having to claim such a representative role for themselves) means that the statements lose their individual-based singularity and are contextualized so that they become more than a particular communicative event and point to larger social issues beyond themselves. That is, statements as manifest discourse are interpreted, rationalized, and criticized after first having been immersed in what Michel Foucault called 'sub-text', the media approaching them as if those expressions necessarily emerged through layers of representation that would supplement articulated discourse and intention with a multiplicity of otherwise silent subjects giving voice to the statements through representation. In his work, Foucault denied discursive objects a representative function beyond themselves ('There is no sub-text', Foucault 2002: 135) and effectively localized all representative qualities in strategic and subsequent attributions exterior to the statements themselves. In representation by synecdoche, as I use that concept here, statements are ordered and indexed according to similarities or dissimilarities with other statements and made to appear as necessary and natural expressions of different groups. Representative attribution happens *after* the statement, and group attribution is semi-arbitrary and subject to variation without affecting the overall logic of

5 *Duo-sang* is a Chinese-language appropriation of the Japanese *tō-san* (父さん, 'daddy').

synecdochical representation itself. Xu and Cai were made to represent people other than themselves in order to stimulate public demand for their opponents' spectacular responses, but it did not make any particular formal difference if that group was identified as people who shared their profession, their age, their nationality, etc. When one characteristic of the speaking subject can be identified as the foundational common denominator of a large collection of people, his statements on whatever topic suddenly acquire the rhetorical potential to represent them as a group.

Protests and Motive Ascription

Synecdochical representation in public discourse functions as a way of connecting individual acts to larger social phenomena, but it also potentially allows publicly staged reactions to those acts to find legitimacy through representative logic. Clear examples of such reactions during the *On Taiwan* controversy were the protest initiatives of the NP legislators, Feng Huxiang (Elmer Fung 馮滬祥) and Zheng Longshui (Cheng Long-sha 鄭龍水), which were launched five days after Xie Jida, a party colleague, had publicly denounced the moral standards of Taiwanese entrepreneurs:

Yesterday morning, Feng Huxiang set fire to the Japanese flag and [copies of] On Taiwan *in front of Eslite bookstore's Dunhua South Road entrance in Taibei, calling on the masses to refuse to buy the book and on booksellers to refuse to sell it. In front of Jilong train station, Zheng Longshui then launched a boycott campaign against Chi Mei food products, hoping that people would stop buying Chi Mei products until Xu Wenlong comes forward to clarify and apologize* (United Daily News, 26 Feb. 2001b).

Both the initiatives – acts of iconoclasm in public space and encouragement of consumer boycott – are typical examples of protest activism and functioned as responses to representation perceived synecdochically. As Kobayashi Yoshinori and his book represented Japan part for whole, and Japan was again represented part for whole in the symbol of its national flag, Fung's desecration of the *Hinomaru* along with copies of *On Taiwan* became a symbolic act of liberation from Japanese oppression through the burning of two synecdochical representations of the country. Zheng's much more complex call for consumers to boycott Chi Mei foods also attempted to draw on synecdoche, first by making Chi Mei's products represent the corporation part for whole (*pars pro toto*), and then having the entire industrial conglomerate represent its chairman, Xu Wenlong, whole for part (*totum pro parte*). The rationale must be that the chain of representations could be actively retraced step by step in a reverse motion, according to which Xu would be targeted by targeting Chi Mei by targeting its products. As far as the synecdochical elements alone are concerned, Zheng's reasoning was fairly consistent, but this type of representation that exclusively locks an individual and a social entity to each other reveals its limits in the illogical and strained connection it ultimately drew between the comfort women and Chi Mei's food products.

The formal rhetorical reason for the connection's appearing to be strained was that it was not synecdochical at all, but metonymic, in that it did not describe a relation between 'a more comprehensive and a less comprehensive category' (Seto, 1999:92) but one of associative contiguity, here between Xu's different roles as Kobayashi's informant on the one hand and as a business professional on the other. The rest of the representative structure being firmly based on synecdochical logic, Zheng's attempted crossover into metonymy disturbed the overall rhetorical structure, and the campaign therefore needed repeated explanation in order to function. Although the whole being targeted (Chi Mei) could only with considerable associative abstraction be said to represent Xu's statements on comfort women, Zheng nonetheless specifically encouraged the consumer to connect two *parts* (food products on supermarket shelves and Xu as company chairman) to generate pressure on a whole that could not in itself 'come forward to clarify and apologize' for statements it did not make. Although perhaps superficially meaningful, this boycott had the serious communicative flaw that it was concerned only with affecting one part through its relation to another part and viewed the whole as a mere conduit between the two. The connection was so farfetched that, in fact, it would correspond to the NP's encouraging people to continue criticizing *On Taiwan* until Chi Mei took certain undesirable food products off the market. In contrast, Feng Huxiang's happening on the same day remained firmly within a system of synecdochical representation, calling upon people merely to 'refuse to buy' the book and booksellers to 'refuse to sell' it. Communicatively much more coherently structured than that championed by Zheng, this campaign targeted *On Taiwan* directly, especially since Feng refrained from taking the metonymic leap equivalent to Zheng's against Chi Mei, which would have been to encourage people not to buy books at the Eslite (誠品) store at all, or to urge Eslite to stop selling books altogether, until *On Taiwan* had disappeared from all Taiwanese bookstores.[6]

As these protest initiatives were unfolding, Xu Wenlong actively tried to dissolve the different representative roles attributed to him by calling a press conference. There he denied having said that becoming a comfort woman was 'a major step upwards for those girls' (one of the most quoted formulations from *On Taiwan* during the whole controversy) but maintained that they had been sold off by their families: 'they were indeed victims, but it was their parents who had harmed them'. He had the following explanation for why he had not previously spoken out in public since the story broke:

Xu Wenlong said he has not responded because he thinks this issue is political, but since some people have been throwing eggs at Chi Mei's Taibei office, and his statement and the company have nothing to do with each other, he wanted to take this opportunity to clarify things. Xu said that these last few days he has been out fishing as usual and neither the Office of the President, the Executive Yuan, nor the DPP have contacted him on this matter (United Daily News, 26 Feb. 2001a).

Xu's communicative task was to distance his controversial remarks from his professional roles as Chi Mei chairman and advisor to the ROC president, and the purpose of his press conference was to 'clarify' his not having spoken in *On Taiwan* either as a representative of his company (wherefore, according to his argument, the activity of throwing eggs at Chi Mei's Taibei office was a misunderstanding and quite meaningless) or in any political capacity. He underlined this point by professing not to have been contacted 'on this matter' (*jiu zhe jianshi* 就這件事) by the ruling party or by any central government bodies under

---

[6] I am not arguing that metonymically structured activist campaigns necessarily fail; I am merely suggesting that in order to succeed they require target-group receptivity to interconnections that operates at a significantly higher level of abstraction than that required by synecdochical campaigns. Confusing metonymy with synecdoche (as in the NP's anti-Chi Mei campaign) only raises the level of associative complexity even further, drastically increasing the need for supplementary communicative and mediating efforts to foster, expand, and maintain target-group mobilization. The more figuratively complex the message, the more demanding the PR effort – and, of course, the more vulnerable the entire venture to an opponent's corresponding defensive strategy to relativize or dissolve the claimed interconnections altogether.

its control (president and cabinet) and by identifying the entire issue as 'political' (*zhengzhi xing de* 政治性的). Thus, a key part of his damage-control strategy was to dissolve the basis for directing political aggression against his official role, his company, and the government by establishing himself as having spoken in a strictly private capacity without any representative roles or obligations. The contrast between Xu serenely and 'as usual' pursuing his free-time hobby in seemingly splendid isolation and the 'political' storm raging elsewhere served as a conceptual barrier between the political sphere, where he insisted his statements did not belong, and the private sphere from which he spoke and in which he represented only himself.

Xu's first attempt to bury the controversy by holding on to the core of his remarks in *On Taiwan* while denying any representative role seems not to have had the desired effect, because the very next day he issued a statement of apology for his remarks in Kobayashi's book. However, despite their emotive and pathos-filled launches, the two NP campaigns were not very successful, either. The *United Daily News* checked some of the major supermarkets in Taibei and concluded that the boycott of Chi Mei products had 'not drawn very much response', citing a retail distributor as saying that Chi Mei 'sales have not been affected by these last few days' crisis over *On Taiwan*' (*United Daily News*, 26 Feb. 2001c). In contrast, Feng's activist campaign – the day after the event in front of the Eslite bookstore, he repeated his flag-burning protest in front of Kobayashi's Taiwanese publisher's (Avanguard's) headquarters (*China Times*, 26 Feb. 2001) – seemed to be having some initial success. However, Fung's momentum was short-lived, and even the next day, the book began to appear on bestseller charts. Ironically, instead of keeping consumers away, the media hype and the NP happenings seemed to be stimulating curiosity and accelerating sales (*China Times*, 27 Feb. 2001). By 2 March, more than 40,000 copies of the Chinese-language version of *On Taiwan* had hit the market, and Avanguard was now out of stock and had problems meeting retailers' orders (*United Daily News*, 2 March 2001). On that day, the Minister of the Interior, Zhang Boya (Chang Po-ya 張博雅), announced an entry ban on Kobayashi, inadvertently causing the public debate to shift dramatically towards questions of freedom of speech, a theme that made the NP's two still unsuccessful boycott campaigns suddenly appear dangerously at odds with fundamental democratic and civil values. For was Kobayashi not entitled to his opinion and free to publicize it in democratic Taiwan without incurring restrictions or harassment from ROC officials?

The media coverage of the Kobayashi affair having taken a new turn, the NP's original intention to (perhaps even score a few points in the upcoming Legislative Yuan election by managing to) force Xu to take responsibility for his statements in public and to prevent Kobayashi from profiting from the Chinese-language edition of *On Taiwan* found itself transformed through the news media into a semi-authoritarian assault on democracy and civil rights. Their strategy having already failed, since both campaigns were unsuccessful in terms of their stated objectives, the NP legislators and their political opponent, the Interior Minister, Zhang Boya, now all became targets of intense media aggression due to their alleged intolerance and disrespect for civil liberties. And if these street protests and boycott initiatives were intended to help the NP appear more attractive to ROC voters, they were not successful in that respect, either: for various reasons, the December 2001 election to the legislature turned out to be a disaster for the NP, with the decimated party returning only a single legislator, elected not in Taiwan proper but in the tiny Jinmen (Kinmen) archipelago off the mainland coast. Xie Jida, Feng Huxiang, and Zheng Longshui all lost their parliamentary seats.

As I have demonstrated above, the strategy of assigning representative functions to controversial agents takes different forms since the groups represented may differ from situation to situation, and the same speaker can be pictured as part of and therefore representing a number of groups in connection with the same statement without hindering the effective operation of representative logic. However, in each case, any specific group being allegedly represented opens specific avenues of possible strategic action, depending on the already established public image or sub-textual understanding of each group, ideas that can be activated and drawn upon as a framework for dealing with the speaking agent. Specific group attribution depends on the purpose of establishing someone as a synecdochical representative – roughly, whether one wants to explain the statement and condemn the group, or explain the group and condemn the statement – and the principle at work is that the perceived character of the group defines the quality of the controversial speaker's representation skills: if the group is negatively perceived, the controversial agent represents it well, and, conversely, if the group is considered in positive terms, he represents it badly. Thus, Xu comes across as an adequate representative of morally flawed and greedy 'Taiwanese entrepreneurs' as well as of 'certain' people of the Japanese-language generation educated under the colonial system and therefore apparently 'unmoved' by Taiwanese suffering, etc., while he is an incompetent representative of Taiwanese society in general. In the first role, Xu functions as a *symptom* of a generally wrongful orientation thought to reside in those groups (wherefore his statements are 'naturally' wrongful and could have been no different), while in the second role, he personifies an *aberration* from the 'natural' inclination of Taiwanese individuals to represent Taiwan in certain ways (wherefore his statements are 'unnaturally' wrongful and should have been different). In other words, when a given agent is pictured as representing others well, this serves strategically as a basis for explaining and motivating his acts, and, conversely, when he represents others badly, that is, *misrepresents* his own group, that becomes a social imperative for passing strategic moral judgments on his acts.[7]

The irony of the pro-unification bloc attacking Kobayashi's sources for lacking 'Taiwanese' qualities was not lost on the pan-greens, and the DPP legislator, Zhang Chuantian (Chang Chuan-tien 張川田), made a direct effort to undermine this sudden pan-blue interest in proper 'Taiwaneseness' during a debate in the Legislative Yuan:

DPP legislator Zhang Chuantian (...) stressed that in the past, the GMD, NP, and PFP legislators criticizing On Taiwan *all used to consider themselves 'Chinese', but now these people have all turned 'Taiwanese'. He said that real Taiwanese do not need to call Xu Wenlong and [others] names, because real Taiwanese read* On Taiwan *from a Taiwanese perspective (*China Times, *6 March 2001).*

Portraying the pan-blue bloc as having switched positions on such a supposedly stable matter as the national identity of the individual, Zhang differentiated between two mutually exclusive categories of 'real' (*zhenzheng de* 真正的) and non-real Taiwanese. The 'real' Taiwanese 'do not need' to react hysterically to a Japanese cartoon book, they rest in their

---

7 Although there are no notable examples in these cases, one could also easily conceive of two other possible types of synecdochical representation: one of a 'good' representative of a 'good' group (a hero, for example), and one of a 'bad' representative of a 'bad' group: someone who, contrary to expectations, acts in a positive way, thereby misrepresenting his 'bad' group (certain types of role models, for example).

national identity and perceive the world 'from a Taiwanese perspective', a lofty viewpoint apparently unattainable for the fake pan-blue Taiwanese who even until very recently thought they were Chinese. Zhang's statement was a refusal to recognize pan-blue parties as synecdochical representatives of Taiwanese society, and once again we see enacted how the alleged misrepresentation of a positively conceived group allows moral judgment (this time on the pan-blues who falsely claimed to represent a group they did not belong to), and, conversely, how the orchestration of competent representation of a negatively conceived group allows explanation and motivation of the representatives' acts (because in fact they represent something completely different from 'real Taiwanese' and cannot really help themselves).

Zhang's vision of what it means to be Taiwanese was a direct counter-image to the one that the GMD's Guo and Xiao had fielded just a couple of weeks earlier. Operating with a genus notion of 'real Taiwanese' as the definition of the species category 'Taiwanese', Zhang's perception was every bit as synecdochical and exclusionary as Guo and Xiao's propagation of the certain mental qualities needed for being 'qualified to be a Taiwanese'. Thus, in exactly the same rhetorical manner, both camps sported politically opportune models for defining the general in the narrowest possible sense, eagerly resorting to mutually exclusive but structurally identical synecdochical constructions. At the same time, Zhang's statement was an attempt to remove the controversial DPP-friendly agents from the game of representation by synecdoche by stripping them of representative sub-text: without sub-text and synecdochical representation, Xu and Cai's controversial statements would lose their political significance – especially as Zhang conveniently failed to mention their close connections to President Chen and his government.

Very importantly, the political strategy of portraying agents as representatives of either negatively or positively perceived groups without their having to claim that role for themselves is intimately connected to a tendency in the media to speculate on the motives of those agents for having acted the way they did. In *Oneself as Another*, Paul Ricoeur discusses precisely the implications of others thus ascribing what he calls 'a retrospective motive' to an agent:

As concerns the notion of motive, to the extent that it is distinguished from the intention with which one acts, principally as a retrospective motive, the fact of its belonging to an agent is just as much a part of the meaning of the motive as its logical tie to the action of which it is the cause. It can legitimately be asked: 'Why did A do X?' 'What made A do X?' To mention the motive is to mention the agent as well. This relation has something particularly strange, even paradoxical about it. On the one hand, searching for the author is a terminable investigation which stops with the designation of the agent, usually by citing his or her name: 'Who did that? So and so.' On the other hand, searching for the motives of an action is an interminable investigation, the chain of motivations losing itself in the unfathomable haze of internal and external influences (...) (Ricoeur 1994: 95).

Ricoeur's distinction between *intention* and *motive* is highly significant, and the difference between them is rather like the difference between aim and reason. A few simple illustrations might be useful here: in a statement such as 'he robbed her because he needed money', his intention is to acquire her valuables and his motive is a lack of money. Similarly, in 'she murdered him out of jealousy', her intention is to kill him and her motive is the unhappiness that he causes her. In other words, the intention is the immediate aim of the act, while the motive is the reason or complex of reasons that propel the agent into acting. While the intention is, ideally speaking, conscious and manifest in the agent when acting, the agent or others identify the motive retrospectively, which is to say that, unlike an intention, a motive is identified analytically.[8] The 'interminable' nature of searching for motives finds reflection, I would argue, in opponents' rhetorical ability to attribute the same agent to different groups, an operation that in each case generates different motives although it formally always follows exactly the same logic. In this way, Ricoeur's concept of motive can be said to relate to what Foucault referred to as 'sub-text', in so far as it concerns third-party speculations about the unexpressed constitutive factors that might lie behind or beneath a given act or statement. To follow Ricoeur's distinction, I argue that in these sources controversy is structured so that intention is distributed individually and without representative value, while motive is distributed typologically through synecdochical representation.

My contention that, in this type of public discourse, intention is construed as personal, and motive as social and synecdochical, is further underlined by the rhetorical structure of Kobayashi's response to the controversy that his book had aroused in Taiwan. In an interview with *China Times,* Kobayashi said:

It is really difficult for me to understand. It seems to me that out of all the cartoons in the book, it is only a certain number that have been put to political use, which is a very unusual thing, and this hysterical reaction is very far from what my real intentions were for wanting to write the book; the reason why I wrote On Taiwan *was because I wanted to make Japanese people aware of the Taiwanese going to great lengths in order to seek their own identity* (China Times, 25 Feb. 2001).

Lamenting the 'political use' of the short passage on comfort women in *On Taiwan*, Kobayashi stressed that his 'real intentions for wanting to write' (*zhenzheng xiang xie de benyi* 真正想寫的本意) were bound up with the aim of informing his fellow countrymen of the 'great lengths' that Taiwanese went to 'in order to seek their own identity'. Thus, Kobayashi 'intended' to set up a mirror for Japan in Taiwan so that the efforts of the Taiwanese would inspire the Japanese to repeat the pattern and likewise 'seek their own identity', that is, effectively, to incite Japanese national pride on the basis of Taiwan-nationalist rejections of Chinese identity through the whitewashing and legitimisation of imperialist Japan's colonial and wartime conduct on the island. Kobayashi's argument was essentially that the 'hysterical reaction' was illegitimate ('really difficult for me to understand') because what should be reacted to was not 'only a certain number' of drawings but Kobayashi's 'real intention', which was apparently to be considered distinct from and unexpressed in the specific passage under public criticism. Again, the difference between intention and motive becomes central: agents may well be aware of or profess to have a certain intention when doing something, but political opponents and the mass media prefer to frame the act as a product of a motive ascribed to the agent after the fact by way of synecdochical representation. The rationale is: why Kobayashi (thinks he) did it is not so interesting – the public wants to know *what made him do it*. However, Kobayashi's argument would logically imply that legitimate criticism of *On Taiwan* would necessarily also mean criticism, or even negation, of Taiwanese efforts

[8] This, of course, does not mean that an agent's intention is immediately clear to observers. The mass media may speculate as well on possible intentions for an act, but motive by synecdochical representation is *necessarily* ascribed by others and readily done so without regard for what the agent may or may not admit to have been his intention.

'to seek their own identity' (the affirmation of such 'efforts' being his 'real intention' considered in its proper totality), his argument thereby attempting to spin two separate and unconnected fields of public debate into existence: firstly, one of Taiwanese criticism which should deal only with Taiwan itself and the island's domestic political differences, and secondly, a more important one where his book and internal Japanese identity issues interrelate and where Taiwan is nothing, *represents* nothing, but a mirror image: a surface reflecting a Japan that can act to a Japan without awareness.

Self-judgment and Misrepresentation

Certain formal rhetorical conditions apply for successful use of the synecdochical representation formula. The very limited success of the NP's consumer boycott initiatives have suggested that the more associatively demanding the link between the (controversial) part and the (positively or negatively perceived) whole, the weaker the representation effect. Effective ascription requires that the part be linked exclusively to one specific whole in order to provide it strategically, through its representative function, with either a motive or a social imperative for moral judgment. And precisely this requirement turned out to be difficult to fulfill for the Taibei Mayor (and later two-term ROC President), Ma Yingjiu (Ma Yingjiu 馬英九) of the GMD, as the *Paradise Taiwan* controversy unfolded in January 2002. A Japanese guidebook to the prostitution scene in Taibei and in Gaoxiong, *Paradise Taiwan* attracted attention in Taiwan in 2002, when the Japanese bookstore Kinokuniya (紀伊国屋) started selling it in Taibei. Calling the book 'an insult to all Taiwanese women', Mayor Ma swore to apprehend any Japanese tourist visiting Taiwan to buy sex, reported the local Kinokuniya manager, Sekine Daisuke (関根大輔), to the police for criminal investigation, and had city police forces perform crackdowns at addresses listed in the guidebook. As the situation developed, the general attitude to the issue found in Taiwanese newspapers was that Ma was overreacting, and the media accused him of hypocrisy after it became clear that the majority of customers at Taiwanese brothels were, in fact, Taiwanese (Sejrup 2012: 761).

After instigating the media fuss himself, Ma then seized the opportunity, at a farewell reception for the outgoing Japanese representative to Taiwan, to express his indignation over the prostitution guidebook:

Yesterday, when Director of Japan Interchange Association Taipei Yamashita Shintar ō bid farewell to the city government, Ma Yingjiu (...) took the opportunity to express the city government's serious dissatisfaction, saying that the explicit images of women contained in the book constituted a violation of Taiwanese society as a whole, that all Taibei citizens including himself felt offended, and that he would like Yamashita Shintar ō to convey that message on his behalf when he got back to Japan. Yamashita immediately promised to do so (United Daily News, 12 Jan. 2002c).

The scene, which the *China Times* described as 'very awkward' (*China Times*, 12 Jan. 2002a), featured the delivery of a protest message from one representative body (the Taibei city government) to another (the Japanese foreign ministry) through their respective representatives (Ma Yingjiu and Yamashita Shintar ō 山下新太郎). The reason for his protest, Ma claimed, was the 'offense' felt by 'all Taibei citizens' and the 'violation of Taiwanese society as a whole' constituted by images in the book. Emphasizing his membership of the group of those allegedly offended ('including himself', *baokuo ta benren* 包括他本人), Ma portrayed Taiwanese society as adopting one united stance in this matter and speaking directly through him. That notion was problematic, because the general public reaction to the book in Taiwan turned out not to match Ma's indignation (Sejrup 2012: 763), but there was a serious communicative problem in the opposite direction, as well. In order for the protest to the Japanese authorities to make logical sense, Ma's assumption must have been that the book represented Japan or, at least, was Japan's official responsibility somehow, since one would hardly lodge protests with anyone perceived to be without influence over that which one finds offensive. In the same article, readers were told that Ma believed that the 'Tokyo government should strongly condemn' the book as well as the 'groups of Japanese prostitution clients' implying that the Japanese would construct a chain of representative responsibility corresponding to the one Ma saw: the book and the tourist 'groups' that supposedly used it should appear to Japanese authorities to somehow represent them and they should then feel resentment and 'condemn' (*qianze* 譴責) them as, effectively, synecdochical *misrepresentations* of Japan. Ma's idea followed the logic described earlier of citizens being somehow naturally obliged to represent their society to the outside world in certain positive ways. Following this line of reasoning, not condemning its part would prove the whole to be considering itself well represented by the book, and Japanese society thereby signal that it be best conceived of in negative terms. But that structure would only work if 'Japan' thought like Ma.

The complicated representative logic underlying Ma's position was quickly undermined from both sides: it soon became clear that he did not speak for all Taiwanese, and the desired reaction from Tokyo was not forthcoming, either. On the very same day, the GMD legislator, Chen Hongji (Chen Hung-chi 陳鴻基), said in an interview with *United Daily News* that Japan worked differently from Taiwan, that books like *Paradise Taiwan* were published in Japan about Japanese locations as well, and that the guidebook was simply a 'garbage book' not worth wasting all this attention on. Explaining further, Chen drew on his personal experiences in Japan:

Chen Hongji pointed out that Japanese social customs are relatively open. Twenty or thirty years ago when he was studying in Japan, Japanese SM novels and comic books were already very common, and although prostitution is illegal in Japan, there are still lots of messy things going on. But the Japanese tend to think that such things don't matter and that you cannot make such issues an indication of what the Japanese are like as a nation or as human beings (United Daily News, 12 Jan. 2002b).

In Japan, Chen suggested, there is no direct link between what an individual may do privately and what defines Japan's national character or the general nature of Japanese people. That is, any Japanese individual engaged in whatever activity cannot be made to automatically represent all Japanese people, contrary to what Ma must be imagining by making precisely such a representative structure the basis of his demand. According to Chen, the Japanese simply make distinctions (or, if you like, fail to draw connections) unlike the Taiwanese, which makes it senseless to demand specific symbolic reactions from a perceived whole if the acting part and represented whole do not consider themselves synecdochically connected at all in the context of a particular statement. The rhetorical problem resides in the fact that Ma wanted 'Tokyo' to *do* something ('Tokyo should condemn'), that is, to pass moral judgment on its wrongful part for representing 'Tokyo' badly. If, conversely, Ma had used the synecdochical representation formula merely to produce a motive for the book as a statement ('the book is like that because it is Japanese'), no Japanese reaction would have been necessary, but that would have been a completely different message (Ma judging Japan) to the one that he wanted to communicate: 'Japan' should judge its representatives, or it would judge itself.

Ma having reported the case, the Taiwanese police set about 'closely examining' *Paradise Taiwan* to determine the extent of its criminality under ROC law. This piece of investigative labour yielded interesting analytical insights: firstly, a large part of the practical information in the book turned out to be inaccurate or even false, and secondly, many of the 'so-called lewd and explicit photographs' were highly ambiguous with regard to their actual national provenance: not only did the pictures contain bits of Japanese text here and there, but 'the women were wearing Japanese sandals and kimonos, and the background display was also a Japanese-style décor'. These findings led the police to conclude that 'many of the girls in the nude photos were simply Japanese' passing themselves off as Taiwanese (*United Daily News*, 12 Jan. 2002d). While such a publication could well be said to operate on postcolonial terms and was picturing Taiwan through Japanese pornographic iconography, the important thing to note is the additional complexity that this element introduced into the already strained representative logic that Ma and likeminded individuals had spun around *Paradise Taiwan*. It became even more difficult to pinpoint exactly what was being represented in the book, and it certainly relativized Ma's contention 'that the explicit images of women contained in the book constituted a violation of the entire Taiwanese society'. If the women in the pictures were Japanese (which is what the police concluded) or, I suppose what is equally possible, Taiwanese women dressed up to look like Japanese women in a Japanese setting, it is no easy thing to convincingly communicate the message through the mass media that the book unquestionably 'violated' all of Taiwan. Other possibilities emerged – it could conceivably have been a 'violation' of Japanese women instead, of the consumer's ethical right to accurate information as advertised, etc. – and the greater the number of alternative possibilities at play, the less effective the allocation of a particular representative function to the book would be.

While 'Tokyo' did not take steps to deal with the guidebook, its publisher, Tsukasa Shob ō , (司書房) adopted a defence strategy that was aimed at dissolving the representative function that Ma had ascribed to *Paradise Taiwan*. In an interview, a Tsukasa editor expressed surprise at the stir the book had caused in Taiwan:

This editor said that Tsukasa Shob ō has published a collection of books in the Paradise *series before this one, each one introducing the 'adult entertainment' business in countries like the Philippines, Thailand, Vietnam, and South Korea, and they even published a* Paradise Los Angeles*, but they never experienced any major problems. Only this release of* Paradise Taiwan *has caused so much upheaval. (...) He stressed that this is an 'interest-based' publication, the book only provides information and does not encourage the reader to go ahead and engage in what it describes* (United Daily News, 12 Jan. 2002a).

Stressing that *Paradise Taiwan* belonged to a series of similar publications, Tsukasa's editor argued that the 'upheaval' (*fengbo* 風波) surrounding the Taiwan volume was uncalled for since other volumes had not caused any similar reaction in the respective public spheres of those countries. The list of countries functioned as a rhetorical mechanism to isolate the Taiwanese reaction, because not only were less economically developed countries in the region that were heavily dependent on tourism (the Philippines, Thailand, Vietnam) unaffected by their respective editions of a harmless 'interest-based' publication, but South Korea – also a former Japanese colony, and fellow 'tiger' economy – apparently did not see any reason to take 'major' offense, either. This connection suggested that the 'upheaval' could not be attributed to Taiwan's colonial past and recent economic development. Indeed, 'even' in the United States there had not been any similar reaction, a point which worked to exclude any possible assumptions that Taiwan might be reacting as would a western society. What was left was an image of the Taiwanese response as utterly mysterious – an image that excused the publisher who could not possibly have anticipated it because it did not follow any established pattern and did not resemble anything else. This depiction marked an attempt to outweigh the charges that Ma and likeminded individuals had levelled against the book: that *Paradise Taiwan* represented (by synecdoche) a particularly Japanese attitude and sexual practice in need of correction and deserving of official condemnation. Instead, it was Taiwan that was erratic, the Tsukasa editor implied, not the guidebook to prostitution in Taiwan.

Ma's campaign against *Paradise Taiwan* was successful in the sense that Tsukasa Shobō eventually halted sales of the book and voluntarily removed the book from the market (*Asahi Shimbun*, 9 Jan. 2003); a Taibei court later found Mr. Sekine guilty of a criminal offense against public morals (*United Daily News*, 22 Aug. 2003). However, the campaign was unsuccessful in its wider aspirations to position Ma as a spokesperson for 'Taiwanese society as a whole.' Not only did the media cover the story within a thematic framework that made Ma look like a hypocrite, but there was also strong editorial opposition to his insistence that the publication had 'violated' Taiwanese society in any wider sense than that of its having violated a specific piece of ROC public decency legislation. A *China Times* editorial noted:

As for claiming that the book hurt the image of Taibei City and insulted Taiwanese women, that was a wild exaggeration. The Netherlands is a country that has legalized the sex trade, and, formulated in all the languages of the world, ideas of 'Paradise Netherlands' circulate globally, but no one considers that an insult to Dutch women or thinks that the country's image is hurt (China Times, 12 Jan. 2002b).

The *China Times* thus rejected Ma's idea of a collectively harmed Taiwan by making the very distinction that Chen Hongji claimed above to characterize the Japanese: one cannot simply take any element of social practice in a country and claim it as representative of the country as a whole. The city of Taibei and the women of Taiwan had not been hurt, what was described in *Paradise Taiwan* was not a part of which they were the whole, things could not be connected this way. Under such circumstances, synecdochical representation cannot function: without sub-text, synecdoche, and representative roles, the book became nothing more than a vulgar publication that happened to be illegal.

Conclusion

This paper has demonstrated how synecdoche and representation intersect in forming strategic notions of inclusivity or exclusivity, group formation, and social identification in the Taiwanese political and mass-media discourses on Japan-related controversies. The paper has pinpointed the arbitrary synecdochical ascription of representative functions to individual agents, thus questioning the underlying representative logic inherent in deployments of this rhetorical technique. Synecdochical representation operates so that groups can be portrayed as being spoken for by any agent perceived as one of its members, and it does not matter whether the same act is presented as representative of a number of different groups at the same time or whether the group in question is organized at all in any formal way. What matters is that the group can be shown to be composed of people with some fundamental trait in common, represented groups being selected on the basis of the established associations they carry in the public discourse. Attributing representative functions to specific agents lifts their acts from an individual (unrepresentative) onto a social level, making the acts susceptible to politicization, rationalization, and demands for reaction on a far more spectacular and newsworthy scale. When the act is controversial, the representative agent is shown either to be exercising his role competently (if the represented group is conceived of in negative terms) or incompetently (in the opposite case). Competent representation of 'bad' groups serves as a way to explain or motivate the act beyond the agent's personal and conscious intention in performing it, and incompetent representation of 'good' groups provides a greater social imperative to pass moral judgment and condemnation on the agent. Synecdochical representation requires 'sub-text' to be added to the individual act *a posteriori*, and it ceases to function if the agent manages communicatively to slip from the macro-social back onto the individual level. Private individuals do not represent others simply by acting or speaking, they are autonomous and non-transparent, and their stated intentions become the explanations of their motives. Undermining the thrust of their opponents' attempts to confront them as embodiments of a greater Other, agents operating at the individual level cannot represent by synecdoche.

An analytical focus on rhetorical strategies illuminates the operation of figures and tropes in political and mass-media discourses, revealing how group generalization, self-making, and othering finds strategic expression in manifest statements. This paper argues that generalization and group attribution follow a specific pattern, have a repeated form and a distinct structure that can be analytically captured through the rhetorical concept of synecdoche. Although the term is drawn from classical western rhetoric, the studied cases clearly document its use in the public discourse of a prominent East Asian society, as well as its usefulness for studies of discursive practices there. This present study analyses textual sources in two individual cases with a very specific geographical and temporal focus, all of which are factors that naturally limit, to some extent, the findings being extrapolated to other issues and societies. Further research is required to increase understanding of the role played by rhetoric and representation for projections and exclusionary notions of selfhood and otherness, not only in Taiwan but also in Japan and other societies in the region and elsewhere.

The paper makes two main contributions to this field of research: at a theoretical level, I introduce the concept and applicability of synecdoche to analyses of the East Asian public discourse in an effort to situate the polemic and ideological propagation of the nature and character of specific or general groups within a proper terminological and conceptual framework. At a practical level, I attempt to provide effective tools for both the media and news consumers to deconstruct and critically reflect on such propagation, since I highlight precisely how exclusionary notions of intrinsic qualities or dispositions thought to reside in certain groups or societies become connected to specific controversial statements through a logic of socially distributed motives and synecdochical representation. Such discursive manoeuvers, I contend, are eminently *strategic* and follow a very specific, continuously repeated, rhetorical pattern. This perspective seems to me especially relevant in the case of Taiwan, where the highly sensitive and mutually antagonistic questions of selfhood, otherness, nation, and history permeate so many aspects of the island's political, social, and cultural life – not only in its postcolonial relationship to Japan, of course, but also in relation to China and to Taiwan's ambiguous place and identity in the Chinese world. [9]

References

Asahi Shimbun 朝日新聞 (9 Jan. 2003) 'Taihoku kensatsu, hōjin kiso – Sei-fūzoku shōkai-hon o hanbai' 台北検察、邦人起訴　性風俗紹介本を販売 [Taibei prosecutor indicts overseas Japanese for selling book introducing sexual entertainment scene], morning ed., 33.

China Times 中國時報 (22 Feb. 2001a) 'Taiwanlun niuqu wei'anfu shishi, qunqingjifen' 台灣論扭曲慰安婦史實，群情激憤 [Mounting public indignation over distortion of historical facts about comfort women in *On Taiwan*], morning ed.

China Times (22 Feb. 2001b) 'Taiwanren zhi chi' 台灣人之恥 [A disgrace to the Taiwanese], evening ed.

China Times (25 Feb. 2001) 'Benbao zhuanfang Xiaolin Shanji: wei'anfu chutou rendi fei Xu Wenlong suo yan' 本報專訪小林善紀：慰安婦出頭人地非許文龍所言 [Exclusive interview with Kobayashi Yoshinori: Xu Wenlong did not say that being a comfort woman was a way to get ahead], morning ed.

China Times (26 Feb. 2001) 'Zaiye geng huo pi Xu yao qian buyao zunyan, nuhuo shao xiang 'Qianwei' cu tingzhi chuban Taiwanlun' 在野更火批許要錢不要尊嚴，怒火燒向'前衛'促停止出版台灣論 [Opposition intensifies excoriation of Xu for putting money above dignity – Engulfed in flames of fury, Avanguard urged to cease distribution of *On Taiwan*], evening ed.

China Times (27 Feb. 2001) 'Meiti rechao 'Taiwanlun' da mai, dengshang Jinshitang changxiao paihang' 媒體熱炒「台灣論」大賣，登上金石堂暢銷排行 [Media-hyped 'On Taiwan' a hit – Climbs Kingstone's bestseller chart], morning ed.

China Times (6 March 2001) 'Zhang Boya gaokou, Xiaolin jinzu re zhengyi, chongti rujing zai shenyi' 張博雅改口，小林禁足惹爭議，重提入境再審議 [Zhang Boya changes her tune – Grounding of Kobayashi having caused controversy, entry (ban) to be reconsidered], morning ed.

China Times (12 Jan. 2002a) 'Jile Taiwan zhenhan Taiwan, Bei-Gao jue antusuoji, zhu jia saodang' 極樂台灣震撼台灣，北高決按圖索驥，逐家掃蕩 [*Paradise Taiwan* shocks Taiwan, Taibei and Gaoxiong decide to follow directions to locate brothels and clear them out], morning ed.

China Times (12 Jan. 2002b) 'Zhengfeng yu chunfeng' 政風與春風 [Sex and government], morning ed

Foucault, Michel (2002) *The Archaeology of Knowledge*, London: Routledge.

Hamilton, Peter M (2003) 'The Saliency of Synecdoche: The Part and the Whole of Employment Relations,' in *Journal of Management Studies* 40:7, 1569-1585.

---

[9] I thankfully acknowledge the valuable comments and constructive suggestions I received from Beata Bochorodycz, Thomas Garcin, Roger Greatrex, Karl Gustafsson, Aline Henninger, Pekka Korhonen, Ewa Machotka, Marie Roesgaard, Sven Saaler, Torsten Weber, Aurelijus Zykas and many others in connection with *this paper. I am very grateful also to the anonymous reviewers as well as the editors of this volume.

Hwang, Yih-Jye (2010) 'Japan as 'Self' or 'the Other' in Yoshinori Kobayashi's *On Taiwan*,' in *China Information* 24:1, 75-98.

Kobayashi Yoshinori 小林よしのり (2000) *Shin-gōmanizumu sengen special: Taiwanron* 新ゴーマニズム宣言 Special: 台湾論 [New insolent-ist manifesto special: On Taiwan], Tokyo: Shōgakkan.

Nerlich, Brigitte (2010) 'Synecdoche: A trope, a whole trope, and nothing but a trope?' in Armin Burkhardt and Brigitte Nerlich (eds) *Tropical Truth(s): The Epistemology of Metaphor and other Tropes*, Berlin: De Gruyter, 297-319.

Ricoeur, Paul (1994) *Oneself as Another*, Chicago: University of Chicago Press.

Schubert, Gunter (2004) 'Taiwan's Political Parties and National Identity: The Rise of an Overarching Consensus,' in *Asian Survey* 44:4, 534-54.

Sejrup, Jens (2012) 'Instrumentalized History and the Motif of Repetition in News Coverage of Japan-Taiwan Relations,' in *Pacific Affairs* 85:4, 745-765.

Sejrup, Jens (2014) 'Awakening the Sufferers: Reflections on Public Relations, Activism, and Subalternity in Postcolonial Controversies between Taiwan and Japan,' in *Public Relations Inquiry* 3:1, 51-68.

Seto, Ken-ichi (1999) 'Distinguishing Metonymy from Synecdoche' in Klaus-Uwe Panther and Günter Radden (eds) *Metonymy in Language and Thought*, Amsterdam: John Benjamins, 91-120.

Suzuki, Shogo (2011) 'The Competition to Attain Justice for Past Wrongs: The 'Comfort Women' Issue in Taiwan,' in *Pacific Affairs* 84:2, 223-244.

United Daily News 聯合報 (23 Feb. 2001) 'Wei'anfu xuelei: cong minzu enyuan dao renquan guanhuai' 慰安婦血淚：從民族恩怨到人權關懷 [Comfort Women's tears of blood: From resentment of the people to concern for human rights], morning ed., p. 2.

United Daily News (26 Feb. 2001a) 'Xu Wenlong dapo shenmo: wei'anfu, shi fumu mai nü'er'文龍打破沈默：慰安婦，是父母賣女兒 [Xu Wenlong breaks the silence: Comfort women were sold by their parents], morning ed., p. 3.

United Daily News (26 Feb. 2001b) 'Fan zhi – Taiwanlun, Qi Mei shipin, Xindang liwei yu ju mai ju mai' 反制 - 台灣論、奇美食品 新黨立委籲拒買拒賣 [Oppositionalism – NP legislators call for consumer, retailer boycott of *On Taiwan* and Chi Mei products], morning ed., p. 3.

United Daily News (26 Feb. 2001c) 'Taiwanlun fengbo, shangxing a-mo: buxi pin laoming jingzuo kangyi' 台灣論風波 傷心阿嬤：不惜拚老命靜坐抗議 [*On Taiwan* crisis, grieved former comfort woman: I'm ready to risk my old life taking part in sit-in demonstration], evening ed., p. 2.

United Daily News (2 March 2001) 'Taiwanlun, chuqi re mai – Zuo you pu chu yiwan ce, gongsi yi wu cunshu, minglie changxiao bang' 台灣論 出奇熱賣 - 昨又鋪出一萬冊 公司已無存書 名列暢銷榜 [*On Taiwan* a surprising hit – Yesterday stores put out another 10,000 copies, publisher has no copies left in stock, book appears on bestseller charts], evening ed., p. 7.

United Daily News (12 Jan. 2001a) 'Riben chushu de 'chu gei Riren kan, zenme xian fengbo''日本出書的「出給日人看 怎麼掀風波」[Japanese publisher says 'it was released to give Japanese an insight, it's nothing to get so worked up about'], morning ed., p. 3.

United Daily News (12 Jan. 2002b) 'Chen Hongji: laji shu, genben buzhiyiti' 陳鴻基：垃圾書，根本不值一提 [Chen Hongji: Garbage book, not worth mentioning at all], Morning ed., p. 3.

United Daily News (12 Jan. 2002c), 'Xiang Riben Jiaoliu Xiehui biaoda buman – Ma Yingjiu: wo he shimin dou juede bei maofan' 向日本交流協會表達不滿 - 馬英九：我

和市民都覺得被冒犯 [Ma expresses his displeasure to the Japan Interchange Association: the citizens and I feel offended], morning ed., p. 3.

United Daily News (12 Jan. 2002d), 'Luolu nüzi genben shi Ribenren – Jingfang 'yandu', huaiyi yihuajiemu' 裸露女子根本是日本人 - 警方「研讀」懷疑移花接木 [The naked women are simply Japanese – Having 'studied the book intensively,' police suspects pictures have been palmed off as something they're not], morning ed., p. 3.

United Daily News (22 Aug. 2003), 'Fan shou Jile Taiwan, Ri shushang panxing liuyue' 販售極樂台灣 日書商判刑六月 [(Manager of) Japanese bookstore that sold *Paradise Taiwan* sentenced to six months imprisonment], morning ed., Taibei news sect., p. 4.

Barbora Platzerova

Bigamy in Chinese Law in the 20th Century: Conflict between Laws and Special Cases of Bigamy

At the end of the 1980s, both the People's Republic of China (mainland China/PRC) and, to some extent, the Taiwan authorities (Republic of China, ROC) adopted policies to promote cross-Strait contacts. Starting with contacts between relatives, cross-Strait tourist and business visits increased significantly and many legal questions arose for the first time, especially regarding the conflicts between the ROC and PRC laws. (Zhao Bingzhi 1989: 245). Conflicting laws led to problems, such as, which court had jurisdiction, which sovereign law would be applied, and whether one court would recognize and enforce the judgment or arbitral awards of its cross-Strait counterpart (Chen, Rong-Chwan 1997-1998: 602). Some conflicts also involved questions related to criminal jurisdiction over crimes committed by Taiwanese citizens in Mainland China, including crimes committed before 1949, and civil and criminal proceedings regarding bigamy committed after 1950, since the renewed contact between residents of the Mainland and Taiwan also revived the issue of spouses left behind in Mainland China during the evacuation in 1948-1949. After connections were re-established, challenges to the existing marital bonds arose because the former spouses in Mainland China as well as the new spouses and children in Taiwan had to deal with the situation (Chen, Shibo 1988: 36). Finally, the authorities on both sides of the Strait created formal procedures for dealing with the challenge, each of them in quite informal ways.
The issue of possible civil law consequences arose in Taiwan in 1987 and led to many academic discussions. The problem was partially resolved in Taiwan by Interpretation No. 242 of the Judicial Yuan of 23 June 1989, regarding the dissolution of bigamous marriages under Art. 992 of the Civil Code (Wang Zhenshao 1990: 57). In this case, the Judicial Yuan declared a ROC Supreme Court judgment unconstitutional for the first time in the ROC history (Wang Hongzhi 2010: 98). The case concerned a husband who had married his first wife in 1941 in Mainland China and had left for Taiwan in 1949, leaving his wife behind. She later left for Hong Kong where, in 1986, she sued for the dissolution of her husband's second marriage, which had taken place in 1960 in Taiwan, using her right as a 'person concerned' under Art. 992 of the Civil Code. The law did not state any statute of limitations to this right or any other relevant limitation. After two judgments in favour of the wife, the defendant petitioned the Judicial Yuan, which finally decided not to protect the wife's right to apply for dissolution.
The ruling was quite broad, and covered not only this specific case of bigamy – one of many in the national tragedy of spouses lost or abandoned in wartime – but also any other case of bigamy occurring under similar circumstances when spouses were separated without any possibility of communication or knowledge of the other spouse's whereabouts. The Judicial Yuan leaned on the necessity of providing constitutional protection for the family rights of the second wife/husband, and also noted that there was no public interest at stake in the dissolution of the marriage, since the purpose of the provision was to uphold a monogamous marriage system and ensure the equality of men and women. Thus the Judicial Yuan refused to protect the right to dissolution in this case simply because it was in conflict with the original purpose of the provision (Wang Hongzhi 2010: 98). The decision did not specify whether the first marriage was still held to exist, and therefore whether the first marriage

Berliner China-Hefte/Chinese History and Society 47 (2016), 105-122

had ceased to exist after this ruling, or whether there were now two marriages existing simultaneously, but there is no reason to believe the first marriage was dissolved.

The ROC authorities first issued a draft in October 1989 and on 31 July 1992 finally promulgated the Mainland Relations Act dealing with the conflict of laws and also with both civil and criminal law issues following restored cross-Strait contacts (*Taiwan diqu yu Dalu diqu renmin guanxi tiaoli*). Art. 74 withdrew the right of the person concerned to sue for the dissolution of a bigamous marriage entered into before 4 June 1985 (when the provision of the Civil Code relating to bigamy was amended), and also stipulated that, in the case of bigamy committed between 5 June 1985 and 1 November 1987, the second, thus bigamous, marriage was valid as well as the former marriage. Only if both parties had committed bigamy would the former marriage be held as dissolved. Art. 76 gave the perpetrators of bigamy committed before the mutual relations between Taiwan and Mainland were re-established (i.e. 1 November 1987) immunity from prosecution for bigamy or adultery (Ke 1993: 57).

The Mainland authorities, on 16 April 1988, issued a circular on the validity of marriages and on the way in which marriages involving those who had left for Taiwan before 1949 would be treated by the Mainland. First, it indicated the usual attitude towards marital disputes: no interference in the absence of any complaint by one of the spouses. In case of a complaint, the principle of 'one husband, one wife' *(yifuyiqi 一夫一妻)* was vaguely upheld, but at the same time a preference was declared for dealing with disputes through mediation (at that time, this was the main method of dealing with marital disputes). The rest of the declaration dealt only with the situations when both spouses wanted to continue with the former marriage relationship (*Minzhengbu, Sifabu* 16 April 1988).

On 9 August of the same year, the vice-president of the PRC Supreme Court, Ma Yuan (馬原), issued a general statement that covered the civil lawsuits arising from the new cross-Strait developments and provided guidance for the courts. Concerning marital disputes, the court required solutions based on the principles of stable marital relationships, monogamy and no interference in the absence of a complaint by one of the spouses. The guidance provided was based on the current law at that time, except for one situation – bigamy committed by one or both spouses after they had been separated by historical circumstances – when the court refused to treat these marriages as bigamous (*Zuigao Renmin Fayuan Ma Yuan Fuyuanzhang* 9 August 1988; Zhao, Bingzhi 1989: 230; Yang 1989).

The PRC judiciary and prosecution adopted a lenient attitude towards historical crimes in the interests of easing future reunification, promised not to prosecute Taiwan residents and considered them subject to the statute of limitations (*Zuigao Renmin Fayuan, Zuigao Renmin Jianchayuan* 14 March 1988). A similarly lenient attitude was proclaimed by the PRC Supreme Court in June 1988 with regard to the crime of bigamy committed because of the separation of the spouses after 1949: not only were these cases different from ordinary bigamy, and could not therefore be treated alike, but they also would not be subject to criminal prosecution. This was clearly a compromise (Ke 1993: 5), a surprisingly simple and appropriate solution for a situation which could have led to thousands of family tragedies, years of judicial proceedings and unnecessary hostility between the two states. The reason the PRC adopted this position is quite clear – the urge to avoid stirring up memories of the 1948-1949 historical circumstances because this could have led to difficulties in the attempts to re-establish connections with Taiwan, which was supposed to lead to reunification in the future. In addition, any disputes over the conflict between the laws of the PRC and those of Taiwan could have jeopardized the position of the PRC in international relations: the PRC was at that time trying to re-establish itself on the international stage and any doubts that might have emerged about the capability of the PRC to enforce its laws in the territories that it claimed to have under its control could have caused the PRC to lose face.

The question is why society and the judiciary in Taiwan were willing to accept that a significant number of marriages entered into after 1949 were in fact bigamous and that the wives and children from former marriages were still actually living on the other side of the Strait. To answer this question, it is necessary to take a look at the tradition of *naqie* (納妾) and the attitude towards bigamy as stipulated in the previous Chinese legislation.

Monogamy, Bigamy and Polygamy in Chinese Law

First of all, it is necessary to define the basic terms that will be employed in this article. When we try to define monogamy, bigamy and polygamy in the context of the Chinese family, problems can arise in connection with the character in the Chinese language that is used to refer to 'marriage', since legal and sociological terms are usually mixed up, legal terms are sometimes understood in different ways and Western and Chinese legal terms are sometimes improperly interchanged.

In this article, I will use the terms that are found in the legislation that was applicable in 19th century Europe, since the influence of the European civil codes, the ABGB, BGB and the Civil Code on the Chinese laws of the 20th century should not be disregarded and the legal reforms at the end of the 19th century and the beginning of the 20th century actually tried to adapt this legislation to the real situation in China, although this was attempted through the Japanese model. In most European countries in the 19th century, family law was still governed by canon law which had its origins in Roman law; the new civil codes granted the state the right to create marriage, but still maintained the same attitude towards the legal formation of marriage as promoted by canon law: marriage was created only by a decision, or at least with the assistance, of the public (state, religious) authority, required some form of registration and preliminary proof of the nonexistence of other marriages. Marriage could not be created by a simple decision made by the people concerned or simply by cohabitation. An already existing marriage acted as a legal obstacle to any new marriage and bigamy was committed only by the act of entering into a marriage with one person while still legally married to another. Cohabitation, sexual relationships or 'de-facto marriage' did not constitute bigamy, but different (usually criminal) offenses such as adultery, fornication, debauchery, etc. might occur, since these acts were usually held to be illegal. This idea is not so different from the attitude to bigamy reflected in Qing law; the problem is that Western law did not recognize any relationship similar to *naqie* and obliged even the husband to fulfil the requirement of sexual fidelity, which Qing law never did. This tradition was still supported by the majority of people in the patriarchal society, where women still had an unequal position, and the new legislation did not interfere with its continuing existence.

Therefore, the term 'bigamy' used in this article is based on the following characteristics: it refers only to a marriage created (or to the attempt to create a marriage) during the existence of a former marriage. The term is restricted to a legal marriage, does not have any requirements concerning sexual fidelity, and is still considered to constitute bigamy no matter how many subsequent putative marriages were concluded. According to Chinese tradition, a bigamous marriage encompassed marriage only where there were two 'principal wives' *qi,* but did not include any form of cohabitation with other women who did not have the same status as *qi* and were traditionally subordinated to the so-called *qie* (妾), usually translated as concubine, which is misleading from the point of view of Western legal terminology.[55] The term 'polygamy' is not a legal term; it is usually used in sociology to refer to stable ongoing sexual relationships regardless of their legal status, and will therefore be used in this way in this article.

Bigamy in the 1930 Civil Code

In the case of the 1930 Civil Code, significant efforts were made to reform and modernize the 'traditional' family in line with Western standards, while at the same time trying to avoid any direct confrontation with existing social practices (see also Huang, Philip C. 2001, Part One).This attitude resulted in the simplest solution: the most problematic parts of Qing family law and known social practices were omitted from the Code, but not abolished. This is the most significant feature of the practice of *naqie*.

Naqie and Bigamy

According to Qing legislation and judicial practice, *naqie* contained a character that was close to that of marriage, but was not considered marriage and thus did not interfere with the principle of monogamous marriage where only one woman might act as *qi*, despite the fact that it allowed men to have polygamous sexual relations. The reforms of the civil law between 1909 and 1930 introduced a strict requirement for monogamous marriage but in practice, *naqie* still existed alongside marriage, still contained a factual and quasi-legal character and was still not considered to be bigamy in legal terms. These points were nevertheless contested and were obviously considered problematic from the point of view of Christian marriage (for more details, see Glosser 2003, Tran 2009). This attitude was also confirmed by the *Daliyuan* (大理院), which on the one hand confirmed the ban on bigamy, but on the other, refused to recognize *naqie* as having any relation to marriage, and therefore allowed its continued existence (Bernhard 1999: 211).[56] During this period the ban on bigamy echoed Qing law – there could be only one *qi*, but as many *qie* as the husband was able to support. *Naqie* was not considered to be bigamy and thus did not provide grounds for divorce or constitute a breach in the idea of the formally monogamous marriage.

The 1930 Civil Code, still in force in Taiwan in an amended version, adhered to the same principle as the former Qing Code: that bigamy is committed only when an individual enters into marriage while already legally married to a *qi*, no matter what other *de facto* relationships or circumstances might exist. The protected object is the monogamous character of

---

55 The precise translation of the term *qie* (妾) as 'concubine' is not suitable, since the status of concubines under Roman law and, later, Canon law was completely different to their status in Chinese society. The English language does not offer a more appropriate term, so I will continue to use the Chinese term *qie*. *Naqie* (納妾) is sometimes translated as 'taking concubines'; the problem is that even if 'taking a concubine' is considered to be similar in some way to *naqie*, a relationship with a concubine according to the Classic and Post-Classic Roman law, not to mention the Canon law, excluded marriage and vice versa, but under Qing law, *naqie* did not interfere with marriage at all.

56 Courts determined that although *qie* and her 'husband' had rights and responsibilities similar to the rights reserved to the husband and to the *qi*, such as the duty of cohabitation, they were legally unenforceable (Wang Hongzhi 2010:81)

marriage as an institution with one husband and one *qi*, thus naqie does not constitute bigamy (Shi 2000: 238). The law and judicial practice strictly separated bigamy from any form of adultery or polygamous sexual relationships - the provisions related to bigamy were not meant to protect the newly established obligation of mutual sexual fidelity between the spouses. On the other hand, the law did not seek to abolish *naqie* or any other sexual relationship outside marriage, provided neither of the spouses complained.

The existence of *naqie,* however, is of course the product of a strictly patriarchal society, where the status of women is significantly lower than the status of men and any rights and interests pertaining to women must be subordinated to the requirements of men. The transfer from the patrilineal family structure to the patriarchal conjugal family in the Civil Code also led to the emergence of a new perspective regarding the purpose of marriage, and social acceptance of *naqie* was considered to be decreasing. As Lisa Tran remarked, the new inheritance rights for daughters, the freedom to adopt his or her descendants and to make a last will and testament weakened the urgency to have sons, and *naqie* started to be seen in a new light: it was no longer necessary for the continuation of the patrilineal family or the transfer of the family property nor for society, and was thus in conflict with the official GMD ideology influenced by the Christian concept of marriage. The practice did not of course simply disappear from everyday life, in spite of the fact that it was not legally regulated (Tran 2009: 203). Due to the need to resolve civil disputes, judicial practice defined the relationship as an innominate contract which included a physical relationship between a man and his *qie* without the legal consequences of marriage or divorce (Shi 2000: 528). Courts considered a *qie* as a *jiashu* (家屬), as a member of the man's household, but also refused to admit any interpretation which would allow *naqie* to constitute bigamy, thus allowing families to maintain the idea of formally monogamous marriages.[57]

Formation of Marriage

The character of marriage in the Civil Code became more contractual, emphasizing the roles to be played by spouses upon entering the married state as well as their mutual rights and responsibilities. Irrespective of limitations to the freedom of both parties, the roles played to be played by the parents and senior relatives in the marriage were also limited - a valid marriage now required the consent of both spouses, allowed spouses to negotiate and set the scope and disposition of marital property, and also introduced the mutual obligation of sexual fidelity, stipulating bigamy and adultery as grounds for divorce for both spouses and also as criminal offenses.[58]

Marriage was now formalized by the performance of a 'public ceremony in the presence of two witnesses' to establish a legal marriage. Thereafter, neither consent nor cohabitation was considered as a sufficient legal means of creating a marriage, and the courts paid close

---

[57] *Qinshu fa jicheng fa lifa yuanze, qinshu fa xian jue ge dian shencha yijian shu.* [Statement of Opinion on Preliminary Problems of Family Law sent to the Judicial Yuan on 23 July 1930] (Valk 1939: 175). For more details on this topic, see Tran 2015.

[58] Art. 256 of the Criminal Code of 1928 (Burdett 1928); Art. 237, 239 of the Criminal Code of 1935 (*Zhongguo Fagui Kanxing she Bianshen Weiyuanhui* 1945). Moreover, Art. 986 of the Civil Code until 1998 forbade marriage between the adulterous spouse and the accomplice, if divorced or prosecuted for adultery. Until 1936, married men could not be charged for the crime of adultery, only as accomplices in cases of adultery committed by a married woman. For more details, see Tran 2009:203.

attention to the ceremony performed in an attempt to find out whether it was the 'public ceremony' required by the Code, or another ceremony that only celebrated *naqie.* While a second 'public ceremony would constitute a second and therefore putative marriage and would mean the crime of bigamy had been committed, other forms of celebration would not have such legal consequences.[59] On the other hand, in the case of a marriage that took the form of the above-mentioned public ceremony, it was considered bigamy even if it was called *naqie* by the parties involved (Shi 2000: 235).

Legal Consequences of Bigamous Marriage

Dissolution of the Putative Marriage

The legal means by which the *qi* could restrict her husband's bigamous marriage with another *qi* were very limited.[60] One possibility was to undertake an action for dissolution of the putative – bigamous – marriage, which would allow the *qi* to end the subsequent marriage concluded between her husband and another woman. Although bigamy was still prohibited, the new legislation also led to a shift in the Qing legislation with regard to the attitude towards putative marriages: the law did not adopt the principle of the bigamous marriage that was considered to be invalid from its inception. On the contrary: Art. 998 of the Civil Code clearly acknowledged the existence and continuation of the bigamous marriage until its dissolution.[61] Moreover, Art. 992 made it necessary to sue for dissolution, limiting the number of plaintiffs to the 'persons concerned', and allowing the bigamous marriage to be dissolved only after a ruling by a court. The definition of 'person concerned' that had been lacking was finally clarified by Decision No. 3000 of the Judicial Yuan (司法院) in 1945, when the court specified that the term would apply to any person having a legal concern in the dissolution of a bigamous marriage. But the right to apply for the dissolution of a bigamous marriage was not only limited by the standing of the person concerned, but also by the existence of the former marriage; if the first marriage ceased to exist, for example, after a divorce, it was not possible to sue for the dissolution of the subsequent marriage (Art. 992 of the Civil Code). Moreover, according to Art. 998 the effect of the dissolution (*chexiao* 撤銷) was not retroactive, so that the bigamous marriage, with all its

---

59 Art. 982 of Civil Code. The 'public ceremony' provision was not centered on the ceremony itself, but on the public nature of the ceremony. Thus any ceremony was held to be valid, if the public were allowed to attend the rites, investigate their validity and point out possible discrepancies, such as, for example, an already existing marriage of one of the participants, and to inform affected persons, such as an already existing *qi* or her family. The stress on the public nature of the wedding ceremony, whether Chinese, Christian, Buddhist or other, was held as to be sufficient to avoid breaches of the law. According to the courts, fulfilling the condition of a public ceremony required that the wedding feast be in some way accessible to the public (through windows, open doors, etc.), and that the circumstances must make it obvious even to outsiders that a marriage ceremony is being held. If these conditions were not fulfilled, e.g. in the case of a *de facto* marriage based only on cohabitation, the marriage would not be considered valid in legal terms, but might be considered to be *naqie*. For more details, see Zhao, Ma 2007: 86.

60 This refers to the means available to the innocent spouse to interfere with the bigamous marriage entered into by her husband with another *qi* (vice versa, also applicable in the case of a bigamous marriage concluded between a *qi* and another man); with the exception of filing for divorce on the grounds of adultery, the *qi* did not have any other legal means of interfering with her husband's relationship with *qie.*

61 Except for soldiers; if soldier's wife committed bigamy, the second marriage was null and void (Shi 2000: 238).

legal consequences, continued to exist until dissolved by the court, and the rights of the third person were protected. This attitude, along with the unclear definition of the 'public ceremony' provided the basis for two issues: it allowed men to conclude several marriages and still enabled them to insist that any of the subsequent marriages did not constitute marriage, but *naqie*, and also allowed the social position of *qi* and *qie* to become closer and closer, especially in the case that they were each unaware of the existence of the other (See also Zhao and Ma 2007: 86).

The amendment to the Civil Code on 25 May 1985 signified a major change in the legal perception of bigamous marriages and their existence: it declared that bigamy, as in the case of any other legal act '*contra bonos mores*' was to be considered null and void from its very inception (Art. 72, 988). Thus, the invalid status of a bigamous marriage was added to Art. 988, and Art. 992 was dissolved. Any bigamous marriage concluded after the promulgation of the amendment was judged to be invalid irrespective of the circumstances and was held to have been non-existent from the very beginning. This obviated the need to sue for its dissolution or to obtain confirmation from the court. In addition, the amendment added a second paragraph to Art. 985, which did not only forbid bigamy, but now also provided a more precise definition of bigamy, namely, being married to two or more spouses at the same time, without making any distinction between *qi* or *qie*.

In practice, the above-mentioned amendment was considered to be too strict, especially in the case of putative marriages concluded in good faith where there was no knowledge of previous marriages, either because of a clerical error during the registration of a divorce, or because a final divorce decree was overruled by a superior court, or any other special circumstances (*Sifa Yuan*, 29 August 1994; *Sifa Yuan* 13 December 2002). The 2007 amendment to the Civil Code reduced the severity of the original article; Art. 988 was reformulated to indicate that bigamous marriages were null and void, but in the case of 'specific' bigamy being committed without malicious intent and in the belief that the previous marriage had ceased to exist because of divorce, the second marriage would be held to be valid and the previous marriage would be viewed as already terminated.

Divorce and Separation

The other possibility for *qi* who were not satisfied when their husbands took a second wife, was to file for divorce according to the provisions of the 1930 Civil Code. But although committing bigamy constituted the grounds for divorce, it was not an easy procedure. First, the statute of limitations was quite harsh – the right to sue for divorce was limited to six months after the discovery of the bigamy, or two years after it had occurred. If the *qi* had given her consent or had forgiven the husband after she had discovered the fact, the right to sue for divorce expired immediately (Art. 1053 of the Civil Code). Also, if she successfully applied for divorce, she could not apply for dissolution of the bigamous marriage (see below) and it thus remained valid (Art. 985, 992, 998, 1052 of the Civil Code). If she applied for the dissolution of the bigamous marriage/s, her right to sue for divorce remained intact, as long as she applied for divorce within the above-mentioned time limit. With regard to the other party to the bigamous marriage, she did not have the right to apply for divorce, but had the right to apply for the dissolution (*chexiao*) of the marriage.[62]

[62] Shi 2000: 471. Divorce was not a suitable solution for most women, who usually lacked the necessary psychological and financial support of their families. The role of marriage in Chinese society was clearly

Another possibility was the judicial separation of spouses without divorce (*fenju* 分居, divorce from bed and board) according to Art. 1001. In this situation, the *qi* did not need to prove that she had not consented to her husband's bigamy, and did not have to apply within a limited period of time, as she would have to if she were suing for divorce. She could avoid the stigma of divorce, her husband would still be responsible for her maintenance, and finally the *qi* was allowed to inhabit a separate residence (Shi 2000: 525; see also Kuo 2010: Chapter 7).

Taiwan Before 1945

At the beginning of the 20th century, Taiwan was excluded from the Qing's attempts to modernize the civil law, since the island had been ceded to the Japanese in 1895 under the Treaty of Shimonoseki, and was therefore not influenced by the Western legal theories that had been introduced into Mainland China. On the other hand, the Japanese colonial authorities gradually introduced their own civil law, which was based on European legislation and very similar to the (later) reformed ROC civil law and was actually one of its main sources. Thus the civil law in Taiwan, except in the case of the family and inheritance laws as mentioned below, was in reality reformed even earlier than the civil law in mainland China.

On the other hand, the Japanese civil law did not influence the family law in Taiwan (that is, the family law of the Han majority) directly, since family law and inheritance law were excluded from the scope of the 1896 Civil Code, which was otherwise gradually implemented in Japan and later, after 1923, directly applied in Taiwan.[63] The Japanese authorities allowed the family to be governed by local customs, i.e. the unreformed Qing law.[64] Family law in Taiwan was, however, influenced indirectly; the Taiwanese population had access to the courts and they were allowed to submit their disputes to be decided according to the customary Taiwanese laws, but the judges were usually Japanese or locals who had studied law in Japan, were therefore influenced by the continental law, and introduced Western legal terminology and concepts into Taiwan. The judges were also allowed to modify or even abolish local customs which were held to infringe against public order or good morals. One of these modifications, for example, was the gradual introduction of the theory that marriage required the consent of the future spouses (Wang Tay-sheng 2013: 100).

These judicial modifications of family law in colonial Taiwan also affected the institution of *naqie*. The *qie* was finally granted a certain level of equality with her husband since she was now allowed to leave him, quoting the same reasons for which she could previously have been expelled from his household, but at the same time she was not considered to be

determined as a way of providing for a woman's livelihood, with the husband providing this livelihood and the wife depending on him completely; most women did not have paid employment or professional skills. Even after 1930, the wife's access to the marital property (including property that she herself brought to the marriage) was highly restricted, both during a marriage and also in any property settlement after a divorce. In addition, on entering into a marriage, a woman became a stable part of her husband's agnatic family, so that divorce meant breaking off this relationship and incurring significant social stigmatization. Divorce was therefore a choice of last resort for a woman who had no other means of providing a livelihood for herself, such as returning to her birth family or remarrying after divorce. For more details, see Kuo 2010.

[63] The Japanese family and succession law was to be finally introduced in 1945, but was never applied because of historical developments after the Japanese capitulation.

[64] This also allows us to consider the character of the Japanese rule over Taiwan.

a *qi*. From the perspective of the colonial authorities, *naqie* was held to be a local custom in Taiwan which did not infringe against public order, and thus was inviolable (Wang Tay-sheng 2010: 357, 359).

When the Nationalist troops from the Mainland arrived in 1945, the 1930 Civil Code of the ROC was introduced into Taiwan, which led to the full introduction of all the principles of continental law governing family law and inheritance law into the residents' everyday lives; up to then, these had been applied only indirectly, and in an unsystematic way.

Origin of the 'Special Case' of Bigamy

The problems related to these 'special' cases of bigamy, i.e. putative marriages entered into on the basis of justifiable motives, started to emerge at the end of the 1940s, but when it was not so surprising in the 1980s, since the first signs of impending troubles appeared at the end of the 1970s.

Divorcing a Missing Spouse

In the PRC, the New Marriage Law that was passed by the Central People's Government Committee on 13 April 1950 explicitly banned bigamy, including *naqie,* completely outlawed it and also implied that both relationships were of the same character. The law was not retroactive - towards existing bigamous marriages and *qie* who were married before the law came into force, judicial practice favoured tolerance, if the respective woman did not complain (*bugaobuli* 不告不理) (Wang Naicong 1951: 21; Zhongying renmin zhengfu fazhi weiyuanhui youguan hunyinfa shixing de ruogan wenti yu jieda). In the case of a complaint or a lawsuit brought by *qi* or *qie*, judicial practice was to expect that the marriage would be dissolved (Zuigao Renmin Fayuan October 1950). Marriage or even cohabitation with men or women other than with the lawful spouse was considered to constitute bigamy or adultery and was punished accordingly, as will be discussed below (Wang Naicong 1951: 69). The public was also encouraged to report any cases of bigamy and a 'policy of interference' was promoted concerning bigamy, no matter what the form, if it was committed after the promulgation (Zuigao Renmin Fayuan 16 May 1957).

Concerning the refugees who arrived in Taiwan at the end of the 1940s, the situation in the PRC was clear: bigamy (in any form as mentioned above) was not to be tolerated even if one spouse was not living in the same country, no matter whether he (or she) had taken up residence in Taiwan, Hong Kong or Japan. The courts presented a clear attitude towards intentional bigamy: if the deserted spouse wanted to enter into another marriage, she (or he) must be divorced first. On the other hand, if the spouse did not begin divorce proceedings or was not granted a divorce, marrying another person might lead to prosecution for bigamy and the related punishment, although the punishment would vary depending on the circumstances of the individual cases (Wang, Naicong 1951: 63-71. *Zuigao Renmin Fayuan* 13 May 1951).

Since it was not possible, in the divided country, for both spouses to appear for the registration of the divorce, consensual divorce was not possible; legal representation or consent granted via notarial deed was usually not accepted, and thus the deserted spouse was referred to the procedure for obtaining a judicial divorce. Obtaining a judicial divorce was not easy: in general, it required procedures at two levels, the first at the local people's government, the second, at the court.[65] At the first level, the local authorities initiated a mediation procedure and launched an investigation into the circumstances related to the divorce petition (see also Huang Philip C. 2010). But in the case of a proven desertion, the procedure was much simpler; since there was no one to mediate with, the procedure might start at the judicial level instead of at the local people's government. Both parties had to be summoned to the court, and nonattendance could be held as proof of desertion. If necessary, evidence was presented to the court, and then a decision regarding the dissolution of the marriage was issued.

Because the law and judicial practice both required the delivery of the court's resolution, the courts had to find a way to deliver the judgment to the missing spouse. The method of publicizing divorce proceedings in the newspaper, popular during the 1930s and 1940s, was not held to be sufficient. Finally, judicial practice was adapted to allow an attempt to deliver the decision instead of proof of the delivery. The divorce was considered final after a proven attempt to deliver the decision, and the abandoned spouse might marry as she or he wished, even if the other spouse had not been served with the court decision. However, if communication was possible, some courts required much more effort on the side of the spouse seeking a divorce. If the deserting spouse had not committed a serious crime of a counterrevolutionary nature, the abandoned spouse was urged as far as possible to wait until the Communist government regained control over Taiwan before filing for divorce. If the spouse did not wish to wait, a letter containing an explanation had to be sent and a reasonable period would then be allowed for the soldier to return and participate in divorce proceedings; only then might a divorce be granted (*Zuigao Renmin Fayuan Xinan fen yuan* 1 December 1951. Wang, Naicong 1951: 67, 120).

The situation of those who left the Mainland to go to Taiwan was even more complicated: before 1985, only 10 grounds for divorce were stipulated in the ROC Civil Code, but none of these were appropriate for the actual situation. As a result, newcomers from the Mainland, who were separated from their legal spouses and in many cases were without any means of communication, were left without any legal route to file for divorce. They might believe their spouses were dead, but did not have any means of having this confirmed. The majority of the people who were in this situation therefore entered into marriage with other people after arriving in Taiwan, and subsequently established new homes and families there.

As mentioned above, the signs of an impending crisis resulting from these marriages appeared soon after the PRC started to allow its citizens to travel outside the country. After the end of the 1970s, the PRC gradually re-established relations with its neighbours, communication between Taiwan, Hong Kong and other places was restored and the question of the marriages that had been concluded on the Mainland before the PRC had been established and terminated afterwards for political reasons re-surfaced. The majority of the disputes arose as a result of the re-establishment of marital relations between once divorced spouses (*fuhun* 復婚), in cases when the spouses had not had any means of communication for years and usually the spouse living outside PRC did not have any knowledge of the divorce proceedings carried out before the PRC courts. One of the main reasons for the emergence of these cases was the new opportunity of the Mainland residents to move abroad on the basis

[65] Art. 17 of the Marriage Law (*Zhonghua Renmin Gongheguo Hunyin fa* 中華人民婚姻法) of 13 April 1950 in Wang, Naicong 1951: 1-8.

of a marital relationship. The PRC Supreme Court approached these disputes with caution, since the applicant living in the PRC usually lacked cooperation on the *fuhun* proceeding or even the consent of the spouse living abroad. The probability that the other spouse had re-married while resident outside the Mainland was high, so the court finally allowed the restoration of the marital relationship on condition that both spouses applied and also provided proof of the nonexistence of other marriages entered into by the spouse that was resident abroad (*Zuigao Renmin Fayuan* 28 August 1980).

In 1980, a voluminous recodification of the marriage law was published in the PRC, in an attempt to clarify the new legal and moral code concerning marriage and family. In addition to reinforcing the institution of marriage as the only acceptable living arrangements of men and women and prohibiting bigamy, the amendment, surprisingly enough, did not stipulate the prohibition of former 'feudal' misdemeanours that had been mentioned in the 1950 Marriage Law, namely, the prohibition of *naqie* or *tongyangxi* (童養媳), although these delicts were not rare (*Zuigao Renmin Fayuan* 2 February 1979, Part One, Section Two). Also, the law did not determine the character of bigamous marriage – whether it was null and void or voidable and if so, who had the right to sue for dissolution. The law again lacked any definition of bigamy (*chonghun* 重婚), but the definition provided by the Criminal Code, although quite extensive, since it also covered adultery committed with the spouses of military personnel, could suffice. The problem of defining bigamy, however, remained the same - the still non-existent official way of entering into marriage, and the inability of the state authorities to maintain any centralized and complex records of marriages.[66]

The Marriage Law of 1980 marked a further attempt to finally eliminate unregistered *de facto* marriages (*shishi hunyin* 事實婚姻): these were marriages that were entered into without registration, usually only on the basis of traditional rituals, and often without the consent of the spouses. The 'married' couples would then be forced to register their marriages under the penalty of the legal nonexistence of the marriage, a penalty which would include their children being declared illegitimate. This development become final in 1994, when the new marriage registration regulations were issued; from that moment onwards, every new marriage had to be registered to be judged valid, at least in theory. In practice, the situation was (and still is) different, especially in rural areas, since the increasing mobility of the population, the loosening of marriage approval rules, the difficulty or sometimes impossibility of divorce, the nonexistence of a central register of citizens, the decreasing role and influence of social organizations, and the decline of public authorities, such as schools or employers as arbiters of personal behaviour, all made it easier to maintain relationships outside marriage. Within the PRC family law traditions of the previous 50 years, the moment of formation of a marriage and the registration of that marriage had always been two completely different things; the registration of marriage was usually a strictly administrative procedure and did not include any ceremony at all; the marriage itself, at least from the popular point of view, was concluded by the performance of traditional rituals depending on the religion and nationality of the spouses, and the registration was usually performed some time before

---

66 Marriage registration was introduced in the areas controlled by the Communists during the 1930s and was one of the main elements of the family law reforms carried out during the 1950s. Before 1994, however, in practice, marriage registration was never held to be necessary for the legal formation of marriage in and the government is still not able to enforce the obligatory registration of marriage in rural areas.

or after the ceremony (usually if the spouses were under marriage age). Unregistered marriage, from the popular standpoint, could therefore be considered completely valid. [67]

As mentioned above, the Marriage Law of 1980 did not require the mutual sexual fidelity of spouses and also did not explicitly prohibit *naqie.* The 1979 Criminal Code did not designate adultery as a crime and, therefore, keeping mistresses, or having short term love affairs, or even establishing secondary households in the place where one spouse had temporary residence during business trips, were theoretically legal as long as they did not cross the line of *de facto* marriage.[68] The requirement to redefine bigamy and to use the Marriage Law as a means of enforcing marital fidelity was not directly addressed by an extensive amendment to the Marriage Law in 2001, although the necessity had been raised during discussions previous to the enactment of the amendment (Wu Haihong 2000).

The 2001 amendment listed some breaches of the marital contract which always constituted sufficient grounds for divorce, and specifically included bigamy and cohabitation with a person other than one's spouse among these (Art. 3, 32, 46 of the Marriage Law, amended). It also declared the right of the other party to claim damages resulting from these breaches of the marital contract, including bigamy and adultery (Art. 46 of the Marriage Law, amended). The amendment further introduced the mutual obligation of sexual fidelity, although the Supreme Court refused to enforce this (*Zuigao Renmin Fayuan* 25 December 2001 in *Zhonghua Renmin Gongheguo Hunyin Fa* 2012: 47).

The amendment clearly considered bigamous marriage null and void from its beginning (Art. 10 of the Marriage Law as amended in 2001 in *Zhonghua Renmin Gongheguo Hunyin Fa*; Huang, Li'e 2003: 23). Art. 45 of the law stated that the bigamy cases could be initiated as either public or private prosecutions, according to the respective sections of the Criminal Procedure Law (Ronald and Zhiqiu 2006: 78), thus giving the other spouse the right to sue the perpetrator on her own, with or without the assistance of public prosecutors.[69]

Conclusion

The legal systems in both Taiwan (ROC) and in the PRC prohibited bigamy on the same basis: the definition is derived from the 19th and early 20th century European legislation under which bigamy, according to civil law and criminal law, was constituted by the act of concluding a marriage during the existence of a former marriage. This idea was quite close to the attitude towards bigamy that was reflected in the Qing Code, but here the perception of bigamy and enforcement of the law colluded with the *naqie*, the custom of keeping *qie* and secondary 'wives' with a legally unclear status.

The split in the legal definition of bigamy was caused by the differences in the perception of what constituted a marriage; after 1949, the definition of bigamy in Taiwan remained the same as it had been during the 1930s, but in mainland China, the definition became broader

[67] Extensive case law on this topic developed during the 1950s, for example, see *Zuigao Renmin Fayuan Huadong fen yuan*: 29 July 1953 and *Zuigao Renmin Fayuan* 27 August 1958.

[68] Cohabitation required the fulfilment of criteria usually applicable in the case of *de facto* marriages: long-term, stable relationship of unlimited duration of time between two persons of different sex, where they themselves as well as the people around them considered them to be a married couple. Thus, common extramarital affairs were not considered to constitute bigamy. *Zuigao Renmin Fayuan* 21 November 1989.

[69] Art. 204, 205, 206 of Criminal Procedure as amended in 2012 (*Zhonghua Renmin Gongheguo Xingshi Susong fa* 中華人民共和國刑事訴訟法).

in scope- not only was *naqie* considered to constitute bigamy, but also any other relationship that was similar to marriage. The reason for this broader definition is difficult to trace, but there are two circumstances which probably influenced this development: 1) the positions of *qi* and *qie* during the republican period, which after the reform of the Civil Code in 1930 became much closer to each other, and 2) at least until 1994, the formation of marriage in the PRC did not require any specific form, therefore any form was acceptable, even cohabitation as 'husband and wife' without any marriage rites at all was considered to constitute a valid marriage, and could therefore also constitute the crime of bigamy. At the same time, in Taiwan, the amendments to the ROC Civil Code led to more severe attitudes being adopted towards bigamy; the legislation still adhered to the narrow definition of bigamy, but clearly stated that a bigamous marriage was null and void.

Legislation and judicial practice in both Taiwan and the PRC prioritized the stability of marriage and the permanent character of marriage. Bigamy was prohibited in both Mainland China and in Taiwan, and constituted a criminal offense; bigamous marriage was pronounced null and void, bigamy constituted legal grounds for divorce and for claiming damages under civil law.

Therefore, the collusion of the legal systems of the Mainland and Taiwan after the restoration of mutual relations after 1987, when the question of bigamous marriages concluded by Taiwanese residents after the cross-Strait separation occurred, led to quite favourable conditions for finding a mutually acceptable and appropriate solution, although only based on facts. Both the ROC and the PRC finally adopted measures to protect Taiwanese residents from criminal prosecution or civil liability and excluded these marriages from the scope of legislation applicable to ordinary cases of bigamy, thus avoiding any crisis which might occur. It was not the first time that the authorities on both sides of the Strait showed a considerable degree of pragmatism as well as the ability to find a quick and efficacious solution to a problem.

References

An Li, Nigel N. T. and Joyce Fan (1990) 'Uncommon Case of Bigamy; An Uncommon Constitutional Interpretation,' in *Journal of Chinese Law*, 69(4), 69-81.

Bernhardt, Kathryn (1999) Women and Property in China: 1960-1949, Stanford, Calif: Stanford University Press.

Burdett S. L. (1928) *Zhonghua Minguo xingfa* 中華民國刑法 [The criminal code of the Republic of China], Shanghai: Shanghai Linshi Fayuan.

Chen, Rong-Chwan (1997-1998) 'Boat on a Troubled Strait: The Interregional Private Law of the Republic of China on Taiwan,' *A. 16 Wis. Int'l L.J.*, 599-638.

Chen, Shibo 陳石波 (1988) 'She Tai hunyin guanxi wenti tantao,' 涉台婚姻關係問題探討 [Exploring the marriage issues related to Taiwan] in *Faxue Zazhi* 法學雜誌 [Law science magazine], 3, 36-38.

Fu Bingchang 傅秉常 and Dingyu Zhou 周定宇 (1964) *Zhonghua Minguo Liufa liyou panjie huibian* 中華民國六法理由判解彙編 [Case law related to the six laws of the ROC], Taibei: Xinlu.

Glosser, Susan L. (2003) *Chinese Visions of Family and State, 1915-1953,* Berkeley: University of California Press.

Honig, Emily (2003) 'Socialist Sex: The Cultural Revolution Revisited,' *Modern China,* 29(2), 143-175.

Huang Li'e 黃麗娥 (2003) 'Haixie Liang'an chonghun falü wenti bijiao' 海峽兩岸重婚法律問題比較 [Cross-Strait comparison of attitude to legal issues related to bigamy], *Jiamusi daxue shehui kexue xuebao* 佳木斯大學社會科學學報 [Journal of social science of Jiamusi University], 21(3), 22-24.

Huang, Philip C. (2001) *Code, Custom and Legal Practice in China, The Qing and Republic Compared*, Stanford California, Stanford University Press.

Huang, Philip C. (2010) *Chinese Civil Justice, Past and Present,* Lanham, Md: Rowman & Littlefield.

Jones, William C. (1994) *The Great Qing Code*, Oxford: Clarendon Press.

Johnson, Kay Ann. (1983) *Women, the Family and Peasant Revolution in China*, Chicago: University of Chicago Press.

Ke, Gezhuang 柯葛壯 (1993) 'Taiwan liang'an guanxi tiaoli zhong de xingshi falü wenti' 臺灣'兩岸關係條例'中的刑事法律問題 [Taiwan's 'Mainland Relations Act' in the criminal legal issues], *Zhengzhi yu falü* 政治與法律 [Political Science and Law], 5, 56-58.

Kuo, Margaret (2012) *Intolerable Cruelty: Marriage, Law, and Society in Early Twentieth-Century China,* Lanham: Rowman & Littlefield Publishers, Inc.

Meijer, Marinus Johan (1971) *Marriage Law and Policy in the Chinese People's Republic,* Hong Kong University Press, Hong Kong.

Palmer, Michael (1995) 'The Re-emergence of Family Law in Post-Mao China: Marriage, Divorce and Reproduction', *The China Quarterly*, 141, 110-134.

Palmer, Michael (2007), 'Transforming Family Law in Post-Deng China: Marriage, Divorce and Reproduction,' *The China Quarterly*, 191, 675-695.

Ronald Keith C. and Lin Zhiqiu (2006) *New Crime in China: Public Order and Human Rights,* Routledge.

Shi, Shangkuan 史尚寬 (2000) *Qinshu falun* 親屬法論 [Family law], Beijing: Zhongguo Zhengfa Daxue chubanshe.

Tran, Lisa (2009) 'Sex and Equality in Republican China: The Debate over the Adultery Law,' *Modern China*, 35(2) March, 191-223

Tran, Lisa (2015) *Concubines in Court: Marriage and Monogamy in Twentieth-Century China*, Rowman & Littlefield.

Valk, Marc van der (1939) *An Outline of Modern Chinese Family Law,* Peking: Henri Vecht.

Wang, Hongzhi 王宏志 (2010) *Deguo hunyin fazhi dui chonghun zhi guiding yu woguo chonghun guiding zhi bijiao* 德國婚姻法制對重婚之規定與我國重婚規定之比較 [The study of bigamy regulations: A comparison between Germany and Taiwan], Master's Thesis Nanhua University.

Wang, Naicong 王乃聰 (1951) *Hunyinfa wenti jieda huibian* 婚姻問題解答彙編 [Questions and answers related to marriage], Wenhua Gongying Shichuban.

Wang Taisheng [Wang, Tay-sheng 王泰升] (2010) *Taiwan Rizhi shiqi de falü gaige* 臺灣日治時期的法律改革 [Legal reform in Taiwan under Japanese colonial rule], Taipei: Lianjing.

Wang Taisheng [Wang, Tay-sheng 王泰升] (2013) 'The Modernization of Civil Justice in Colonial Taiwan, 1885-1945,' in *Journal of Japanese Law* 36, 95-116.

Wang Zhenshao 王貞韶 (1990) 'Taiwan diqu yu dalu diqu renmin guanxi zanxing tiaoli cao'an zhong de hunyin guifan pingshu' 《臺灣地區與大陸地區人民關係暫行條例草案》中的婚姻規範評述, in *Zhengzhi yu falü* 政治與法律 [Political science and law], 4, 57-59.

Watson, Rubie S. and Patricia Buckley Ebrey (eds.) (1991) *Marriage and Inequality in Chinese Society*, Berkeley: University of California Press.

Xia Yinlan 夏吟蘭 (2012) *Hunyin jiating jicheng fa* 婚姻家庭繼承法 [Family law], Beijing: Zhongguo Zhengfa Daxue Chubanshe.

Yang Zhufu 楊主福 (1989) 'Cong san ge anli kan zhengque chuli qu Tai renyuan chonghun wenti,' 從三個案例看正確處理去台人員重婚問題 [Correct handling of the issue of bigamy based on the three cases of those who left for Taiwan], in *Faxue* 法學 [Legal Science], 93(8), 29-31.

Zhao Bingzhi (1989) 'Issues in Criminal Law across the Taiwan Strait' in 3 *J. Chinese. L*, 227-249.

Zhao Ma (2007) *On the Run: Women, City, and the Law in Beijing 1937-1949*. Doctoral Thesis. Johns Hopkins University, UMI 3288612.

Zhongguo fagui kanxing she bianshen weiyuanhui 中國法規刊行社編審委員會編纂 (1946) Zuixin Liufa Quanshu 最新六法全書 [Latest Six Laws], Shanghai: Zhongguo fagui kanxing chuban.

Zhonghua Renmin Gongheguo guowuyuan gongbao 中華人民共和國國務院公報 [Bulletin of the State Council of the People's Republic of China] (1955) No. 9 (Summer 20).

Zhonghua Renmin Gongheguo Hunyin Fa, 中華人民共和國婚姻法 [Marriage Law of the People's Republic of China] (2012) Beijing: Falü Chubanshi.

Zhongyang zhengfa gongbao 中央政法公報 [Central political bulletin] (1950), 12/13.

Internet References

Beida Fabao 北大法寶 [Legal information center of Peking University] <www.pkulaw.cn>, Accessed 31 January 2015.

Minzhengbu, Sifabu 民政部, 司法部 (16 April 1988) Guanyu qu Tai renyuan yuqi liu zai dalu de pei'ou zhijian hunyin guanxi wenti chuli yijian tongzhi 關於去台人員與其留在大陸的配偶之間婚姻關係問題處理意見的通知 [Ministry of Civil Affairs, Ministry of Justice Announcement on issues related to marriage relationships between the Mainland spouses and those who left for Taiwan]. <http://www.people.com.cn/item/bflfgk/gwyfg/1988/213111198803.html>, accessed 31 January 2015.

Sifa Yuan 司法院 (23 June 1989) Shi zi di 242 hao 釋字第 242 號 [Interpretations of Judicial Yuan no. 242], <www.judicial.gov.tw/constitutionalcourt/p03_01.asp?expno=242>, accessed 31 January 2015.

Sifa Yuan 司法院 (13 December 2002) Shi zi di 552 hao 司法院釋字第 552 號 [Interpretations of Judicial Yuan no. 552] of. <http://www.judicial.gov.tw/constitutionalcourt/p03 01.asp?expno=552>, accessed 31 January 2015.

Sifa Yuan 司法院 (29 August 1994) Shi zi di 363 hao 司法院釋字第 363 號 [Interpretations of Judicial Yuan no. 363] <www.judicial.gov.tw/constitutionalcourt/p03_01.asp?expno=363>, accessed 31 January 2015.

Wu Haihong 吳海虹(2000) 'Hunyinfa xiuding jiaodian fencheng 婚姻法修訂焦點紛呈 [Focus on the amendment to the Marriage Law], Beijing Qingnian Bao 北京青年報 [Beijing Youth Daily]. <www.people.com.cn/GB/channel1/11/20000809/180005.html>, accessed 31 January 2015.

Zhonggong zuhongyang wei gongbu guo gong hezuo xuanyan 中共中央為公佈國共合作宣言 [Declaration of Cooperation] (1937),<cpc.people.com.cn/GB/69112/75843/75874/75991/5175429.html>, accessed 31 January 2015.

Zuigao Renmin Fayuan 最高人民法院 (October 1950) Dui Meng Lisheng suo ti hunyin wenti ji qi chuli yijian de dafu 對孟力生所提婚姻問題及其處理意見的答覆 [Supreme People's Court on Questions on how to handle marital disputes raised by judge Meng

Lisheng]. <http://www.people.com.cn/item/flfgk/gwyfg/1950/113202195003.html>, accessed 31 January 2015.

Zuigao Renmin Fayuan 最高人民法院 (31 May 1951) Duiyu hunyin jicheng deng youguan wenti de lai wen zhi jieda 對於婚姻繼承等有關問題的來問之解答 [Supreme People's Court Reply on issues related to marriage and inheritance]. <http://www.people.com.cn/item/flfgk/gwyfg/1951/113202195143.html>, accessed 31 January 2015.

Zuigao Renmin Fayuan 最高人民法院 (19 July 1963) Guanyu chonghun zui shifou qin gao cai chuli de pi fu, 關於重婚罪是否親告才處理的批復 [Supreme People's Court on Whether should be bigamy prosecuted only after complaint of relatives]. <http://www.people.com.cn/item/flfgk/gwyfg/1963/113602196305.html>, accessed 31 January 2015.

Zuigao Renmin Fayuan 最高人民法院 (28 August 1980) Guanyu chuli peiou yi fang zai Gang-Ao-Tai huo guowai, Renmin fayuan yijing panjue lihun, xian dangshiren yaoqiu fuhun wenti de fuhan 關於處理配偶一方在港澳臺或國外，人民法院已經判決離婚，現當事人要求重婚問題的復函 [Supreme People's Court on How to handle cases where one of the spouses is living in Hong Kong, Macao, Taiwan or other, when they had divorced and now apply for remarriage]. <http://www.people.com.cn/item/flfgk/gwyfg/1980/113202198002.html>, accessed 31 January 2015.

Zuigao Renmin Fayuan 最高人民法院 (13 May 1951) Guanyu gedi Renmin fayuan hunyin anjian pei shen qingkuang de zonghe tongbao, 關於各地人民法院婚姻案件陪審情況的綜合通報 [Supreme People's Court Circular on juries dealing with the marital disputes] <http://www.people.com.cn/item/flfgk/gwyfg/1951/113703195101.html>, accessed 31 January 2015, accessed 31 January 2015.

Zuigao Renmin Fayuan 最高人民法院 (2 February 1979) Guanyu guanche zhixing minshi zhengce falü de yijian (jie lu) 關於貫徹執行民事政策法律的意見（節錄） [Supreme People's Court on Implementation of civil law policy]. <www.law-lib.com/law/law view.asp?id=43872>, accessed 31 January 2015.

Zuigao Renmin Fayuan 最高人民法院 (16 May 1957) Guanyu Hunyinfa shishi hou he guanche Hunyinfa yundong hou de chonghun jing qunzhong jianju Renmin fayuan ying fou zhijie shou li wenti pi fu, 關於婚姻法實施後和貫徹婚姻法運動後的重婚經群眾檢舉人民法院應否直接受理問題的批復 [Reply of the Supreme Court whether after the implementation of the Marriage Law and the related campaign took place the courts should prosecute bigamy according to complaints lodged by the masses] <http://www.people.com.cn/item/flfgk/gwyfg/1957/113602195705.html>, accessed 31 January 2015.

Zuigao Renmin Fayuan 最高人民法院 (21 November 1989) Guanyu Renmin fayuan shenli lihun anjian ruhe rending fuqi ganqing que yi polie de ruogan juti yijian 關於人民法院審理離婚案件如何認定夫妻感情確已破裂的若干具體意見 [Supreme People's Court opinion on How the people's courts should determine that the marital affection has been broken]. <http://www.people.com.cn/item/flfgk/gwyfg/1989/113202198901.html>, accessed 31 January 2015.

Zuigao Renmin Fayuan 最高人民法院 (27 August 1958): Guanyu ruhe rending chonghun xingwei wenti de pi fu, 關於如何認定重婚行為問題的批復 [Supreme People's Court on What behaviour should be considered bigamy] <http://www.people.com.cn/item/flfgk/gwyfg/1958/113113195801.html>, accessed 31 January 2015.

Zuigao Renmin Fayuan Huadong fen yuan 最高人民法院華東分院 (29 July 1953): Guanyu guanche Hunyinfa yundong hou bu dengji jiehun zhe qingqiu lihun shifou an lihun banli wenti de pi fu, 關於貫徹婚姻法運動後不登記結婚者請求離婚是否按離婚辦理問題的批復[East Branch of the Supreme People's Court Reply to How should be handled divorces of marriages unregistered despite the Marriage Law Campaign]; <http://www.people.com.cn/item/flfgk/gwyfg/1953/113202195336.html>, accessed 31 January 2015.

Zuigao Renmin Fayuan Ma Yuan Fuyuanzhang 最高人民法院馬原副院長 (9 August 1988): Guanyu Renmin Fayuan chuli she Tai minshi anjian de jige falü wenti 關於人民法院處理涉台民事案件的幾個法律問題 [Vice president of the Supreme People's Court On several legal issues related to Taiwan and how should the people's courts deal with related civil cases]. <http://www.people.com.cn/item/flfgk/gwyfg/1988/113117198803.html>, accessed 31 January 2015.

Zuigao Renmin Fayuan xinan fen yuan 最高人民法院西南分院 (1 December 1951) Guanyu hunyin anjian beigao xian zhu guowai huo Taiwan wufa chuanxun ruhe chuli wenti de pi fu 關於婚姻案件被告現住國外或臺灣無法傳訊如何處理問題的批復 [Southwest Branch of the Supreme People's Court On situations when defendant is inaccessible abroad or in Taiwan] <http://www.people.com.cn/item/flfgk/gwyfg/1951/113202195141.html> Accessed 31 January 2015.

Zuigao Renmin Fayuan, Zuigao Renmin Jianchayuan 最高人民法院最高人民檢察院 (14 March 1988): Guanyu buzai zhuisu quTai renyuan zai Zhonghua Renmin Gongheguo chengli qian de fanzui xingwei gonggao 關於不再追訴去台人員在中華人民共和國成立前的犯罪行為的公告 [Supreme People's Court and the Supreme People's Procuratorate Announcement on not prosecuting criminal acts committed before the establishment of the People's Republic of China]. <http://www.people.com.cn/item/flfgk/gwyfg/1988/113117198803.html>, accessed 31 January 2015

Jens Damm

The Contemporary Political and Public Discourse on the Xinhai Revolution in Taiwan in the Context of the Centennial Celebration of the ROC

This paper provides a nuanced description of main aspects concerning the interpretations and understandings of the Xinhai Revolution in the context of the centennial celebration of the founding of the ROC in Taiwan. The paper focuses on 'omissions' and ahistorical rationalizations in the sources' smoothed-out depictions of Taiwanese and ROC history and thus provides a critical inquiry into the highly political and semi-propagandistic sources it analyses. Especially after the most recent political changes in Taiwan, with the 'green camp', that is, the independence-leaning camp coming to power in both the presidential and the parliamentary elections, it is interesting to see how the GMD president Ma Yingjiu employed a ROC identity to create a continuous history of Taiwan and the ROC, despite the fact that Taiwan in 1911 was not part of the ROC and had already been under Japanese rule for almost two decades.

Introduction

The Xinhai Revolution, also known as the Revolution of 1911, which overthrew the Manchurian Qing dynasty and established the Republic of China (ROC), became a topic of interest in Taiwan's academic world during the 100 years' celebrations, but only through the lens of the political and public discourse can a clear picture of the role played by these events be obtained. For example, the pan-blue camp, including political parties such as the Guomindang (GMD, Kuomintang), the People First Party (PFP, Qinmindang), and the New Party (NP Xindang), and some media such as the *United Daily News*, the *China Times*, and TVBS) offered a smoothly polished version of the historical events of 1911–1912 that dovetailed neatly with the political discourse on integration across the Taiwan Strait, 'Chineseness with Taiwanese characteristics', and the modernization of the island linked with democratic achievements in order (it could be argued) to legitimize the rule of the GMD. The pan-green camp, including political parties such as the Democratic Progressive Party (DPP, Minzhu jinbu dang) and the Taiwan Solidarity Union (TSU, Taiwan tuanjie lianmeng), and some media such as the *Liberty Times*, on the other hand, prefer to downplay the importance, for Taiwan, of the historical developments of the 1911–1912 period in mainland China but without attacking or openly questioning the centennial celebrations, so that an impression emerges of outspoken indifference.

In Taiwan, in contrast to the situation in mainland China, the Xinhai Revolution has not become a major focus of academic research. It has, however, been mentioned in official speeches by leading GMD politicians and the pan-blue camp, generally with the obvious aim of evoking a China-oriented collective historical memory and legitimizing the rule of the GMD. In addition, state-sponsored celebrations of '100 Years' could be seen everywhere on the island in 2011 and 2012.[70] The views of both these camps differ from those

[70] It is questionable whether the 100 years' celebration of the ROC has led to arousing greater interest in the Xinhai Revolution and its consequences for both mainland China and Taiwan in the Taiwanese academic world, despite the wide variety of conferences that were organized under the slogan "100 years." For example, only 50 or 60 people took part in the government-sponsored conference on October 3 that took place at Academia

found in the mainland China discourse where the Xinhai Revolution is perceived as an important national revolutionary event with pan-Chinese implications.

The contradictions inherent in the perception in Taiwan of the historical significance of the events in mainland China a century ago were immediately apparent even to the casual observer: outwardly, signs of the centennial celebrations could be seen everywhere, such as Double Tenth Day with related specific events, competitions for children, and numerous workshops and conferences. A closer look, however, revealed that many of these events had only a tenuous link with the 1911–1912 period; although the titles of many academic workshops in 2011 included a reference to the '100 years', few of these seemed to offer any opportunity for discussion of the Xinhai Revolution. It was difficult to avoid the suspicion that the lure of the financial subsidies offered by the National Science Council, the Ministry of Education, and the Ministry of Foreign Affairs led many researchers to frame plans, projects, and conferences basically unrelated to the 100-year period simply in order to obtain the specific funds being made available. Most of the events linked with the centennial celebrations used the number 100 merely as a lucky number, without going into any detail about what exactly was being celebrated, and unrelated historical events during the ROC period in mainland China and the Japanese period in Taiwan were treated as causally linked.

In addition, the political discourse on the Xinhai Revolution in Taiwan has to be seen in the context of the developments taking place on the other side of the Taiwan Strait: the election of a pan-blue candidate as president in 2008 and his re-election in 2012 served as common ground in the context of the economic and societal integration on both sides of the Taiwan Strait and the political rapprochement between the current leadership in Taiwan and the CCP. This culminated then in the meeting of Ma Yingjiu with the PRC president Xi Jinping in 2015, which nevertheless did not help the GMD to stay in power, and then in 2016 Cai Yingwen (Tsai Ingwen) from the DPP was elected president. Until 2010, there was also broad speculation that joint celebrations might be held for the Xinhai Revolution that would include members of the CCP and the GMD, since both 'Chinese' parties claim the 1911 revolution as part of their history and founding myths and as the 'beginning' of the new China, but these plans failed for several reasons. Beijing insisted that the ROC ceased to exist in 1949, when it was succeeded by the PRC. The ROC constitution, however, which is valid in Taiwan today, states that both the mainland and Taiwan still form part of the

---

Sinica in the presence of President Ma Yingjiu. The number of conferences that mentioned "100 years" in their headings but did not have any tangible connection with the topic was astonishing, but the real motives for the popular use of the slogan were easily traced: according to information obtained during several interviews with conference organizers from National Taiwan Normal University, National Sun Yat-sen university, National Tsinghua University, etc., there was a general understanding that conferences claiming to be part of the centennial celebrations would receive preferential treatment when it came to obtaining official funding, particularly that being offered by government organizations, such as the Ministry of Education. The discrepancies between the titles of the conferences and the content were often obvious: I attended a conference entitled "Democracy and Minority Rights in Taiwan: An Interdisciplinary Conference at the 100th Anniversary of the Hsinhai [Xinhai] Revolution" on April 28–29, 2011, Kaohsiung, NSYSU, which featured only one presentation linked to the Xinhai Revolution (Dr. Jacob Kovalio, Department of History, Carleton University, on "Then, Now and in the Future: Sun Yat-sen and Democracy, Relations with Japan and Pan-Asianism"); all the other papers dealt with more recent developments in Taiwan without making any reference to the Xinhai Revolution.

ROC within the 1947 borders.[71] There are different interpretations of the Xinhai Revolution: Beijing placed an emphasis on the aspect of nationalism and, therefore, on the unification of China (including Taiwan's 'return to the motherland'); and Taibei emphasized the aspects of democracy and livelihood, regarding the ROC ideology based on Sun Yixian's Three Principles of the People as a future model for the whole of China that would be better than the communist model. Thus, demonstrations in China on the evening of October 10 were dissolved by the police, and a Sun Yixian opera, which should have been performed simultaneously in Hong Kong and Beijing, was postponed on the grounds that it did not fall in line with the official emphasis on nationalism.[72] Officials from the ROC (on Taiwan) would not have been able to attend the celebratory events on the mainland in an official capacity; the events would have had to be held as two-party celebrations, and this was an unacceptable condition for the majority of the Taiwanese. The GMD government in Taipei had to take into consideration various upcoming elections; joint celebrations would have exposed the GMD to criticism, not only from the green camp but also probably from the great majority of people in Taiwan who prefer to see the political status quo maintained while, at the same time, they continue to claim Taiwanese identity or dual Taiwanese/Chinese identity. Ma Yingjiu was frequently criticized for leaning too far in the direction of Beijing and for neglecting questions related to sovereignty.
The following hypotheses can be formulated with regard to the centennial celebrations in Taiwan in 2011 and 2012: With the exception of the official speeches (mainly given by the president, Ma Yingjiu), the meaning of '100 years' remained obscure, and references to actual political developments were lacking in the official celebrations. In the presidential addresses, the ideas of Sun Yixian were discursively linked to the implementation of these ideas by Ma Yingjiu, while the roles played by other presidents, that is to say, by the two Jiangs (Jiang Jieshi and Jiang Jingguo) as well as Li Denghui (Lee Teng-hui), were either downplayed or entirely omitted. Sun Yixian's 'Three Principles of the People' (Sanmin zhuyi) were again frequently mentioned, but with regard to the three principles, democracy (*minzhu*) was given high priority, livelihood and welfare (*minsheng*) were mentioned, and nationalism (*minzu*) (the central argument in Sun's writing) was downplayed.

Methodology and Procedure

This paper will examine official addresses given by prominent politicians, substantiated by reports found in the old and new media, in order to establish the significance accruing to Sun Yixian. The official addresses in this paper include Chinese- and English-language versions of speeches given by Ma Yingjiu that were subsequently published on the presidential website (www.president.gov.tw), in particular, those given at the Double Tenth Day and the New Year celebrations and, in addition, specific addresses on the importance of Sun Yixian or on the 100 years of the ROC celebrations. Other political speeches, for example, those

---

71 Interestingly enough, the entire speech given by Ma Yingjiu on the Double Tenth Day in 2011 was available on China's Internet (on Sina Weibo, "Ma's National Day Speech Wins Plaudits from China's Netizens"), although usually the use of the term "Republic of China" in relation to Taiwan today would lead immediately to the blocking of the Web content.

72 Accessed at http://www.nytimes.com/2011/10/12/arts/music/the-opera-dr-sun-yat-sen-is-canceled-in-china.html?pagewanted=all, http://atimes.com/atimes/China/MJ14Ad01.html (All following links to newspaper articles were accessed on 14 November 2011).

given by opposition leaders, are selectively included, but as will be shown later, the opposition generally did not respond to the '100 years' commemorative events and usually regarded any reference to either the ROC or the l00 years' celebrations as unnecessary, unlike the previously mentioned 'pan-green leaning' historians.

Two popular works on the 100 years of ROC history were also included. The book *Celebrating 100 Years*, edited by the Government Information Office of the Republic of China (Taiwan),[73] presented 170 topics drawn from the last 100 years of ROC history. According to a report in the *Taipei Times*, there were originally 20,000 submissions, and the 170 topics were selected by a review panel consisting of four people: Huang Kewu (Huang Ke-wu), director of the Institute of Modern History at Academia Sinica; Qiu Xiuzhi (Ciou Siou-jhih), from the Chiu Ko Publishing Co; Cai Shiping (Tsai Shih-ping), executive director of the ROC (Taiwan) Centenary Foundation; and Ping Lu, an author.[74] The second book was *Expose the Truth of 100 Years ROC,* edited by the Taiwan Historical Association.[75]

This paper will focus, in particular, on the political discourse on the Xinhai Revolution and the significance of Sun Yixian, including related speeches given by prominent politicians, reports found in the old and new media, and popular publications. This will show the complex linkages in the current political mainstream discourse between the Xinhai Revolution, the accomplishments of Sun Yixian, the 100 years' existence of the ROC and issues related to Taiwan's democratization, the creation of a specific Taiwanese identity, and the accomplishments of 100 years of GMD rule. In the counter-discourse, Sun Yixian's achievements were, however, seen as irrelevant for Taiwan, first of all, because the island was a Japanese colony which was spared the chaos of the Warlord Period on the mainland and, secondly, because the (postwar) GMD government should be regarded as a 'government in exile' or a de facto colonial regime. Nevertheless, any sharp criticism of the rewriting of history in the mainstream counter-discourse was mainly restricted to political activists outside the DPP or in the non-mainstream faction of the DPP as well to pan-green academics. It has, however, evoked an indifferent response from the broader population and little or no reaction from the majority of the pan-green camp. The new leadership of the DPP, particularly the newly elected president Cai Yingwen, having officially come to terms with the idea of the ROC system in Taiwan, was trying to present a much more moderate stance and avoid being seen as striving to establish a Republic of Taiwan.

This study employs a modified critical discourse analysis (Dijk 2008, 1989; Fairclough 1992) to explore how, in official statements made by the current ROC government and, in particular, in addresses and speeches delivered by Ma Yingjiu, the Xinhai Revolution, the Wuchang uprising, and the founding of the ROC are linked to more recent developments in Taiwan and cross-Strait relations in order to highlight the particularities of this political discourse by exploring dominant rhetorical clusters and omissions. A particular focus is

73 *Bainian fenghua* 百年風華 (Celebrating 100 Years [Subtitle 100 年文華光影光影，100 年的勤奮進程，100 年的溫馨記憶, 100 年的中華民族] edited by the Government Information Office of the Republic of China (Taiwan).

74 The number 20,000 for submitted articles was questioned by Huang Ko-wu, Director of the Institute of Modern history, Academia Sinica, interview November 14, 2011. Cover of the afterword "The ROC Centennial: Celebrating a Dream Come True" taken from the inaugural address given by Ma Yingjiu, May 20, 2008.

75 *Jiechuan Zhonghua minguo bainian zhenxiang* 揭穿中華民國百年真相 (Expose the Truth of 100 Years ROC), edited by the Taiwan Historical Association 台灣歷史學會首會, in 116 short chapters.

placed on commemorative speeches, especially the National Day presidential addresses and the New Year speeches: 'Such addresses are discursive sites where the president's representative function finds its best expression; reconfirms general norms and values to the public; and creates a sense of societal coherence and consensus' (Chang and Holt 2009: 303). According to Ensink (1997), these usually invoke and produce national meanings. This is of particular interest in the case of Taiwan where two national identities (ROC and Taiwan) occur in competition with each other. Official addresses can therefore reinforce the one or the other national meaning or help to bring two meanings together, and the surrounding symbolic implications provide essential tools for natural identity construction (see also, Chang and Holt 2009: 303–304). In Taiwan's vibrant media landscape today, the presidential addresses and their inherent symbolism are spread through various forms of traditional media (newspapers, TV), through new media (websites), and through the new social media (Facebook, downloadable and streaming video, microblogs such as Twitter and Sina Weibo) in Chinese and in official English translations to a wide audience. They are intended not only for the people in Taiwan but also for foreign governments involved in securing Taiwan's status (for example, the United States and Japan) and mainland China.

These official addresses are not usually concerned with examples of (good) governance; they do, however, provide broader and more general legitimacy and are therefore often linked to historical events and set a public agenda without going into detail (Cohen 1995): 'Presidents are also obliged to sustain established national symbols and meanings' (Chang and Holt 2009: 304). But the question remains, what is going to happen in a place where national identity is contested, historical memory uneven and unequal, and even the basic idea of who belongs to the nation is a matter of dispute, if this nation is understood to be the ROC? Bakhtin, Holquist, and Emerson (1986) also make a distinction between what they refer to as monogolism and dialogism: monogolism is represented by an appeal to what are recognized as established cultural values where claims concerning an ultimate truth do not allow space for alternative interpretations; dialogism is represented by new courses of action that introduce and offer the potential for transgression. In the case of Taiwan and the ROC, questions related to the use of 'Taiwan' or 'the ROC' remain a delicate issue. 'Since the nation can be conceived of as an imagined community constructed and enacted through various symbolic acts that unite members and mark its boundaries . . ., construction of national identity requires one to subjectively see oneself as part of a collectivity' (Chang and Holt 2009: 305). 'The very selection of a term . . . puts invisible boundaries for human perception and suggests attitudes for its evaluation' (Kiewe 1998: 81). 'Different terms have evolved through a variety of idiosyncratic historical-political contexts. As these names travel through social life, they draw to themselves specific meanings and strength; reflect and define alternative political ideologies; and participate in the construction of political realities' (Chang and Holt 2009: 305).

The Speeches of Former Presidents

Current presidential addresses also have to take into consideration the speeches made by former presidents and the rhetoric that they have employed. In Taiwan, these presidents are Jiang Jieshi (Chiang Kai-shek), Jiang Jingguo (Chiang Ching-kuo), and Li Denghui (Lee Teng-hui) from the GMD and Chen Shuibian from the DPP.

During the rule of Jiang Jieshi and the early years of Jiang Jingguo, the nation addressed was always the ROC, and Taiwan was seen as only one part of the larger construct of the

Republic of China which had continued to exist after 1949; the 'mainland' was regarded, analogously to the interpretation of the PRC in Taiwan, as an occupied area which had to be brought back under the control of the ROC. 'The principle of 'Nationalism', which Sun himself reinterpreted to suit changing circumstances, has been enshrined in the 'National Polity' to liberate the mainland from the agents of international communism and reunify it under Nationalist rule (Chu and Lin 2001; Harrison 1988; Israel 1963).

During Li Denghui's presidency, the main emphasis was on a reconsideration of the relationship between Taiwan and China. After being elected president for a second term, Li made various references to, for example, 'a community of 21 million with a shared fate', 'managing a great Taiwan', and 'the new Taiwanese' (Shi 2005: 148), which showed that his main focus was on Taiwan. He did not show any interest in the Three People's Principles (Clough 1996: 1068), and by the end of the 1987–1997 decade, any references to the 'Father of the Republic' and the *Sanmin zhuyi* had totally vanished from Taiwan's political speeches (Corcuff 2002: 79).

During the rule of Chen, in all the official speeches given on National Day or at New Year (with the exception of the 2002 New Year speech), the term 'Taiwan' was used more often than 'Republic of China' (Chang and Holt 2009: 307). In addition, Chen used the term to construct a history of Taiwan that was different or even unconnected to the history of the ROC (Chang and Holt 2009: 308). Democracy and democratic achievements, for example, were mentioned in the context of the courageous battle fought by the people of Taiwan against authoritarian rule (Chang and Holt 2009; Lams and Liao 2011).

Analysis of the Public and Political Discourses: State Addresses Delivered by the Current Ma Administration

First of all, a brief look at the speeches made by Ma Yingjiu after his inauguration in 2008, in comparison with later speeches, reveals great differences not only in content and in the use of crucial terms such as 'Taiwan' and 'Republic of China' but also in the time period covered. The recurrent use of the term 'Republic of China' (*Zhonghua minguo*) in official speeches made by Ma Yingjiu emerges as a new phenomenon with strong links to the 100 years of ROC celebrations. For example, at the beginning of his New Year address, on January 1, 2009, Ma only uses the term 'Republic of China' in connection with the 'Year of the Republic 98.'[76] In the following part of his speech, the year is described as being of 'specific importance for Taiwan', no matter whether with regard to the economy ('to refortify Taiwan's economic strength'), politics and history ('Taiwan entered a new and historic era of political development in 2008'), or the future ('without doubt Taiwan is advancing into a period marked by more stable democracy and better governance'). Indirectly, Taiwan is even referred to as a nation: '***Nations*** that are unable to effectively re-engineer their economic structure may enter an extended period of stagnation. Therefore, when the global economy rebounds and the economic race begins anew, will ***Taiwan*** be one of those ahead of the game?' (emphasis added). Finally, there is no reference to the history of Taiwan or the ROC before 1949.

In the New Year message delivered two years later, on January 1, 2011,[77] the historical context is important and the emphasis is clearly on the Republic of China rather than on

[76] Accessed at http://english.president.gov.tw/Default.aspx?tabid=1283.

[77] Available at http://www.president.gov.tw/Default.aspx?tabid=131&itemid=23185&rmid=514, and http://

Taiwan. In this first presidential speech in the year 100 of the Republic, Ma starts by giving a brief historical overview, focusing on the role of Sun Yixian in overthrowing the Qing and on Sun's pledge of a strong and prosperous nation—one of the few occasions when Sun can be linked with nation-building. A historical narrative is then unfurled which leads to the Republic of China (on Taiwan) becoming a 'paragon of political and economic progress for developing nations around the world.'

The historical overview follows the GMD interpretation of history, including a brief mention of the Warlord Era, references to the Northern Expedition as a great success story, and a one-sided description of the War of Resistance against Japan ('the ROC crushed Japan's ambitions for China in an eight-year war of resistance') after which 'Taiwan was returned to the fold of the Republic of China.' This interpretation leaves out the CCP's role and the role played by allies such as the United States in the surrender of Japan, which led Japan to relinquish sovereignty over Taiwan. It also disregards the disputed issue of whether Taiwan should belong de jure to the ROC or the PRC or whether Taiwan was actually recolonized by the GMD (the idea of the GMD government as a government in exile).[78]

After the defeat on the mainland, the success story of the ROC on Taiwan continues, with references being made to the land reform, the Ten Major Construction Projects, the education and national insurance programs, the lifting of martial law, and even the redressing of the wrongs perpetrated in the February 28 Incident. Although the 228 Incident is mentioned, the GMD is presented in a positive light, as the party that redressed previous wrongs, but the fact that the GMD committed the wrongs in the first place is neatly sidestepped. In the next paragraph, subtitled in the English version as the 'collective homeland' (a term that is missing in the Chinese version), a specific commitment to a common collective memory and experience is made for 'everybody on Taiwan', but when talking about the ROC national flag (in fact, the upper left part of Taiwan's flag is the Blue Sky with a White Sun, the Kuomintang's [GMD] party flag), the 'Shanghai memory' is mentioned: 'Gave the Eight Hundred Heroes the strength to fight valiantly in defending the Sihang Warehouse in Shanghai back in 1937.' This struggle against the Japanese occupation is certainly celebrated in mainland China and by the mainlanders in Taiwan, but it does not form part of the collective memory of the Taiwanese. The Taiwanese went through a period of strict Japanization during the 1930s, and after the outbreak of the war, many Taiwanese fought in the Imperial Japanese Army (probably more than 200,000, many of whom enlisted as volunteers). The speech continues with Ma's idea of Taiwan as the bearer of Chinese tradition. In this context, he chooses the traditional GMD interpretation of events, which maintains that while the culture was destroyed in mainland China (Cultural Revolution), it was preserved in Taiwan. Ma nevertheless also enlarges upon the idea of an 'Island History', explaining that

---

english.president.gov.tw/Default.aspx?tabid=491&itemid=23186&rmid=2355). The ROC yearbook of 2009 quotes from the inaugural address of Ma Yingjiu are as follows: "Dr. Sun Yat-sen's dream of a constitutional democracy was not realized on the Chinese mainland, but today has taken root, blossomed and borne fruit in Taiwan": this provides a brief but poignant summary of one of the most frequently cited topics in Ma Yingjiu's later speeches, the idea that the far-reaching ideas of Sun Yixian have finally achieved maturity and have come to exist in Taiwan today under the leadership of Ma, after a long struggle by the GMD against various enemies.

78 See, for example, Petzold 2007.

Taiwan's culture has been enriched with additional elements drawn from its maritime culture.[79]

In a news release on October 9, 2011, under the heading 'President Ma attends events to celebrate the ROC's centenary with overseas Chinese compatriots',[80] many keywords featuring in the celebration discourse could be found: the focus on Sun Yixian, the symbolic place, the Sun Yat-sen Memorial Hall, and the ideals of Sun Yixian, named as the 'nation's father' (*guofu*). As in most of the 2011 speeches, Sun's ideals were placed under the headings of democracy and freedom, without any mention of nationalism, but later on there is a reference to the 'equal distribution of wealth.' All the speeches included remarks concerning the relevance of Sun Yixian's ideas in Taiwan today; for example, his ideals were said to have gradually 'been realized since the ROC's government moved to Taiwan' under the current GMD administration. The strong relationship between Sun and Ma is underlined in a short paragraph which reads as follows: 'He (Ma) said that since taking office in May 2008, he has specially moved a bronze statue of Dr. Sun back to the Presidential Building's Entrance Hall and that each day before starting work he bows in front of the statue to pay his respects. The President said he also thinks about the extent to which he has been able to realize the wishes of Dr. Sun here.'[81] The other side, mainland China, which was of course one of the central topics in speeches made during the era of the two Jiangs, is not mentioned, and the final statement remains vague with regard to future developments. 'President Ma said he is confident that the descendants of the ethnic Chinese people will be able to establish a fully free and democratic nation that enjoys equitable distribution of wealth.'

Similar patterns with slight variations can then be found in Ma Yingjiu's 2011 National Day address.[82] Compared with the New Year speech, a few more historical elements appeared, and taking the rapprochement between the two sides of the Taiwan Strait into account, surprisingly old anti-Communist rhetoric was employed such as 'the defense of Taiwan and its outlying islands against the invasion by Communist forces' and the call for the mainland 'to courageously move in the direction of Sun Yixian (Sun Yixian) with regard to establishing a free and democratic nation with equal distribution of wealth' (ibid.). Ma's emphasis, that one should not refer to the Republic of China 'in the past tense' and confront the existence of the Republic of China head-on, also contradicts the interpretation of Beijing, where the continued existence of the ROC (on Taiwan) after 1949 is bluntly denied. Ma repeats his statement that it was the resistance of the GMD in mainland China which led directly to

---

[79] The idea that Taiwan was very different from China when the GMD arrived in 1945 is not discussed. From this perspective, Taiwan was a marginalized island and border province under Qing rule, and only under the last Qing governor, Li Mingchuan, was Taiwan brought more closely under central rule; Taiwan was then colonized and "intensively Japanised" from 1895 to 1945. It is argued that the strict Sinification program of the GMD (that resulted in the renaming of streets (*Boai, Xinyi*, etc), the language education in Mandarin, and a school curriculum which focused only on developments on the mainland) was introduced precisely because Taiwan was so different from China. In addition, the focus on Confucianism and *Sanmin zhuyi* during the authoritarian GMD period is seen as an ideology pushed on Taiwan from above that did not develop deep roots. For the idea of a specific island history, see Heylen 2010.

[80] Accessed at http://english.president.gov.tw/Default.aspx?tabid=491&itemid=25621; http://www.president.gov.tw/Default.aspx?tabid=131&itemid=25508&rmid=514&sd=2011/10/09&ed=2011/10/10.

[81] Accessed at http://english.president.gov.tw/Default.aspx?tabid=491&itemid=25621.

[82] Accessed at http://www.president.gov.tw/Default.aspx?tabid=1103&itemid=25525&rmid=2780; http://english.president.gov.tw/Default.aspx?tabid=1361.

the retrocession of Taiwan: 'It was the sacrifice of 20 million soldiers and civilians of the Republic during the War of Resistance against Japan that enabled Taiwan to end Japan's colonial rule' (ibid.). The One-China discourse is also put in ethnic terms, when he emphasizes that people on both sides of the Taiwan Strait are ethnically Chinese (liang'an renmin tongshu Zhonghua minzu). This again goes against the widespread understanding in Taiwan, that Taiwan is a multi-ethnic society composed of four ethnic groups (Hoklo, Hakka, aborigines, and mainlanders) that form a specific Taiwanese identity, a claim which has taken root since the mid-1990s (Damm 2011a, 2011b; Wang 2003).
The speech starts with references to historical events, and the middle section deals with Taiwan, including Taiwan's economic ties with the mainland, but in the conclusion, Ma returns to Sun Yixian and describes the ROC as representing not only the name of a nation but also a free and democratic way of life and a model for other ethnic Chinese societies (*huaren diqu*). In the context of the relationship between Taiwan and the ROC, Ma ends this speech with the words 'The Republic of China is our nation, and Taiwan is our home (*Zhonghua minguo shi women de guojia, Taiwan shi women de jiayuan*). The nationalist stance of Sun Yixian, however, is only rarely mentioned within the political discourse; Yang Yi from the Taiwan Affairs Office on the mainland is one of the few GMD members who has been quoted as saying, 'The spirit of the Xinhai Revolution is a precious treasure jointly shared by compatriots on both sides of the Strait. The purpose of holding commemorations is to unite compatriots on both sides of the Strait and all Chinese people, and to pass down Dr. Sun Yixian's ideals on revitalizing the Chinese nation.'[83]

Counter-discourses

First of all, I would like to emphasize the fact that in contrast to the Chen Shuibian era, when any attempts made by the president or the minister of education, Tu Chengsheng, to 'Taiwanize' (*bentuhua*) the education system or the history narrative were immediately sharply attacked by the GMD and the pan-blue camp for criticizing 'de-Sinification' and neglecting the collective memory of the mainlanders (for example, the soldiers and their families), the pan-green camp fell silent, more or less ignoring the official celebrations, and accusations linked with a re-Sinification program are seldom to be heard.[84] Cai Yingwen seldom mentioned the term 'ROC' in her speeches, but she did point out recently that, when the Republic of China was established in 1912, Taiwan was not part of its territory and that the ROC, having lost all its territory in 1949, found shelter on Taiwan.[85] She went on to say that after the historical narrative and the territory were separated, the link with the people's feelings was also lost and people's hearts could only be touched with difficulty. Cai did not deny that the Republic of China has specific significance for Taiwan, but she reminded the GMD that Taiwan has its own history. 'Several thousands of years ago, the Aborigines (*yuanzhu minzu*) lived here, and four-hundred years ago, immigrants cultivated the land, political power took turns, that is what has been passed on from generation to generation of Taiwanese people, and what has left its mark in the blood and their memories. This belongs in the history of the people.' In addition, Cai Yingwen pointed out that even though the

83 Accessed at http://www.kmt.org.tw/english/page.aspx?type=article&mnum=112&anum=10256.

84 Accessed at http://justrecently.wordpress.com/2011/10/10/mas-tsais-double-ten-speeches-one-roc-two-interpretations/.

85 This differs slightly from the idea of "a government in exile."

ROC government's arrival on Taiwan had brought with it a very long period of authoritarian rule, now, after the termination of the 'period of mobilization for the suppression of Communist rebellion', with comprehensive parliamentary elections and direct presidential elections, the vast majority of Taiwanese today could acknowledge that 'Taiwan simply is the Republic of China', as the two have merged and taken on a new life in Taiwan. She emphasized that the next president's task was not to take the country back to 1912 but to lead it into a democratic future.

The most striking omission in the discourse is that of the two Jiangs, Jiang Jieshi and Jiang Jingguo, who certainly played a much stronger role in Taiwan after 1949 than Sun Yixian. In an attempt to present history in a positive light, it might of course make sense to mention only 'harmless' figures, but leaving the two Jiangs out of the picture renders the official addresses shallow and uninteresting. The memories of the Taiwanese and their negative connotations with the rule of the two Jiangs also omitted, for example, the period of authoritarian rule, the 228 Massacre, and the White Terror. James Soong (Song Chuyu) from the oppositional PFP[86] criticized Ma Yingjiu for neglecting to mention the Jiangs and accused Ma of 'distorting historical reality and alienating his audience'; Soong also mentioned the distortion of historical facts with regard to the Anti-Japanese Era of Resistance and the retrocession of the island to the ROC.

The dangers of glorifying the rule of the Jiangs, however, become apparent if we consider the reaction to a speech to mainland veteran soldiers given by Hao Bocun, the former disputed premier and general, in which he attempted to justify the period of authoritarian rule and martial law; this led to an immediate outcry from the pan-green camp.[87]

Analysis of Edited Volumes

Recent popular historical publications illustrate the struggle that is going on between the two camps over the importance of the Xinhai Revolution. First of all, the official publication, *Celebrating 100 Years,* edited by the Government Information Office of the Executive Yuan, offers a foreword by Ma Yingjiu.

A single glance at the cover page of this edited volume is enough to reveal the basic dilemma of Taiwan's current historical memory: important historical personalities from 100 years of ROC history are featured here, but most of these belong to the GMD historical memory as GMD and GMD-inclined individuals who held power in mainland China before 1949 and then moved to Taiwan where they remained influential. Only the minority are Taiwanese who were actively fighting against Japanese rule. They form part of the *benshengren* memory, but they can hardly be connected to the rule of the GMD after 1949. Influential 'negative' individuals are omitted: for example, leftist GMD members, such as Wang Jingwei (1983–1944), who opposed the new conservative GMD military elite (for example, Jiang Jieshi) after Sun's death in 1925 and then gave his support to the Japanese collaborationist government in Nanjing in the 1930s; Lei Zhen (1897–1979) and Yin Haiguang (1919–1969, the liberal mainland faction); Thomas Liao (Liao Wenyi, 1910–1986), Peng

---

[86] Accessed at http://www.taipeitimes.com/News/editorials/archives/2011/10/21/2003516269.

[87] Accessed at http://www.taipeitimes.com/News/editorials/archives/2011/11/02/2003517246. The former premier, Hao Bocun, praised "Chiang Kai-shek's dictatorship and the KMT as a necessary prerequisite for Taiwan's democratic and economic development" when talking to veteran soldiers in front of the Chiang Kai-shek Memorial Hall.

Minmin (b. 1923), and Lin Yixiong (b. 1941), representatives of the Taiwan independence movement.

In more detail, the following individuals are included as representing the 100 years of the ROC. If they are classified according to their (national) identity and their stances towards the ROC, the following picture emerges (from left to right, with Sun Yixian sitting at the front):

1) Chinese identity, GMD-inclined, accepts ROC point of view:

Yu Youren (1879–1964), educator, scholar, calligrapher, and politician in the Republic of China. He could probably be seen as fully characterizing the 100 years' history according to the interpretation of the GMD. Born in 1879, he was involved in the anti-Qing activities of the early reformers, although he took part in the imperial examinations. While he was a political refugee in 1906, he met Sun Yixian in Japan and then joined the *Tongmenghui*, the predecessor of the GMD. In 1911, he joined the government of Sun Yixian and remained loyal to the GMD during the following decades. His fame was due to his being well-known as an artist and as a non-corrupt politician (1931, Director of Control Yuan). In 1949, he followed the GMD government to Taiwan where, in his poems, he lamented the impossibility of going home to the mainland. A large bronze statue of Yu Youren was placed, after his death, at the summit of Yushan, or Jade Mountain, the highest mountain in Taiwan, where he could look down on the lost mainland. In 1996, however, the statue was removed by Taiwan independence activists, who wanted to sever any imagined ties between Taiwan and the mainland.

Sun Yun-suan (Sun Yunxuan 1913–2006) is best known for his contributions in the fields of engineering and economics in Taiwan after 1945, but he was also an influential and popular politician who followed the GMD from the mainland to Taiwan. He is one of the chief architects of Taiwan's 'economic miracle' that led Taiwan to become one of the East Asian Dragons after 1978 when he was prime minister.

Kwoh-Ting (Li Guoding 1910–2001) was an economist and politician, known as the 'Father of Taiwan's Economic Miracle' for his work in transforming Taiwan from an agrarian-based society into one of the world's leading producers of information and telecommunications technology. Although he probably possessed a strong ROC Chinese identity, his achievements were restricted solely to Taiwan and he still enjoys wide respect in Taiwan today.

Jiang Jingguo (1910–1988), the son of Jiang Jieshi, definitely belongs in the ROC identity category. He is, however, well-known for his achievements during the last years of his life, when he initiated various measures, such as the lifting of martial law and the first attempts at Taiwanization. He also increased the numbers of Taiwanese in his government and chose Li Denghui as his successor. Unlike Sun, his role is disputed in Taiwan: while the GMD highlights his merits in connection with his achievements in the fields of democratization and economic modernization, the more radical pan-green camp tends to focus on his earlier years in government, when, as chief of the secret police until 1965, he was in charge of carrying out the atrocities associated with the White Terror,

Jiang Jieshi (1887–1975) is placed in the middle of the picture. He represents the ROC identity perfectly, but even today he remains a much disputed figure in Taiwan. The old mainland soldiers, the members of the New Party (Xindang), and some groups with the GMD praise him for fighting against the Japanese and the Communists, while the pan-green camp sees in him the personification of everything they detest about GMD rule: authoritarian rule and the neglecting of Taiwanese subjectivity including the Sinification of the island after 1949.

Soong May-ling (Song Meiling 1898–2003), wife of Jiang Jieshi, who left Taiwan behind (she did not return after 1995) and resided in the United States, is also representative of the ruling GMD elite who fled to Taiwan. Although she represents the modern and Western image of the GMD rulers, she is described in negative terms in the collective Taiwanese memory.

Hu Shih (Hu Shi 1891–1962), the philosopher known in mainland China for his support of the written vernacular Chinese, was the liberal face of the GMD in Taiwan. He became the first president of the prestigious Academia Sinica, and while remaining loyal to the government, he was one of the few who were allowed to express a certain level of criticism without being harassed by the secret police. His political influence, however, remained weak.

2) Apolitical, pan-Asian, cross-Strait:

The inclusion of *Teng Lijun* (Theresa Teng, Deng Lijun, Teresa Teng 1953–1995) as a famous singer is surprising, as she is the only non-politician (or non-political figure). She became famous not only in Taiwan but all over Asia, and particularly in the PRC after the 1980s, although she never had the opportunity to perform on the mainland. Her songs were performed in Japanese, Mandarin, Hoklo, and English. In Taiwan, she was popular with both the mainlanders and the *benshengren*.

3) Taiwan identity:

The remaining individuals are historical figures dating from the Japanese period (1895–1945) in Taiwan, and their links to an imagined 100 years of ROC history covering both the mainland and Taiwan are not easy to construct.

Mona Rudao (1882–1930) was the son of a chief of the Seediq tribe in the Taiwanese indigenous population. Although he had been to Japan briefly, he became famous for his role in the unsuccessful Wushe revolt against Japanese rule in 1930 which led to his execution. At first, his bones were kept in the Taihoku Imperial University as a warning by the Japanese against taking part in any uprising, and even the GMD only allowed a reburial in 1974. Recently, his name was given to a character, a protagonist in the film *Seediq Bale*, which has been praised by representatives of all Taiwanese parties.

Chiang Wei-shui (Jiang Weishui1891–1931), founder of the Taiwan People's Party during the period of Japanese rule, was severely criticized by more conservative elements within Taiwanese society. He is best known for the formation of the Taiwan Local Self-Government League (*Taiwan difang zizhi lianmeng*). Although he is remembered for the positive stance that he adopted towards Sun Yixian (Jiang Weishui has been called the Sun Yixian of Taiwan), he is certainly not directly connected to the ROC. When the Taiwan Cultural Association split up in 1926, Jiang founded the Taiwan People's Party in order to improve the status of the Taiwanese during Japanese rule. The Taiwan People's Party was the first legal party ever to be established in Taiwan.

The cover of the *Bainian Fenghua* edited volume, therefore, also illustrates the dilemma of the current GMD administration with regard to national identity and history; it is difficult to bring a Taiwan-centered history in line with the official ROC-centered history. Taiwan-centered history, based on the geographical location, would include various governments during the last 100 years, such as the Japanese period, the years from 1945 to 1949 when

Taiwan was again a ROC province, and the years of the Republic of China on Taiwan after 1949. The history based on the construct of the ROC, however, has to cover the period from 1911 to 1949, the area of the ROC, including the mainland but excluding Taiwan, and after 1940, Taiwan, Penghu, Jinmen, and Mazu.

One of the reasons for including the edited volume, *Bainian Fenghua*, in the analysis, is the official character of this book. Not only was it edited by the Government Information Office of the Executive Yuan, but Ma Yingjiu, the current president, and Wu Dunyi, the current premier of the ROC, each provided brief forewords: Ma Yingjiu contributed 'The Core Values of 100 Year long tradition', which is followed by Wu Dunyi's 'Witness history in order to see the future' and the general editor Yang Yongming's) 'Growth and transformation.

Ma Yingjiu lays emphasis on the fact that after a long and hard struggle the Republic of China has achieved great successes in the areas of democracy ('from authoritarianism to democratic structures') to become a model in the free world and particularly within ethnic Chinese societies (*huaren shehui*). With regard to culture, Ma draws attention to the hybrid nature of Western and Chinese culture in Taiwan which has led, as he termed it, to 'Taiwan's unique style' (*dute fengge*). The following paragraphs then deal with the current situation in Taiwan, and only in the last paragraph does Ma return to the topic of history. The second foreword by Wu Dunyi focuses on the change from authoritarian structures to democracy which is, however, solely attributed to Jiang Jingguo and thus omits Li Denghui (known in the West as 'Mr. Democracy'), although Li Denghui was a member of the GMD. In addition, Wu also fails to mention the role of the oppositional forces, who fought against the authoritarian rule.[88] In this foreword, we can identify the unusual form of periodization which has become the standard for the current GMD government. Let me first introduce a more detailed form of periodization, which reads as follows:

Mainland China: 1911 to 1949, Republic of China (including periods and areas not under control of the GMD government, such as the Northern Government, areas occupied by Japan, and the areas under control of the CCP); 1949 to now, mainland China, under the control of the CCP.

Taiwan: 1895 to 1945, Japanese rule; 1945 to 1949, Taiwan, a province of the ROC which was ruled from the mainland; 1949 to 1987, the authoritarian rule of the GMD who had moved the central government to Taiwan; finally, 1987 to now, Taiwan, a democracy with the official title Republic of China and de facto rule over Taiwan, Jinmen, Penghu, and Mazu.

The general editor of *Bainian*, however, describes the framework of the volume as follows: 'The subjects are the 100 years of the Republic of China, including the 34 years from 1911 when Taiwan, until 1945, was under the control of the Japanese occupation government, and refers to this as a 'Y-shaped history.'' The years in Taiwan from 1911 to 1945 are therefore included, which from a Taiwanese- centered perspective does not make any sense,

---

[88] Li Denghui has become a much contested figure within the pan-blue camp for a variety of reasons, including the support he showed for Chen Shui-bian and the founding of the Taiwan Solidarity Union. In addition, his own life story (he and members of his family being soldiers of the Japanese Imperial Army) contradicts the official GMD discourse which focuses only on the resistance of the Chinese, including the Taiwanese population, against Japanese rule. See, for example, Keng Shu, "Assessing the Lee Teng-Hui Legacy in Taiwan's Politics," www.tfd.org.tw/docs/d1t1/177-184.pdf.

although of course the Taiwanese elite paid a certain amount of attention to the changes that were taking place in mainland China. Nevertheless, the editor remarks that the different perceptions towards the time from 1911 to 1945 in Taiwan can be found in various entries and that it is up to the authors whether to use *Rizhi* 日治, *Riju* 日據, *Riben zhimin shiqi* 日本殖民時期, or *Riben shidai* 日本時代 (Japanese rule, Japanese occupation, Japanese colonial time, or Japanese time). The content of the edited volume is described as a kind of encyclopaedia that presents 100 years of the ROC in the fields of politics, the economy, society, and culture by focusing on outstanding historical figures, events, and matters.

In addition to the foreword by Ma Yingjiu, the first two chapters written by Pan Guangzhe (Pan Kuang-che), a historian at the Institute of Modern History at Academia Sinica, also deal with Sun Yixian and the founding of the Republic. Chapter 1, Yazhou diyi minzhu Gongheguo: Zhonghua minguo chengli (The first Asian Republic: The Republic of China) presents the day of the founding of the Republic and attributes many of the social changes to the new government, including the ending of the requirement for men to shave their foreheads and wear their hair in 'the queue', the ban on bound feet for women, the ban on opium smoking, the requirement to read the classics, and the *baihua* (page 24). A stark contrast is thus created between the old and new culture, society, and the political situation.[89]

The second chapter, on Sun Yixian, the 'General Engineer of Nation Building' includes one of the most frequently recurring topics in the volume: an attempt to show a connection between Taiwan and Sun Yixian. This starts with the sentences 'The image of Sun Yixian is everywhere in Taiwan. On coins, one can see his smiling face, all over Taiwan are Sun Yixian Streets, Sun Yixian Halls, Sun Yixian Parks and Sun Yixian statues. Sentences and prhrases such as 'humanity' (*boai*) and 'the whole world as one community' (*tianxia wei gong*) are written all over the island, and the *Sanmin zhuyi* ideology (Three Principles of the People) can be found in the first article of the ROC constitution: the ROC constitution is based on the *Sanmin zhuyi*. . . .' It cannot be disputed that many streets and places are named after Sun Yixian, but whether this shows the deep affiliation of the Taiwanese towards Sun, or whether this naming is only a relic left over from the former GMD authoritarian rule, is certainly a matter of debate: the *Sanmin zhuyi* as ideology, for example, in school and university examinations, has been abolished, while all *Sanmin zhuyi* research institutes and university programs have been remodelled and are no longer named after Sun. While the *Bainian Fenghua* generally refrains from making direct comments and providing explanations, it does not present a comprehensive view and, of course, the omission of negative ROC figures and the inclusion of Taiwan before 1945 leave this GMD-centered interpretation of history wide open to criticism.

One of the few examples showing the aggressive promotion of a counter-discourse was the launch of the edited volume, *Expose the Truth of 100 Years ROC*, by the Taiwan Historical Association. During the book's launch, the historians involved promoted a different view of history, with the aim of deconstructing history to reveal inconsistencies and provide an

[89] To put it briefly, the dominant view is that many of the changes propagated by the revolutionaries were, first of all, not really new because they had been discussed for quite some time in China and, secondly, some but not all of the proclaimed aims were only fulfilled later. The social changes brought by the revolution, in particular, are usually seen as marginal.

alternative understanding of history.[90] The volume is divided into 116 short chapters covering various topics of 100 years of history with a focus on Taiwan instead of on the ROC. The first chapters deal with the 'historical facts' related to the Xinhai Revolution: the question of the 'rightful' successor to Sun Yixian, the changes and political ambitions of Jiang Jieshi (including the question of how 'fascist did the GMD become in the 1930s and 1940s?'), and the historical development of Taiwan under ROC rule (such as the 228 Incident and the White Terror). The following chapters then offer various other topics, to name but a few, the situation of local languages, aboriginal culture in Taiwan, the Taiwanese opposition movement, the GMD and religious freedom, a critical evaluation of the Taiwanese land reform, economic developments, including the situation of the impoverished classes, the international legal status of the island, and the new liberal politics during the last decade. Finally, the volume moves on to the Economic Cooperation Framework Agreement (ECFA) and the so-called 1992 Consensus.

Chang Yan-hsien (Zhang Yanxian), the secretary-general of the association introduces the volume with the remarks that although the GMD government expressed the intention of celebrating the 'founding of the ROC 100 years ago', the government chose to employ the term *Jingcai bainian* (great, wonderful 100 years) as a title for the celebrations and avoided the term *jianguo* (establishing a nation). Chang further asks, 'Has the 100-year period of the ROC really been such a wonderful time as is claimed by the Chinese GMD government and President Ma Yingjiu? Or . . . does this term not hide the historical truth and cover up the bad things which happened? Has this period of history really been as wonderful as the Chinese GMD government and President Ma Yingjiu claim? Or are these claims only being made to back up the GMD's own statements in order to obscure the historical facts, to show only the positive side wherever possible while hiding the negative aspects? Are the details deliberately exaggerated, some enlarged and others diminished; are some historical facts actually fabricated, deliberately twisted or even deliberately embellished?' (page VII). Chang also expresses doubt that it is correct to talk about the years of the Republic on the mainland without taking into consideration the fact that, for many years, the GMD did not have any legitimate control over many areas. For example, in 1912, power shifted to the government of Yuan Shikai (the Northern Government) that was legitimate at that time, and after the 1930s, more and more areas came under the control of the Chinese Communist Party and were occupied by the Japanese.

Another main issue dealt with in this volume is the question of whether the role of Sun Yixian is not being deliberately overemphasized in the current GMD discourse. Quotations derived from biographies that are critical of Sun Yixian, such as Wilbur's *Frustrated Patriot* and other works, are used to indicate that Sun Yixian was not alone, that there were many other revolutionaries, such as Song Jiaren and Zhang Binglin. With regard to the evaluation of Sun Yixian, the authors cast doubt on assertions made by the GMD (pages VIII to IX) that the Three Principles of the People or the Five-Power Constitution developed by Sun were really the best remedies for China's problems. They point out that in the democratic Taiwan of today, the fivefold separation of powers (the Executive Yuan, Legislative Yuan, Judicial Yuan, Examination Yuan, and Control Yuan) has in fact been altered to a threefold separation of powers in the constitution (executive, legislative, and judicial) like that found in Western countries and that the *Sanmin zhuyi* is no longer an official doctrine in Taiwan.

[90] Personal observations of the author.

In addition, there is criticism of the orthodox history of the GMD in Taiwan: Jiang Jieshi is described as the natural successor to Sun while, in reality, Hu Hanmin, Wang Jingwei, and Liao Zhenglai would have been preferred by Sun. Jiang, however, succeeded in grasping the opportunity that emerged as a result of the power struggle within the GMD. The authors also support the idea of a government in exile, and stress that it was only the outbreak of the Korean War which led to the strange situation of the GMD government in Taiwan being able to claim legitimacy (pages IX, X). One of the authors, Li Fuzhong, asks whether 'Sun Yixian was an irresponsible dreamer' (*Sun Zhongshan shi bu fuze ren de kongxiangjia*) when discussing the argument that the revolutionary ideas of Sun could be seen as having led to the destruction of China and not to the creation of anything new, an idea which is supported by Li Xiaofeng.

Conclusion

The analysis of the political and public discourse has shown that the broad implications of these historical events and their significance for Taiwan today are far from clear. The centennial celebrations of the ROC (on Taiwan) do not lead to greater unity on Taiwan but expose the deep political and identity rifts that exist in Taiwan.

It seems that the GMD government and President Ma Yingjiu, with the focus on 'celebrating 100 years', deliberately excludes negative aspects of the past 100 years and also omits events and persons related to a specific Taiwanese identity including the history of the Taiwanese independence movement. These omissions include 'negative' persons, such as the leaders of the CCP, who without doubt played a major role during the early years of the ROC on the mainland.[91] In addition, the atrocities carried out during the early period of GMD rule on the mainland are not mentioned at all, and the White Terror in Taiwan after 1945 is referred to in the *Bainian Guanghua* volume but not in official speeches made by President Ma. It is therefore quite understandable that the presidential candidate of the opposition, Tsai Ing-wen, chose to refrain from participating in the official National Day celebrations. On October 9, Tsai stated 'The Republic of China (ROC) is Taiwan and Taiwan is the ROC', but according to an analysis carried out by Jean-Pierre Cabestan, this refers basically to the final years of ROC rule on Taiwan: 'Everybody on the island was aware that there were three ROCs – the republic founded by Dr. Sun Yat-sen [Sun Yixian], the authoritarian period and, later, the democratic ROC [on Taiwan].'

If we concentrate on the official political discourse of the president, several clusters of argumentation can be identified:

Firstly, in his addresses, Ma regards himself as the fulfiller of the ideals of Sun Yixian. He mentions his sentimental attachment to Sun, and by focusing on economic growth and democracy, he shows that he regards the ROC on Taiwan today as being the nation envisioned by Sun and thus deliberately omits Sun's strong emphasis on Chinese nationalism. In Ma's speeches and in *Bainian Guanghua*, a polished GMD version of history is presented which starts with Sun Yixian and ends with Ma Yingjiu, omitting almost all other presidents in between, including of course Jiang Jieshi and Li Denghui. Ma's rhetoric even included his

[91] See, for example, the resignation of Lin Man-houng [Lin Manhong], head of the Academia Historica who stepped down after she had initiated a controversial online poll on the most important ROC figures and had included Mao Zedong and Deng Xiaoping, http://www.taipeitimes.com/News/taiwan/archives/2010/12/17/2003491170).

'getting tearful': the *China Post* reported, in 'Ma Gets Tearful about Dr. Sun Yat-sen', that President Ma 'apparently moved by his own words, wiped his nose with a handkerchief, reiterating his determination to follow Dr. Sun's teachings.'

The second point about Ma's addresses is that the ROC on Taiwan today is presented as the bearer of traditional Chinese culture, including the strong affiliation to Confucian values. Taiwan's development is positively compared to the 'chaos of the Cultural Revolution' on the mainland. For example, in his New Year speech in 2011, Ma also referred to the former rhetoric of Jiang Jieshi and Chiang Ching-kuo who stated that the ROC represents the edge of Chinese culture—a claim which now only rarely appears in official publications and stands in direct contrast to the proclaimed hybridity of Taiwan's culture, in which Chinese culture certainly plays a role but certainly not the only, dominant role.

Thirdly, the collective memory of the mainlanders (Shanghai 1937, ROC flag) is mentioned but not, however, a specific Taiwanese memory. Where reference is made to the Japanese time, the revolts against the Japanese and the pro-Chinese dissidents are highlighted, but the group of Taiwanese who accepted Japanese rule yet continued to strive for equal representation of the Taiwanese is not.

Fourthly, the democratic transformation of Taiwan is perceived as having been founded on Sun Yixian's ideals, which omits the contribution of the Taiwanese opposition movement. Politicians, particularly those belonging to the pan-blue camp, prefer to make only vague references to the 100 years; the many gaps and contradictions in the 100 years of history of both the ROC and Taiwan are glossed over to show how the Xinhai Revolution led straight to today's democratic, pluralistic, gender-aware, and multicultural Taiwan, which is embedded in global structures but nevertheless committed to overcoming the old rivalry with the PRC government.

Fifth, in contrast to mainland China, nationalist discourses (for example, unification) are almost non-existent; only vague references are made to the democratic future of all Chinese societies.

The Xinhai Revolution itself is smoothly linked to the issues related to Taiwan's democratization, the creation of a specific Taiwanese identity, and the accomplishments of 100 years of GMD rule. It is argued that Sun Yixian and the other 1912 revolutionaries were not able to fulfil their dream of the first Republic in Asia due to external aggression and the civil war. There is no mention of any opposition to the democratic ideals deriving from the conservative groups such as Jiang Jieshi, who was very much influenced both by traditional Confucian thinking and later on by Fascist ideas in Europe. The 'authoritarian communism' on the mainland is referred to as the primary reason for the relocation of the GMD government to the 'island province' in 1949. The years under Japanese rule in Taiwan are mentioned but with no reference being made to any societal or economic changes during that period. The dream of a democratic society is then attributed to the developments in Taiwan afterwards, the authoritarian years hidden in the words 'the past quarter-century in particular has seen dramatic progress in political reform, including the direct election of the ROC president and the development of a lively system of multiparty politics.'

For the pan-blue camp, the thoughts of Sun Yixian paved the way for the evolutionary development of democracy (tutelage) and also helped to develop the economic system (the Taiwan Miracle). Sun Yixian is respected in all Chinese places (PRC, Hong Kong, Taiwan, and even in the Chinese diaspora). For the pan-green camp, Sun Yixian is not considered to have been of any importance for Taiwan, because Taiwan was a Japanese colony in 1911 and 1912; Taiwan was spared the chaos of the Warlord Period. After 1949, the Three Principles of the People were misused: the frequent references to the Three Principles formed part of the policy of the authoritarian regime, and for this reason, they are no longer taught in Taiwan schools and do not form part of the university entrance system. Sun Yixian was not an important symbol in the context of democratization, and liberals, such as Lei Zhen and Yin Haiguang, failed in their earlier attempts to establish democratic structures in Taiwan, in contrast with the successful indigenous democratic movement after the late 1970s. On the other hand, the counter-discourse tries to stick more to the established 'facts'; at least this discourse tries to overcome the streamlining of historical events from Sun Yixian to Ma Yingjiu by focusing both on Taiwanese history and the history of the Taiwanese independence movement as well as on the various developments during the first half of the 20th century in mainland China.

References

Bakhtin, M. M., Michael Holquist, and Caryl Emerson (1986) *Speech Genres and Other Late Essays*, Austin: University of Texas Press.

Chang, Hui-Ching, and Rich Holt (2009) 'Taiwan and ROC: A Critical Analysis of President Chen Shui-bien's Construction of Taiwan Identity in National Speeches', *National Identities,* 11(3): 301–330.

Chu, Yun-han, and Jih-wen Lin (2001) 'Political Development in 20th-Century Taiwan: State-Building, Regime Transformation and the Construction of National Identity', *The China Quarterly* 165: 102–129.

Clough, Ralph N. (1996) 'The Enduring Influence of the Republic of China on Taiwan Today', *The China Quarterly* 148 (1054–1071).

Cohen, Jeffery E. (1995) 'Presidential Rhetoric and the Public Agenda', *American Journal of Political Science,* 39: 87–107.

Corcuff, Stéphane (2002) *Memories of the Future: National Identity Issues and the Search for a New Taiwan*, Armonk, N.Y.: M.E. Sharpe.

Damm, Jens (2011a) 'From 'Overseas Chinese' to 'Overseas Taiwanese': Questions of Identity and Belonging, in Damm, Jens and Gunter Schubert (Eds.) *Taiwanese Identities in the 21st Century*, London: Routledge: 218–236.

Damm, Jens (2011b) 'Multiculturalism in Taiwan and the Influence of Europe', in Damm, Jens and Paul Lim (Eds.) *European Perspectives on Taiwan,* Wiesbaden: Springer: 84–106.

Dijk, Teun Adrianus (2008) *Discourse and Context: A Sociocognitive Approach*, Cambridge: Cambridge University Press.

Dijk, Teun Adrianus (Ed.) (1989) *Handbook of Discourse Analysis: Discourse and Dialogue*, London: Academic Press.

Ensink, Titus (1997) 'The Footing of a Royal Address: An Analysis of Representativeness in Political Speech, Exemplified in Queen Beatrix', address to the Knesset on March 28, 1995, in Schäffner, Christina (Ed.) *Analysing Political Speeches*, 5–32.

Fairclough, Norman (1992) 'Discourse and Text: Linguistic and Intertextual Analysis within Discourse Analysis', *Discourse & Society* 3(2): 193–217.

Harrison, Selig S. (1988) 'Taiwan after Chiang Ching-Kuo [Jiang Jingguo]', *Foreign Affairs* 66(4): 790–808.

Heylen, Ann (2010) 'The Transnational in Taiwan History: A Preliminary Exploration', *Concentric: Literary and Cultural Studies* 36(1) March 2010: 9–33.

Israel, John (1963) 'Politics on Formosa', *The China Quarterly* 15: 3–11.

Kiewe, Amos (1998) 'The Crisis Tool in American Political Discourse', in Feldman, Ofer and Christ'l de Landtsheer (Eds.) *Politically Speaking: A Worldwide Examination of Language Used in the Public Sphere*: 79–90.

Lams, Lutgard, and Xavier Li-wen Liao (2011) 'Tracing 'Taiwanization' Processes in Taiwanese Presidential Statements in Times of Cross-Strait Rapprochement', *Journal of Current Chinese Affairs,* 40(1): 63–98.

Petzold, Claudius (2007) *Der völkerrechtliche Status Taiwans, R.O.C.*, Baden Baden: Nomos.

Shi, Zhiyu (Shih Chih-yu) 石之瑜 (2005) 'Hainei Huaren? Taiwanren shenfen zhengzhi zhong de zuxian lunshu 海內華人？台灣人身份政治中的祖先論述 [Overseas Chinese at home? The ancestor discourse in Taiwanese identity politics]', in Zhang Qixiong 張啟雄 (Ed.) *Shidai bianju yu haiwai huaren de zuguo rentong* 時代變局與海外華人的族國認同, Taibei: Zhonghua minguo haiwai huaren yanjiuhui: 71–167.

Wang, Fuchang 王甫昌 (2003) *Dangdai Taiwan shehui de zujun xiangxiang* 當代台灣社會的族群想像 [The ethnic imagination in Taiwan's current society], Taipei: Xuejun.

International Workshop China Studies in a Global Context. Freie Universität Berlin; Konfuzius-Institut an der Freien Universität Berlin, 16.-17. Oktober 2015

Welche disziplinären Herausforderungen stellen sich Sinologie bzw. Chinastudien in einer Zeit wachsender Vernetzung zwischen China und der Welt? Wie verändern die vielfältigen Stimmen und konkurrierenden Perspektiven die Paradigmen eines Faches, dessen europäischen Grundsteine in der Kolonialzeit gelegt wurden? Diesen Fragen widmete sich der Workshop 'China Studies in a Global Context'. Passend zum Thema war auch die Gruppe der Vortragenden international und interdisziplinär, beleuchtete neue Foki der historischen und gegenwartsbezogenen Forschung, sowie die dahinterstehende Ideengeschichte. Eingeladen hatten Mechthild Leutner und Katja Levy von der Freien Universität, sowie Zhang Xudong von der New York University. Da letzterer verhindert war, eröffnete Mechthild Leutner mit ihren Thesen zur Geschichte der Sinologie in Deutschland. Unter anderem am Beispiel der Umstrukturierung der ostdeutschen Universitätslandschaft nach der Wende zugunsten westdeutscher Wissenschaftler zeigte sie, wie Wissen im Zuge ideologischer Arroganz verloren gehen kann. Daran anknüpfend stellte Bettina Gransow-Van Treek (Freie Universität Berlin) die Schwerpunkte chinesischer Soziologen und soziologischer Chinawissenschaftler gegenüber. Dabei wurde klar, dass die simple Dichotomie zwischen „chinesischen' und 'westlichen' Perspektiven zu kurz greift. Die Globalisierung ist längst im Forschungsalltag angekommen: Sprachkompetenzen, Austausch und Kooperationen mehren sich, durch ihre Ausbildung und Arbeit innerhalb und außerhalb Chinas sind heutige Forscher häufig in mehreren Ländern akademisch beheimatet. In diesem Zusammenhang verwies Jens Damm (Chang Jung Christian University, Tainan) insbesondere auf die dynamische asiatisch-chinesische Diaspora. Mit den Netzwerken werden auch Themen global. Darüber hinaus bieten Länder wie Indonesien oder Singapur ein Umfeld chinesischer Forschung jenseits der staatlichen Restriktionen in der Volksrepublik. Damit betonte er jedoch, dass bei aller Annäherung thematische Pfadabhängigkeit und der regionale politische Einfluss nicht zu vernachlässigen seien. Bettina Gransow führte die chinesische 'Guoxue' (Landeskunde) als Beispiel in die Diskussion ein. Die Themen dieses Faches überschneiden sich zum Teil mit der klassischen Sinologie. Doch spiegelt ihre Förderung an den chinesischen Universitäten auch das Interesse Chinas als Nationalstaat wieder, herrschaftssichernde Narrationen produzieren zu lassen. Andererseits zeige sich hier ein berechtigtes Interesse chinesischer Forscher, die Deutungshoheit über die eigene Geschichte gegenüber dem amerikanischen Monopol zurückzugewinnen und chinesische Stimmen gleichberechtigt gelten zu lassen. Eindeutiger präsentierte Paul U. Unschuld (Humboldt Universität zu Berlin) den Fall der Traditionellen Chinesischen Medizin. Diese werde als Gegenentwurf zur westlichen Schulmedizin konzipiert und instutionalisiert. Der nationalistische Fokus erlaube dabei keine Zweifel an der Wirksamkeit und Autorität des als traditionell definierten Wissens. Dabei würden naturwissenschaftliche Kriterien hintangestellt, der letztendliche Erkenntnisgewinn und der Austausch mit Naturwissenschaftlern stark behindert. Doch wie komplex die Grenzen zwischen Annäherung und Distanz in der akademischen Gemeinschaft verlaufen können, zeigte der Vortrag von Huang Haifeng (Beijing Universität). Er sprach über die ökologische 'grüne Revolution' in China aus Sicht der staatlichen Entscheidungsträger. Diese Agenda sei nicht national isoliert, sondern Teil der globalen Diskussion zu Umweltschutz und von dieser beeinflusst. Andererseits war seine Darstellung ausschließlich positiv und kritische Fragen blieben eloquent unbeantwortet. Damit wurde auch

deutlich, wie die politische und kulturelle Färbung der Kommunikationsgewohnheiten weiterhin den wissenschaftlichen Austausch bestimmen.
Umso interessanter war Hauke Neddermanns Präsentation zur Imagination der Jugend in chinesischen Zeitschriften. Die staatliche Diskursdominanz propagiert nicht eine starre Wahrheit, sondern ist zeitlichen Änderungen unterworfen. Dass ihre Rolle in der akademischen Gemeinschaft dabei nicht eindeutig ist, zeigte Jiang Hongsheng (Beijing Universität). Er beschäftigte sich mit der Rolle der Shanghaier Kommune während der Kulturevolution im Blick der chinesischen und englischsprachigen Literatur. Beide entwickelten sich ähnlich, das heißt: Auch westliche Forscher folgten über eine lange Zeit der offiziellen Position, die Kulturrevolution zu verdammen. Im Gegenzug sprechen sich heute auch chinesische Intellektuelle für eine positive Re-Evaluation aus, entgegen der staatlichen Doktrin. Jiangs Sichtung des Diskursmaterials war umfassend und gründlich. Doch bei der Frage nach den französischen Diskussionen, die sein Thema tangierten, musste er auf seine sprachlichen Grenzen verweisen. Wie viele Sprachen und Stimmen kann und muss man als Forscher in einer global vernetzten Disziplin wahrnehmen? Ariel Armony (University of Pittsburgh) zeigte dabei, wie das weltweit agierende China auch in den Fokus anderer Disziplinen rückt - in diesem Fall der Lateinamerikastudien. Um den Blick zu weiten, dürfe die Ausbildung der Forscher diversifizierte Sprach-, Kultur- und Geschichtskenntnisse nicht vernachlässigen. Doch problematisch sei die Vereinbarung mit bestehenden Institutionen, den Fachbereichen und der fachspezifischen Forschungsförderung. Die Frage nach dem Einfluss von Fördergeldern kam dabei immer wieder während des Workshops auf. Paradigmatische Rahmen werden vorgegeben und von Modethemen ergänzt, während das Verwertungsinteresse an den Forschungsergebnissen sowohl chinesische als auch deutsche Geldgeber auszeichnen. Erstere stehen jedoch diesbezüglich häufiger in der Kritik. Neben der Politik, sind es die „economics of research' (Mechthild Leutner) und die spezifischen Netzwerke, die auf der Metaebene die Forschung formen. „China Studies in a Global Context' bringt also nicht nur neue Forschungsfragen hervor, sondern bedarf auch eines wachsenden Bewusstseins, wie und warum Themen aufgegriffen oder ignoriert werden und welche Faktoren welche Narrationen zu China und der Welt begünstigen.

(Ryanne Flock)

Chinas International Relations in Historical Perspective. Konfuzius-Institut an der Freien Universität Berlin. 27.-28. November 2015.

Chinas atemberaubender Aufstieg zur zweitgrößten Volkswirtschaft ist ein in Medien und Wissenschaft häufig diskutiertes Thema. Hand in Hand damit gingen jedoch ebenso bedeutende Veränderungen in Chinas außenpolitischen Beziehungen. Der chinesische Staat, der bis 1997 über Teile seines Territoriums keine Souveränität ausgeübt hat, strebt nun danach, nicht nur in der asiatischen Hemisphäre, sondern global Verantwortung zu übernehmen. Die Tagung im Konfuzius-Institut an der Freien Universität Berlin – organisiert von Prof. Dr. Mechthild Leutner, Prof. Bettina Gransow (Freie Universität Berlin), Prof. Niu Dayong (Peking University) und Prof. Eberhard Sandschneider (Freie Universität Berlin, Deutsche Gesellschaft für Auswärtige Politik) - hatte zum Ziel, sich mit den chinesischen Außenbeziehungen seit den 1950er Jahren zu befassen, wobei der Schwerpunkt auf der Gegenwart lag.

Zu diesem Zweck tauschten sich chinesische, russische und deutsche Sinologen, Historiker und Politikwissenschaftler aus.

Die Grundzüge der aktuellen chinesischen Außenpolitik und Chinas Stellung in der Weltpolitik legte Eberhard Sandschneider (Freie Universität Berlin) dar. Demnach verfolgt China die Ziele der Förderung von wirtschaftlicher Entwicklung bei gleichzeitiger Aufrechterhaltung von sozioökonomischer Stabilität mit allen erdenklichen Mitteln und will auf dieser Grundlage seine globale Rolle noch stärker ausdehnen. Hinter dieser globalen Ausrichtung eröffnen sich für China Fragen, wie der westliche Einfluss begrenzt werden kann, wie internationale Regeln definiert werden können und wer diese in Zukunft verteidigen wird. Mit Chinas Verständnis von Globalisierung beschäftigte sich Lian Yuru (Universität Peking). Sie führte aus, dass der Kern der chinesischen Außenpolitik im 21. Jahrhundert die Schicksalsgemeinschaft (*mingyun gongtongti*) sei. Dieser von Xi Jinping 2013 geprägte Begriff beschreibt die Akzeptanz einer globalisierten Welt bei gleichzeitigem Festhalten am Prinzip staatlicher Souveränität. An die Akzeptanz globaler Werte und an eine globale Weltsicht sind eine Reihe von außenpolitischen Zielen gebunden, wie etwa gegenseitiger Nutzen und damit eine win-Situation für alle Beteiligten. Dass China in seinen internen Diskurs über die internationalen Beziehungen auch auf seine eigenen Denk- und Rechtstraditionen integriert, zeigte der Vortrag von Jens Damm (Chang Jung Christian University, Tainan) über die chinesische kulturelle Diplomatie. Durch den Rückgriff auf die chinesische Kultur, das heißt teilweise modifizierte konfuzianische Werte, aber auch daoistische und buddhistische Versatzstücke, möchte sich China als zivilisierte, verantwortliche und vertrauenswürdige Nation unter Gleichen präsentieren.

Das aktuelle sino-russische Verhältnis skizzierte Nikolay Samaylov (St. Petersburg State University). Seit 2001 besteht zwischen beiden Staaten eine freundschaftliche Kooperation. Angestrebt werden jedoch von Seiten Chinas eine strategische Partnerschaft sowie eine stabile ökonomische Allianz. Die als Folge der Ukraine-Krise 2014 eingeleitete Intensivierung der wirtschaftlichen Kooperation mit Russland war auch Ausdruck gemeinsamer Abneigung gegen die USA. Doch die Interessen überschneiden sich nicht nur. Russland möchte die Beziehungen zu China berechenbar halten, fürchtet aber dessen Dominanz. Dies verringert die Möglichkeit einer tatsächlichen Realisierung einer strategischen Kooperation. Eine neue Partnerschaft bahnt sich hingegen auf humanitärer Ebene an, um das jeweilige Außenbild zu optimieren. In diesen Kontext ist es auch einzuordnen, dass es gerade in jüngster Zeit zu einer Annäherung der sehr kleinen orthodoxen Gemeinde in China mit dem russischen Patriachat gekommen ist.

Die russisch-chinesischen Interessen stoßen in Zentralasien, traditionell eine russische Einflusszone, aufeinander. Beide Nationen versuchen, ihre dortige geopolitische Präsenz auszubalancieren, um den radikalen islamischen Terrorismus zu bekämpfen. Die Bedeutung des Seidenstraßen-Wirtschaftsgürtels für China stellte Bettina Gransow (Freie Universität Berlin) vor. Es handelt sich hierbei um ein transkontinentales Entwicklungsprojekt hinsichtlich Sicherheit und Ökonomie, vom asiatischen Pazifik zur europäischen Ostsee bzw. Venedig, von Zentralasien bis zum Indischen Ozean bzw. Persischen Golf. Doch jeder der beteiligten Staaten in Zentralasien, vor allem aber Russland, möchte über die diesbezüglichen Regeln mitentscheiden. Peter Linke lenkte in seinem Vortrag den Blick auf die arktische Region, wo Spannungen zwischen China und Russland immer deutlicher hervortreten.

Um die Chancen einer Zusammenarbeit mit China zu verbessern, stütze sich Russland hinsichtlich des Arktik-Problems stark auf Japan.
Mit der Frage der augenblicklichen Rivalität zwischen den beiden ostasiatischen Ländern Japan und China in Lateinamerika beschäftigte sich Katja Levy (Freie Universität Berlin). Als Ergebnis ihrer Analyse chinesischer Zeitschriften stellte sie fest, dass es dort zwischen beiden Nationen weder einen Wettbewerb noch Drohung oder gar Feindschaft gebe. Vielmehr profitiert Japan von dem chinesischen Vorgehen in Lateinamerika. China stösst vor allem in Brasilien auf offene Türen, weil alle lateinamerikanischen Staaten derzeit bestrebt sind, den US-amerikanischen Einfluss zu reduzieren. Daniel Cardoso (Freie Universität Berlin) stellte die chinesisch-lateinamerikanische Kooperationen als Herausforderung in einer neuen globalen Weltordnung vor. Ein Hauptproblem ist dabei, dass lateinamerikanische Länder über sehr unterschiedliche Profile verfügen und hinsichtlich ihrer politischen Möglichkeiten und der Ausdehnung ihrer Rolle in den internationalen Beziehungen unterschiedlich auftreten.
Den zweiten Schwerpunkt der Konferenz bildeten Vorträge zu Chinas internationalen Beziehungen im Kalten Krieg, bei denen auch ein besonderes Augenmerk auf die deutsch-chinesischen Beziehungen gelegt wurde. Niu Dayong (Universität Peking) befasste sich mit der Tibet-Frage in den 1950er Jahren, zu der bisher nur eine begrenzte Anzahl von Dokumenten freigegeben ist. Unbestritten ist jedoch, dass in Tibet damals amerikanische und chinesische Interessen aufeinandertrafen. Die USA verfolgten zunächst das Konzept eines autonomen Tibet, um Chinas Einfluss zu schwächen. Erst nachdem militärische Maßnahmen nicht den erhofften Erfolg brachten, wurde das Modell eines „gewaltfreien Tibet' geschaffen. Seit dem Vietnamkrieg, vor allem aber seit den 1969 einsetzenden Verbesserungen der chinesisch-amerikanischen Beziehungen hielten sich die USA in Tibet zurück.
Als einen Detailaspekt der sino-russischen Kooperation in den 1950er Jahren analysierte Izabella Goikhman (Freie Universität Berlin) die akademischen Beziehungen in den Naturwissenschaften am Beispiel chinesischer Studenten und Wissenschaftler in Russland und vice versa russischer Experten in China. Die sowjetische Seite teilte nicht jedes Wissen vorbehaltlos mit China. Vielmehr galten bestimmte Informationen als Staatsgeheimnis, wobei dieser sensible Bereich jedoch nicht genau definiert war. Der Charakter der jeweiligen persönlichen Begegnung war stark abhängig vom jeweiligen Kontext. In der politischen Einordnung dieses Transfers gibt es bis heute Unterschiede: Während die russische Literatur von „sozialistischem Internationalismus' spricht, erkennt die die chinesische „sozialen Imperialismus'. Als eine andere Art der intersozialistischen Wissensübertragung betrachtete Kong Fujun (Universität Peking) den Transfer von China nach Albanien von den 1960er Jahren bis 1978. Nach Beendigung der Moskauer Unterstützung für Tirana entsandte China etwa 6.000 Experten. Diese unterstützten über Hundert Projekte in den Bereichen Eisen-, Stahl und chemische Industrie. Die chinesische Hilfe wurde in dem Moment gedrosselt, als Albanien begann, Maos Theorie der drei Welten zu kritisieren und sich gegen eine Verbesserung der sino-amerikanischen Beziehungen auszusprechen.
Die deutsch-chinesischen Beziehungen während der Zeit des Koreakrieges (1950-53) wurden von Susanne Kuß (Universität Bern) thematisiert. Sie waren damals zwischen China und Westdeutschland sowie zwischen China und der DDR zweigeteilt. Während in der westdeutschen Presselandschaft China zumeist negativ dargestellt wurde, hing die DDR ei-

nem sehr enthusiastischen Chinabild an. Dabei waren die deutsch-chinesischen Beziehungen – wie bereits seit Abschluss des ersten, zwischen China und Preußen 1861 abgeschlossenen Vertrages – Teil eines internationalen Systems, in diesem Fall des als „Kalter Krieg' bezeichneten Systems. Die deutsch-chinesischen Beziehungen in ihrer Gesamtheit vom 17. Jahrhundert bis heute rekonstruierten Mechthild Leutner und Dagmar Yü-Dembski (Freie Universität, Berlin). Die Beschreibungen dieser Beziehungen waren durchgängig gekennzeichnet durch die sich in China bietenden Möglichkeiten für deutsche Wirtschaftsunternehmen bei gleichzeitiger negativer Berichterstattung über China. Wie tief solche negativen Chinabilder verankert sind, zeigen exemplarisch die China-Berichte und –Abbildungen des SPIEGELS seit den 1990er Jahren. Sie stellen die Kehrseite der deutsch-chinesischen wirtschaftlichen Erfolgsgeschichte dar und weisen die Ambivalenz der gegenseitigen Beziehungen hin. An die Stelle ideologischer Auseinandersetzungen während des „Kalten Kriegs' sind heute etwa die Diskussionen um die unterschiedliche Auslegung der Menschenrechte getreten. Die Bedeutung dieser negativen Chinabilder kann kaum hoch genug eingeschätzt werden. Im Gegensatz zu der häufig in den deutschen Medien vertretenen Meinung, dass in China nur ideologisch-aufklärerische Überzeugungsarbeit geleistet werden müsse, um die deutsch-chinesischen Beziehungen zu harmonisieren, sind es die alten negativen Chinabilder, die einer Annäherung entgegenwirken.

(Susanne Kuß)

Isabelle Cheng is a Senior Lecturer at the School of Languages and Area Studies of the University of Portsmouth, UK. Her research concentrates on migration in East Asia, multiculturalism, citizenship and national identity. She is currently conducting a research on the Cold War across the Taiwan Strait with a reference to Chiang Kai-shek's [Jiang Jieshi] war plans on retaking China.

Feng-yi Chu just received his PhD degree in Oriental Studies, University of Oxford. Born and raised in Taipei, Taiwan and experiencing the most agitated era of political reform and nationalist development on the island through 1980s and 1990s, he has developed his research interests focusing on identities, political ideologies, nationalist discourses, and cultural studies in East Asia. He was the convener of Taiwan Studies Programme, Asian Studies Centre of St Antony's College, University of Oxford and one of the founding members of Oxford Taiwan Salon at the university.

Jens Damm is an Associate Professor at the Graduate Institute of Taiwan Studies, Chang Jung University, Tainan, Taiwan. His research interests include the new media and the Internet, the Taiwanese and Chinese diasporas, and gender studies China's cultural diplomacy. He is currently leading a research project at the Oriental Institute, Academy of Science, Czech Republic supportably by the Czech Science Foundation, GACR.

Ryanne Flock studied China Studies, Economics and Sociology at Free University and Humboldt University Berlin. As a doctoral candidate of the East Asian Seminar her research interest concentrates on the social production of urban public space in Guangzhou and the relation to contemporary processes of modernization and urbanization in China. Since February 2016, she has been working as lecturer and coordinator of the Master Program Modern East Asian Studies at the Goethe University Frankfurt.

Susanne Kuss is Privatdozentin in Modern History at the University of Bern (Switzerland). Following her study of History, Philosophy and Berlin and Freiburg (Germany), she took a D.Phil in history from the University of Freiburg in 1988. One focus of her research lies on the German-Chinese relations and the colonial wars in Africa and China. Her last book, also focusing on this topic, was awarded a prize in Germany; the English version will be published by Harvard University Press soon.

Lara Momesso is a post-doctoral researcher at Portstmouth University (UK). Her current research project, funded by the Chiang Ching-kuo Foundation for International Scholarly Exchange, explores the phenomenon of marriage migration and family formation across the Taiwan Strait. Her other research interests include transnational migration, gender studies, migration in East Asia.

Barbora Platzerova is a post-doctoral researcher at the Chiang Ching-kuo International Sinological Center at Charles University in Prague, Czech Republic. Her research interests include the family law and feminist legal history of the Mainland China and Taiwan, as well as Roman law and comparative law.

Ek-hong Ljavakaw Sia is a Ph.D. candidate of Political Science Institute of Tübingen University and a research fellow at the European Research Center of Contemporary Taiwan (ERCCT). His research interest includes nationalism, church-state relations, aboriginal self-rule, and environmental governance.

Jens Sejrup, Jens Sejrup is a postdoctoral research fellow at the Dept. of Anthropology, University of Copenhagen (KU), Denmark. A Japan specialist, he holds a Ph.D. as well as an M.A. in Japanese Studies (KU), and has previously worked as a research fellow at the Centre for East and South-East Asian Studies, Lund University, Sweden. He also serves as a steering committee member of the Nordic Association for the Study of Contemporary Japanese Society.